Jinnah Muslim League and Demand for Pakistan

JINNAH MUSLIM LEAGUE AND DEMAND FOR PAKISTAN

Col. S.C.Dhiman (Retd.)

NEHA PUBLISHERS & DISTRIBUTORS
DELHI

Publisher
NEHA PUBLISHERS & DISTRIBUTORS
4832/24,Prahlad Lane,S-207 Ansari
Road, Daryaganj, Delhi-110002
Ph.: 43570976, 23278261
Email: nehapubdistributors@gmail.com

Edition: 2015

ISBN: 978-93-80318-68-4

Laser Typesetting
JEE-VEE Graphics, Delhi

Price: 1195/-

Printed
Vikas Computers, Delhi

Preface

In 1940 the Muslim League formally endorsed the partitioning of British India and the creation of Pakistan as a separate Muslim state. During pre-independence talks held in 1946, therefore, the British government found that the stand of the Muslim League on separation and that of the Congress on the territorial unity of India were strongly irreconcilable. The British then decided on partition and on August 15, 1947, transferred power dividedly to India and Pakistan. The latter, however, came into existence in two parts: West Pakistan, as Pakistan stands today, and East Pakistan, now known as Bangladesh. The two were divided by 1,600 km (1,000 miles) of Indian territory.

From then onwards, the Muslim League policy was clear and unmistakable. It did not want one India with a clear Hindu majority, which through a parliamentary system of government and so-called democratic process would nullify Muslim rights and interests. The Pakistan Resolution was the Muslim answer to Congress ambitions. The Quaid did not have to define Pakistan. All knew what he meant. Beverley Nichols, visiting India in 1943, asked the Quaid how he would describe the vital principle of Pakistan. "In five words," replied the Quaid, "the Muslims are a nation."

Jinnah demand and divided the subcontinent, created a new nation, Pakistan for Muslims and was ironically ignored by his own colleagues who were in power during his last days.

—*Editor*

Contents

1

Jinnah: Pakistan's Founding Father

To Pakistanis, Muhammad Ali Jinnah is revered, known as Quaid-e-Azam, or 'Great Leader.' He is their George Washington, their de Gaulle, their Churchill. A brilliant lawyer by trade, he rose to the forefront of the struggle for a Muslim nation as India negotiated its independence from Britain.

But his insistence on a separate Muslim state to be carved out of the former British India earned him many enemies. Indeed, the last viceroy of India under British rule, Lord Mountbatten—thwarted by Jinnah's relentless call for partition plans of the future states of India and Pakistan—referred to him variously as a 'lunatic', an 'evil genius,' and a 'bastard'.

Today, many in the West view Jinnah through the eyes of Richard Attenborough's movie 'Gandhi,' in which the Muslim leader was portrayed as a cold villain who wanted a separate Pakistan only for his own political aggrandizement. In truth, Jinnah was a complex man who by his eloquence and perseverance inspired both adulation and condemnation.

Born in 1876, the son of a wealthy Karachi merchant, Jinnah was not a man of the people like Indian nationalist Mahatma Gandhi. Jinnah studied law in England, and after his return to India in 1896 as an advocate for the Bombay High Court, the slender, well-dressed and well-spoken attorney quickly made a name for himself.

According to one contemporary, quoted in a Time Magazine profile, Jinnah was "the best showman of them all. Quick, exceedingly clever, sarcastic and colourful. His greatest delight was to confound the opposing lawyer by confidential asides and to outwit the presiding judge in repartee." In 1906, Jinnah joined the All India Congress. In 1913, while still serving in the Congress, he joined the Muslim League, prompting a leading Congress spokesman of the day to call him the "ambassador of Hindu-Muslim unity." With time, that would change.

Early in his political career, Jinnah was chiefly concerned with achieving independence for a unified India. Increasingly, however, he worried that British oppression would be replaced by Hindu oppression and continued subjugation of India's Muslim minority. In 1919, Jinnah resigned from the Congress and turned his focus to Muslim interests. Over the next two decades he would become the architect of a dream first voiced by Muslim poet-philosopher Muhammad Iqbal that Indian Muslims would someday have their own nation.

By the late 1930s, Jinnah, who had become leader of the Muslim League, was convinced that a partition of India along religious lines was the only way to preserve Muslim political power. In 1940, the Muslim League adopted the 'Lahore Resolution' calling for separate autonomous states in majority-Muslim areas of northeastern and eastern India.

In 1946, violence between Hindus and Muslims broke out after Jinnah called for demonstrations opposing an interim Indian government in which Muslim power would be compromised. The riots spread. In the first weeks of the uprising, more than 3,000 people were killed and thousands wounded.

Against the rising tide of ethnic unrest, Jinnah demanded partition of India. Britain, eager to make a clean break with India, finally relented and Pakistan was born. Jinnah, who by most accounts was not a particularly religious man, called for equal rights for all Pakistani citizens without regard to their religion.

In his inaugural speech as first governor general of Pakistan, Jinnah said: 'You will find that in the course of time, Hindus would cease to be Hindus and Muslims would cease to be Muslims, not in the religious sense because that is the personal faith of each individual, but in the political sense as citizens of the state."

But Jinnah would not live to see the development of his fledging country. He died of tuberculosis just 13 months after the formation of Pakistan. His vision of a secular government was never fully realized, either, with disputes between religious groups marring much of Pakistan's brief history. And later, many of his followers disputed the degree to which he was committed to a secular government. A half-century after his death, controversy stirs over the making of a film about his life. Critics of the film, which stars British actor Christopher Lee, worry that Jinnah will be cast in an unfavourable light. Those involved in the project insist that the film will portray Pakistanis beloved leader accurately.

However history may judge him, his own contribution to history cannot be doubted. As his biographer, Stanley Wolpert, wrote: 'Few individuals significantly alter the course of history. Fewer still modify the map of the world. Hardly anyone can be credited with creating a nation-state. Muhammad Ali Jinnah did all three.'

THE PAKISTANI VIEW

The Sole Statesman

"The government of the United States invariably does the right thing after having exhausted all other possibilities." So said Winston Leonard Spencer Churchill, the premier statesman of last century. Had Churchill been alive today, and still ruminating over the loss of the Empire ("I have not become the King's first minister in order to preside over the liquidation of the British Empire") he would have said of Pakistan of the year 2000 that the government of General Pervez Musharraf makes the right noises but too often swiftly retracts its words when one or more of the unrepresentative obscurantists of the country voices an objection.

Muhammad Ali Jinnah was a proud man, proud for good reason; by the overriding force of his indomitable will, and that alone, he carved out a country for us. Not following the form of his day, Jinnah did not go to jail for a single day, never embarked on a hunger strike, did not encourage rowdy protest marches, he abhorred any form of violence. Liberal-minded and self-confident he did what he liked, ate and drank what he liked, dressed as he liked, encouraged others to do the same, held his head high-and kept to his faith. "Do your duty and have faith in God. There is no power on earth that can undo Pakistan." This conviction was soon to be proved wrong. His buoyant optimism and his firm certitude in the future of this country clouded his perception of the calibre and character of the leaders who would immediately and later follow him. He failed to conceive that through their lack of ability, lack of integrity, their avarice, their unquenchable greed, their hunger for power, pomp, pelf and position, they would be the undoing of Pakistan.

He was the sole statesman this country has had. Those who followed were small men, narrow of thought, fearful of others, who grabbed at today and ignored the morrow. Within a quarter of a century half of Jinnah's Pakistan was lost. What was left slid swiftly down the slithery hill. It is now an overpopulated, illiterate, bankrupt country, the principal aim of its leadership being to fight to acquire a disputed territory. Its main claim to fame, of which it rarely ceases to remind the world at large, is its nuclear prowess.

To repeat (and it bears repetition ad nauseam), when Jinnah addressed the first constituent assembly of the country on August 11 1947 he embodied in his speech the core of his philosophy, his ideas, and his vision for the state he had founded. It was a fine piece of rhetoric; too fine, too moral, too democratic, too liberal, too full of justice, too idealistic for the Philistines. This speech has been interpreted in many different ways, it has been subject to distortion, it has inspired fear in successive governments, which would have been far happier had it never been delivered. It is to the misfortune of the people of this country that their so-called leaders have refused to live with, or up to, the principles by which Jinnah wished them to be guided.

It is a matter of national shame that, from top to bottom, the citizens of this country live in dread of contamination by the truth-such is the measure of self-deception, insecurity, disunity, indiscipline, and faithlessness.

On August 11, 1947, before the flag of Pakistan had even been unfurled, Jinnah told his people and their future legislators: "You are free, free to go to your temples, you are free to go to your mosques or to any other places of worship in this state of Pakistan. You may belong to any religion or caste or creed-that has nothing to do with the business of the State. As you know, history shows that in England conditions some time ago were much worse than those prevailing in India today. The Roman Catholics and the Protestants persecuted each other. Even now there are some states in existence where there are discriminations made and bars imposed against a particular class. Thank God, we are not starting in those days. We are starting in the days when there is no discrimination, no distinction between one caste or creed and another. We are starting with this fundamental principle that we are all citizens and equal citizens of one state. The people of England in course of time had to face the realities of the situation and had to discharge the responsibilities and burdens placed upon them by the government of their country and they went through that fire step by step. Today, you might say with justice that Roman Catholics and Protestants do not exist; what exists now is that every man is a citizen, an equal citizen of Great Britain and they are all members of the nation. Now I think we should keep that in front of us as our ideal.....".

[This particular passage has been subject to deliberate distortion and misinterpretation, inspiring the dishonest dogmatists who misappropriated the country after his death with such fear and unease that in the official biography of Jinnah commissioned by the Government of Pakistan, written by Hector Bolitho, published in 1954, it was censored to falsely read: ".....You may belong to any religion or caste or creed-that has nothing to do with the fundamental principle that we are all citizens and equal citizens of one State..... Now, I think we should keep that in front of us as our ideal....". (Most of the above passages were committed).]

That same August day, he made it clear to the future legislators and administrators that "the first duty of a government is to maintain law and order, so that the life, property and religious beliefs of its subjects are fully protected by the state." He told them he would not tolerate the evils of bribery, corruption, blackmarketeering and "this great evil, the evil of nepotism and jobbery," the daily bread of powermongers. Little did he know that day that these prime evils were to become prerequisites for the survival of the politicians in and out of uniform and of the administrators of all ranks and grades for the maintenance of their power.

In a way, it was fortunate that Jinnah did not live long enough to see the negation of his principles, the perversion of his vision. A man of high ideals, of impeccable moral and material honesty, tolerant, open-minded, liberal to the core, a consummate statesman-his disillusion would have been too great to bear.

This newspaper of record founded by Jinnah carried an editorial on December 25 1989, his 113th official birthday, headed 'Back to Quaid's ideals', from which I quote : "At this juncture, a true appreciation and understanding of the precepts and practices of the Quaid-i-Azam is crucially important. His visionary concepts of statecraft could provide the basic guidelines in charting an unfaltering democratic course for the nation. What is needed is a revivification of the basic postulates that the Father of the Nation enunciated in various speeches and policy statements he made during the struggle for, and immediately after, the creation of Pakistan. A serious effort must be made to rediscover the essence of his message and vision from the plethora of twisted interpretation of his acts and utterances. We have been guilty of passivity in the face of deliberate misrepresentations and selective distortions of the Quaid's precepts by a whole tribe of charlatans, pretenders and crafty autocrats to serve their selfish ends.... It was neither theocracy nor feudalism nor exploitative capitalism that the Quaid ever approved of. What he basically desired was a sovereign state for the Muslims of the subcontinent based on the principles of constitutionalism, democracy, federalism and Islamic social justice in which the civil liberties and human rights of all citizens would be guaranteed without any discrimination on any ground whatsoever..... "

Oxford University Press in its Millenium Series has just published a book of Jinnah's speeches and statements made in

1947-48, with an introduction by S M Burke, historian and writer, successively an ICS judge, a diplomat of Pakistan, and Professor and Consultant on South Asian studies at the University of Minnesota. It is essential reading for the generals and the others who rule over us from Islamabad.

QUAID-I-AZAM MUHAMMAD ALI JINNAH

Father of the Nation Quaid-i-Azam Muhammad Ali Jinnah's achievement as the founder of Pakistan, dominates everything else he did in his long and crowded public life spanning some 42 years. Yet, by any standard, his was an eventful life, his personality multidimensional and his achievements in other fields were many, if not equally great. Indeed, several were the roles he had played with distinction: at one time or another, he was one of the greatest legal luminaries India had produced during the first half of the century, an 'ambassador of Hindu-Muslim unity, a great constitutionalist, a distinguished parliamentarian, a top-notch politician, an indefatigable freedom-fighter, a dynamic Muslim leader, a political strategist and, above all one of the great nation-builders of modern times.

What, however, makes him so remarkable is the fact that while similar other leaders assumed the leadership of traditionally well-defined nations and espoused their cause, or led them to freedom, he created a nation out of an inchoate and down-trodeen minority and established a cultural and national home for it. And all that within a decase. For over three decades before the successful culmination in 1947, of the Muslim struggle for freedom in the South-Asian subcontinent, Jinnah had provided political leadership to the Indian Muslims: initially as one of the leaders, but later, since 1947, as the only prominent leader-the Quaid-i-Azam. For over thirty years, he had guided their affairs; he had given expression, coherence and direction to their ligitimate aspirations and cherished dreams; he had formulated these into concerete demands; and, above all, he had striven all the while to get them conceded by both the ruling British and the numerous Hindus the dominant segment of India's population. And for over thirty years he had fought, relentlessly and inexorably, for the inherent rights of the Muslims for an honourable existence in the subcontinent. Indeed, his life story constitutes, as it were, the story of the rebirth of the Muslims of the subcontinent and their spectacular rise to nationhood, phoenixlike.

Early Life

Born on **December 25, 1876**, in a prominent mercantile family in Karachi and educated at the Sindh Madrassat-ul-Islam and the Christian Mission School at his birth place, Jinnah joined the Lincoln's Inn in 1893 to become the youngest Indian to be called to the Bar, three years later. Starting out in the legal profession withknothing to fall back upon except his native ability and determination, young Jinnah rose to prominence and became Bombay's most successful lawyer, as few did, within a few years. Once he was firmly established in the legal profession, Jinnah formally entered politics in **1905** from the platform of the Indian National Congress. He went to England in that year alongwith Gopal Krishna Gokhale **(1866-1915)**, as a member of a Congress delegation to plead the cause of Indian self-governemnt during the British elections. A year later, he served as Secretary to Dadabhai Naoroji **(1825-1917)**, the then Indian National Congress President, which was considered a great honour for a budding politician. Here, at the Calcutta Congress session **(December 1906)**, he also made his first political speech in support of the resolution on self-government.

FIRST LEADER OF A NEWLY BORN STATE

In recognition of his singular contribution, Quaid-e-Azam Mohammed Ali Jinnah was nominated by the Muslim League as the Governor-General of Pakistan, while the Congress appointed Mountbatten as India's first Governor-General. Pakistan, it has been truly said, was born in virtual chaos. Indeed, few nations in the world have started on their career with less resources and in more treacherous circumstances. The new nation did not inherit a central government, a capital, an administrative core, or an organized defense force. Its social and administrative resources were poor; there was little equipment and still less statistics. The Punjab holocaust had left vast areas in a shambles with communications disrupted. This, along with the en masse migration of the Hindu and Sikh business and managerial classes, left the economy almost shattered.

The treasury was empty, India having denied Pakistan the major share of its cash balances. On top of all this, the still unorganized nation was called upon to feed some eight million refugees who had fled the insecurities and barbarities of the north Indian plains that long, hot summer. If all this was symptomatic of Pakistan's administrative and economic weakness, the Indian annexation, through military action in November 1947, of Junagadh (which had originally acceded to Pakistan) and the Kashmir war over the State's accession (October 1947-December 1948) exposed her military weakness. In the circumstances, therefore, it was nothing short of a miracle that Pakistan survived at all. That it survived and forged ahead was mainly due to one man-Mohammed Ali Jinnah. The nation desperately needed in the person of a charismatic leader at that critical juncture in the nation's history, and he fulfilled that need profoundly. After all, he was more than a mere Governor-General: he was the Quaid-e-Azam who had brought the State into being.

In the ultimate analysis, his very presence at the helm of affairs was responsible for enabling the newly born nation to overcome the terrible crisis on the morrow of its cataclysmic birth. He mustered up the immense prestige and the unquestioning loyalty he commanded among the people to energize them, to raise their morale, land directed the profound feelings of patriotism that the freedom had generated, along constructive channels. Though tired and in poor health, Jinnah yet carried the heaviest part of the burden in that first crucial year. He laid down the policies of the new state, called attention to the immediate problems confronting the nation and told the members of the Constituent Assembly, the civil servants and the Armed Forces what to do and what the nation expected of them. He saw to it that law and order was maintained at all costs, despite the provocation that the large-scale riots in north India had provided. He moved from Karachi to Lahore for a while and supervised the immediate refugee problem in the Punjab. In a time of fierce excitement, he remained sober, cool and steady. He advised his excited audience in Lahore to concentrate on helping the refugees, to avoid retaliation, exercise restraint and protect the minorities. He assured the minorities of a fair deal, assuaged their inured sentiments, and gave them hope and comfort. He toured the various provinces, attended to their particular problems and instilled in the people a sense of belonging. He reversed the British policy in the North-West Frontier and ordered the withdrawal of the troops from the tribal territory of Waziristan, thereby making the Pathans feel themselves an integral part of Pakistan's body-politics. He created a new Ministry of States and Frontier Regions, and assumed responsibility for ushering in a new era in Balochistan. He settled the controversial question of the states of Karachi, secured the accession of States, especially of Kalat which seemed problematical and carried on negotiations with Lord Mountbatten for the settlement of the Kashmir Issue.

Discussion on Jinnah

"Few individuals significantly alter the course of history. Few[er] still modify the map of the world. Hardly any one can be credited with creating a nation state, Muhammad Ali Jinnah did all three. Hailed as 'Great Leader' (Quaid-e-Azam) of Pakistan and its first Governor General, Jinnah virtually conjured that country into statehood by the force of his indomitable will."

—Stanley Walport, "Jinnah of Pakistan"

Stamp issued 11 September 1998

On December 25, 1876 a child was born in a prominent mercantile family of Karachi who was destined to change the course of history in South Asia and to carve out a homeland for the Muslims of India where they could peruse their destiny according to their faith and ideology. From his very childhood, young Jinnah developed the habit of stern independence and self-reliance. In 1892, he was called to the Bar at the very early age of 16. He stayed for four years in England and on his return, started his practice in Bombay. The early period was spent in hard and constant labour. However, he soon came to be looked upon not only as a brilliant lawyer, but also as a man of great integrity and character. He was soon elected to the Imperial legislative Council.

Mr. Jinnah began by accommodating the Congress point of view, and was called 'Ambassador of Hindu-Muslim Unity' when he brought about rapprochement between the Congress and the Muslim league in 1916. He soon felt, however, that the Congress was merely a camouflage for consolidating Hindu India at the expense of Muslim, and it was at the London meetings of the Round Table Conference during 1930-32 that he received the shock of his life. "In the face of danger" he said, "the Hindu sentiment, the Hindu mind, the Hindu attitude led me to the conclusion that there was no hope of unity".

Mr. Jinnah returned from England in 1934, and set out to galvanizing the Muslim League into a most dynamic organization. "We are a Nation" he asserted, "with our own distinctive culture and civilization, language and literature, art and architecture, names and nomenclature, sense of value and proportion, legal laws and moral code, custom and calendar, history and tradition, aptitude and ambitions; in short, we have our own distinctive outlook on life and of life. By all canons of international law we are a Nation." In subsequent years, Mr. Jinnah, popularly known by the title "Quaid-e-Azam" (the Great Leader), came to symbolize the Muslim aspirations for a separate independent homeland, and in 1940 the Muslim League, under his inspiring leadership, demanded that India should be partitioned and the Muslim majority areas should constitute the sovereign, independent State of Pakistan. It was his ardent advocacy and unbending character, his unshakable determination and his power of persuasion that brought about the successful fruition of the Muslim struggle in the shape of Pakistan.

Quaid-e-Azam performed the opening ceremony of the establishment of State Bank of Pakistan on 1st July, 1948. The Quaid-e-Azam was accompanied by Mohtarma Fatima Jinnah. On arrival, he was greeted by State Bank's first Governor, Mr. Zahid Husain. After having inspected a Guard of Honour of a detachment of Pakistan Army, Quaid- e-Azam took the salute.

The function, among others, was attended by the members of Central Board of Directors of State Bank of Pakistan Sir Maratab Ali Shah, Mr. Wabiduz-Zaman, Mr. Hatim A. Alavi, Mr. Jogesh

Das and Mr. Kasim Hussain Kassam Dada. The freedom fighters, Pirzada Abdul Sattar, Sir Gbulam Hussain Hedayatullah, Khawaja Shababuddin. Mr. I.I. Chundrigar, Raja Ghazanfar Ali Khan, Sardar Abdur Rab Nishtar, Sir Zafarullah Khan and Mr. Liaquat Ali Khan were also present to witness the creation of the Bank. Inaugurating the Bank, Quaid-e-Azam began his historic, and what turned out to be his last public address by saying "the opening of the State Bank symbolizes the sovereignty of our State in the financial sphere'. Quaid-e-Azam has specially come to Karachi by interrupting his stay in Ziarat for the occasion of national importance. With his characteristic foresight he could see as early as that, as the put it in the concluding portion of his inaugural speech, that the Bank "will develop into one of our greatest national institutions".

The three other stamps epitomize Quaid-e-Azarn Muhammad Ali Jinnah's visit to 5 Heavy Anti Aircraft Regiment (Artillery) on 21st February, 1948 and 2/15 Punjab on 15- 4-1948. The 5 Heavy Anti Aircraft Regiment (Artillery) was given the unique honour of being the first Armed Forces unit to be visited by Quaid-e-Azam. Regimental parade was held in Quaid's honour. When Quaid-e-Azam reached the saluting dais the Regiment gave a general salute. While the Regiment was still at 'present arm' Quaid was requested by Lieut. (later Admiral) Ahsan, his ADC, to move to review the parade.

The parade commander just could not decide to order the Regiment to 'order arm' as Quaid was then moving. Thus Quaid reviewed the Regiment at 'present arm'. A tradition was thus born on Quaid's first visit to the Unit. Since then the 5 Heavy Anti Aircraft Regiment has been claiming the right to be inspected at 'present arm' as Quaid had inspected it at 'present arm' on his first visit. The claim of 5 Heavy Anti Aircraft Regiment was examined and re-examined many a time when finally it was approved by the Chief of Army Staff General Mirza Aslam Baig and Maj. Gen. Agha Masood Hasan, GOC Army Air Defence Command, inspected the 5 AD Regiment guard at 'present arm' at Quetta for the first time, when Lieut Colonel (now Major General) Tahir Mahmud Qazi was the Commanding Officer.

Since then the Regiment has a unique honour of being reviewed at 'present arm' and using the motto "Fakhr-e-Quaid." The stamp places the visit of Quaid to 5 Heavy Anti Aircraft Regiment in Philatelic history.

The Quaid was seventy-one when Pakistan was born. He was spared by Almighty only for one year to set the ship of the new State on its keel. In spite of his immense prestige and popularity he conducted himself strictly as a constitutional Head of the state and never deviated from democratic conventions and constitutional Propriety.

He died on September 11, 1948 deeply mourned by a grateful Nation but as one of the great immortals of history. Jinnah first entered politics by participating in the 1906 Calcutta session of the Indian National Congress, the party that called for dominion status and later for independence for India. Four years later he was elected to the Imperial Legislative Council—the beginning of a long and distinguished parliamentary career.

In Bombay he came to know, among other important Congress personalities, Gopal Krishna Gokhale, the eminent Maratha leader. Greatly influenced by these nationalist politicians, Jinnah aspired during the early part of his political life to become "a Muslim Gokhale." Admiration for British political institutions and an eagerness to raise the status of India in the international community and to develop a sense of Indian nationhood among the peoples of India were the chief elements of his politics. At that time, he still looked upon Muslim interests in the context of Indian nationalism. But, by the beginning of the 20th century, the conviction had been growing among the Muslims that their interests demanded the preservation of their separate identity rather than amalgamation in the Indian nation that would for all practical purposes be Hindu. Largely to safeguard Muslim interests, the All-India Muslim League was founded in 1906. But Jinnah remained aloof from it. Only in 1913, when authoritatively assured that the league was as devoted as the Congress to the political emancipation of India, did Jinnah join the league. When the Indian Home Rule League was formed, he became its chief organizer in Bombay and was elected president of the Bombay branch.

"Ambassador of Hindu-Muslim unity." Jinnah's endeavours to bring about the political union of Hindus and Muslims earned him the title of "the best ambassador of Hindu-Muslim unity," an epithet coined by Gokhale.

It was largely through his efforts that the Congress and the Muslim League began to hold their annual sessions jointly, to facilitate mutual consultation and participation. In 1915 the two organizations held their meetings in Bombay and in 1916 in Lucknow, where the Lucknow Pact was concluded. Under the terms of the pact, the two organizations put their seal to a scheme of constitutional reform that became their joint demand vis-a-vis the British government. There was a good deal of give and take, but the Muslims obtained one important concession in the shape of separate electorates, already conceded to them by the government in 1909 but hitherto resisted by the Congress.

Meanwhile, a new force in Indian politics had appeared in the person of Mohandas K. Gandhi. Both the Home Rule League and the Indian National Congress had come under his sway. Opposed to Gandhi's Noncooperation Movement and his essentially Hindu approach to politics, Jinnah left both the League and the Congress in 1920.

For a few years he kept himself aloof from the main political movements. He continued to be a firm believer in Hindu-Muslim unity and constitutional methods for the achievement of political ends. After his withdrawal from the Congress, he used the Muslim League platform for the propagation of his views. But during the 1920s the Muslim League, and with it Jinnah, had been overshadowed by the Congress and the religiously oriented Muslim Khilafat committee. When the failure of the Noncooperation Movement and the emergence of Hindu revivalist movements led to antagonism and riots between the Hindus and Muslims, the league gradually began to come into its own. Jinnah's problem during the following years was to convert the league into an enlightened political body prepared to cooperate with other organizations working for the good of India. In addition, he had to convince the Congress, as a prerequisite for political progress, of the necessity of settling the Hindu-Muslim conflict.

To bring about such a rapprochement was Jinnah's chief purpose during the late 1920s and early 1930s. He worked toward this end within the legislative assembly, at the Round Table Conferences in London (1930-32), and through his 14 points, which included proposals for a federal form of government, greater rights for minorities, one-third representation for Muslims in the central legislature, separation of the predominantly Muslim Sind region from the rest of the Bombay province, and the introduction of reforms in the North-West Frontier Province.

But he failed. His failure to bring about even minor amendments in the Nehru Committee proposals (1928) over the question of separate electorates and reservation of seats for Muslims in the legislatures frustrated him.

He found himself in a peculiar position at this time; many Muslims thought that he was too nationalistic in his policy and that Muslim interests were not safe in his hands, while the Indian National Congress would not even meet the moderate Muslim demands halfway.

Indeed, the Muslim League was a house divided against itself. The Punjab Muslim League repudiated Jinnah's leadership and organized itself separately. In disgust, Jinnah decided to settle in England. From 1930 to 1935 he remained in London, devoting himself to practice before the Privy Council. But when constitutional changes were in the offing, he was persuaded to return home to head a reconstituted Muslim League.

Soon preparations started for the elections under the Government of India Act of 1935. Jinnah was still thinking in terms of cooperation between the Muslim League and the Hindu Congress and with coalition governments in the provinces. But the elections of 1937 proved to be a turning point in the relations between the two organizations.

The Congress obtained an absolute majority in six provinces, and the league did not do particularly well. The Congress decided not to include the league in the formation of provincial governments, and exclusive all-Congress governments were the result. Relations between Hindus and Muslims started to deteriorate, and soon Muslim discontent became boundless.

QUID-E-AZAM MUHAMMAD ALI JINNAH—THE FATHER OF THE NATION

In the endless corridors of history, a name was added in August 1947. It was that of Quid-e-Azam Muhammad Ali Jinnah, the Founder of Pakistan. Born into a Karachi mercantile family on December 25, 1876, Quid-e-Azam Muhammad Ali Jinnah had his early schooling at Karachi. Later,he joined the Lincolin's Inn, to become the youngest Indian barrister to be called to the bar. By sheer native ability and determination,young Jinnah rose quickly to prominence,and soon became a successful lawyer.

In 1910 he was elected by Bombay Muslims to the newly constituted Imperial Legislative Council. All through his parliamentary career, which spanned some four decades, he supported or opposed measures solely on their marits. His was also among the most powerful voices on the cause of India's freedom, Indian rights and freedom. By 1917, Quid-e-Azam Muhammad Ali Jinnah's reputation as one of the outstanding and highly respected leaders of South-Asian subcontinent was firmly established. He was a prominent member of Congress Party and an outspoken champion India's freedom in the Imperial Legislative Council. Simultaneously, he was the President of all India Muslim-League. He brought the Congress and the League together, and was chiefly responsible for the Congress-League pact (1916), a joint scheme for postwar reforms. For his untiring efforts to effect a communal settlement,he was hailed as the "ambassador of Hindu-Muslim Unity".

Since he stud for civic freedoms, he resigned from the Imperial Council in 1919, when the Rowlatt Bill was passed into law; and since he stood for "Ordered Progress", moderation, gradualism, and constitutionalism, he left the Congress in 1920 when it opted for M.K. Gandhi's direction action and noncooperation plank. Jinnah's ascendency to national leadership had received a serious setback.

Returning to active politics after three years, Quid-e-Azam Muhammad Ali Jinnah reorganizes League of which he was President since 1916, and devoted the next seven years to bringing about unity among Muslim ranks. To him a Hindu-Muslim settlement was still a precondition for Indian freedom. He attended several unity conferences, authored the Delhi Muslim proposals (1927), pledged for the incorporation of basic Muslim demands in the Nehru report (1928), formulated the "fourteen points" (1929), as minimum Muslim demands for any constitutional settlement and as a riposte to Nehru report,and participated in the Round Table conference (1930) in London,called the British to formulate a new constitution of India.

Despaired alike of the "negative" Congress attitude and a chronic disunity in Muslim ranks, he was into self-exile in London (1931), but returned to India. In 1934 at the fervent appeal of Muslims, became the President of reunited Muslim League, and assumed its leadership. When Quid-e-Azam Muhammad Ali Jinnah took up the leadership of the Muslims in 1936, they were a mass of demoralised men and women, politically disorganized and without a clear-cut political programme. During the next three years, Quid-e-Azam Muhammad Ali Jinnah made energetic efforts to broaden his mass support,bringing the Muslims on the one platform, breating new life into the moribund League, democrating its structure and organizational network, giving it a coherent all-India policy and programme, and made Muslim India a power to be reckoned with. By 1939 he had become the sole spokesman of the Indian Muslims, their Quid-e-Azam ("the Great Leader").

In 1940 he spelled out the concept of Muslim nationhood,asserting that "We are a nation,with our own distinctive culture and civilization,language and literature,art and architecture, names and nomen culture, sense of value and proportion, legal laws and moral code, customs and calendar, history and traditions,aptitudes and ambitions,in short, we have our own distinctive outlook on and of life. By all canons of international law we are a nation". And on that basis of demand the setting up of an independent Muslim homeland in the predominantly Muslim northwestern and eastern India.

Despite the vehement opposition of the Congress and the antipathy of the British to his demand, Quid-e-Azam Muhammad Ali Jinnah organized his movement gathered momentum within a few years,became the central issue in all subsequent constitutional proposals, and was overwhelmingly voted for by Muslims in the 1945-46 general elections. Pakistan was finally established on 14th August, 1947, and Quid-e-Azam Muhammad Ali Jinnah, then became the first Governor General.

Indeed, few nations in the world started on their career with less resources and in more difficult circumstances than Pakistan. That it survived at all was largely the hardwork of one man Quid-e-Azam Muhammad Ali Jinnah, who filled in need for a charismatic leader at the critical juncture in the nation's history. He deftly exploited the immense prestige and utmost loyalty he commanded among the people to energize them, to raise their morals,and canalise the profound feelings of patriotism the coming of freedom had generated, along constructive channels. Though tired and in poor health, Quid-e-Azam Muhammad Ali Jinnah carried the heaviest part of the burden in that first, critical year. He devoted the last year of his life to the onrous task of consolidating Pakistan and securing its survival. He died on 11th September, 1948.

Quid-e-Azam Muhammad Ali Jinnah believed in peace within and without,and in the principle of "live and let live". Actually, the Pakistan demand itself, as defined by him,was based on this principle : "let the two major nations, Hindus and Muslims, manage their affairs in their respective a read according to their own rights and traditions and unthwarted by the instruction of each other, thus paving the way for two nations to live in peace and good neighbourliness with each other in the Subcontinent. "Pakistan presupposed freedom for the Subcontinent as a whole". His passion for freedom was,however not restricted either to Muslims or Hindus; It extended to all the enslaved people of the world struggling to liberate themselves from foreign yoke. While engrossed all the while in the consuming task of wresting freedom for Muslims of the South-Asian Subcontinent, he took timeout on various occasions to lend his and Muslim India's moral support to freedom movements in other Asian and African countries.

One of the great nation builders, Quid-e-Azam Muhammad Ali Jinnah, invites comparison with some of the greatest names in modern times : Washington, Bismark, Cavour, Gribaldi, Lenin, Ataturk, What, however, makes him so remarkable even in the galaxy of nation- builders is the fact that while others assumed the leadership of traditionally well-defined nations and led them to freedom, he created a nation out of an inchoate and backward minority and established a cultural and national home for it. And all that within a decade.

The Quid was the recipient of some of the greatest tributes paid to any one in modern times,some of them even from those who held a polarized viewpoint, The Agha Khan considered him "the greatest man he ever met"; Beverly Nichols, the auther of virdict of India, called him "the most important man in Asia"; and Dr. Kailasnath Katju, the West Bengal Governor in 1948, thought of him as "an outstanding figure of this century, not only in India but in whole world"; While Adul Rehman Azzam Pasha, Secretary General of Arab League, called him "one of the greatest leader in the Muslim world", the Grand Mufti of Palestine considered his death as a "great loss" for the entire world of Islam. It was, however, given to Sarat Chandra Bose, leader of the forward block Wing of the Indian National Congress to sum up his personal and political achievements. "Mr. Jinnah" he said on his death on 1948, "was great as a lawyer, once great as a Congressman, great as a Leader of Muslims, great as a world politician and diplomat, and greatest as of all as a man of action. By Mr. Jinnah's passing away, the world has lost one of the greatest statesmen and Pakistan its life-giver, philosopher and guide." Such was Quid-e-Azam Muhammad Ali Jinnah, the man and his mission; such the range of accomplishment and achievements.

On Gandhi and Jinnah

I can give only my impressions of them, for what they are worth. The first thing that strikes me is that it would be difficult to find two persons who would rival them for their colossal egotism, to whom personal ascendancy is everything and the cause of the country a mere counter on the table. They have made Indian politics a matter of personal feud. Consequences have no terror for them; indeed they do not occur to them until they happen. When they do happen they either forget the cause, or if they remember it, they overlook it with a complacency which saves them from any remorse. They choose to stand on a pedestal of splendid isolation. They wall themselves off from their equals. They prefer to open themselves to their inferiors. They are very unhappy at and impatient of criticism, but are very happy to be fawned upon by flunkeys. Both have developed a wonderful stagecraft and arrange things in such a way that they are always in the limelight wherever they go. Each of course claims to be supreme. If supremacy was their only claim, it would be a small wonder. In addition to supremacy each claims infallibility for himself. Pius IX during whose sacred regime as Pope the issue of infallibility was raging said— " Before I was Pope I believed in Papal infallibility, now I feel it." This is exactly the attitude of the two leaders whom Providence—may I say in his unguarded moments—has appointed to lead us.

One Response to "On Gandhi and Jinnah"

And few quotes of Gandhi. Mahatma Gandhi, a racist - extracted from various sources. If the Shudras (low castes) leave their ancestral profession and take up others, ambition will rouse in them and their peace of mind will be spoiled. Even their family peace will be disturbed. (Hind Swaraj).

I believe in Varnashrama (caste system) which is the law of life. The law of Varna (colour and/or caste) is nothing but the law of conservation of energy. Why should my son not be scavenger if I am one? (Harijan, 3-6-1947). He (Shudra, low caste) may not be called a Brahmin (uppermost caste), though he (Shudra) may have all the qualities of a Brahmin in this birth. And it is a good thing for him (Shudra) not to arrogate a Varna (caste) to which he is not born. It is a sign of true humility. (Young India, 11-24-1927).

According to Hindu belief, he who practices a profession which does not belong to him by birth, does violence to himself and becomes a degraded being by not living up to the Varna (caste) of his birth. (Young India, 11-14-1927).

As years go by, the conviction is daily growing upon me that Varna (caste) is the law of man's being, and therefore, caste is necessary for Christians and Muslims as it has been necessary for Hinduism, and has been its saving grace. (Speech at Trivandrum,

(Collection of Speeches), Ramanath Suman (1932)). I would resist with my life the separation of "Untouchables" from the caste Hindus. The problems of the "Untouchable" community is of comparatively little importance. (London Round Table Conference 1931.) I call myself a Snatana man, one who firmly believes in the caste system. (Dharma Manthan, p 4).

I believe in caste division determined by birth and the very root of caste division lies in birth. (Varna Vyavastha, p 76-77). The four castes and the four stages of life are things to be attained by birth alone. (Dharma Manthan, p 5). Caste means the predetermination of a man's profession. Caste implies that a man must practice only the profession of his ancestors for his livelihood. (Varna Vyavstha, p 28, 56, 68). Shudra only serves the higher castes as a matter of religious duty and who will never own any property. The gods will shower down flowers on him. (Varna Vyavastha, p 15).

I have noticed that the very basis of our thought have been severely shaken by Western civilization which is the creation of the Satan. (Dharma Manthan, p 65). How is it possible that the Antyaja (outcastes) should have the right to enter all the existing temples? As long as the law of caste and karma has the chief place in the Hindu religion, to say that every Hindu can enter every temple is a thing that is not possible today. (Gandhi Sikshan, Vol. 11, p 132).

There are I am sorry to say, many Hindu temples in our midst in this country, which are no better than brothels. The caste system can't be said to be bad because it does not allow inter-dining and inter-marriages in different castes. (Gandhi by Shiru, p129). The caste system, in my opinion, has a scientific basis. Reason does not revolt against it. It has disadvantages. Caste creates a social and moral restraint - I can find no reason for their abolition. To abolish caste is to demolish Hinduism. There is nothing to fight against the Varnasharma (caste system). I don't believe the caste system to be an odious and vicious dogma. It has its limitations and defects, but there is nothing sinful about it. (Harijan, 1933). You can also spread this word. Let world knows if we apply his thoughts in American context, Gandhi can be termed as racist.

Jinnah was against the Name 'Pakistan' at First

There is a very interesting but little known fact about the use of the term 'Pakistan' by Muslim League leaders including its supreme leader M.A. Jinnah-that they did not like it in the beginning so that for nearly two years they avoided using it, as Jinnah was against it.

They only called it 'Lahore Resolution' demanding division of India on communal lines as it was passed at the League's Lahore session on March 23, 1940.

They did not want to give the impression that they were demanding the creation of a PURE Muslim land, which the word Pakistan implied, as 'Pak' means 'pure'.

Its use also implied ethnic cleansing and expulsion of all non-Muslims from it to make it a pure Muslim land. They wanted to avoid this impression to soften its opposition among the Hindus especially. K.K. Aziz, Pakistan's official historian throws interesting light on this episode as follows:

> *"Mr Jinnah's definite dislike of the term was conveyed to a League leader of Lahore, Mian Kifait Ali who writing under the pen-name 'Punjabi' wrote a book in 1939 making a most detailed case for the Partition and creation of a Muslim state in North West India. He named the book Pakistan and took the final manuscript to Abdullah Haroon, the Muslim League leader of Sind and also showed it to Nawab of Mamdot, the League leader of Punjab. The two offered to finance it, Mamdot's offer was accepted. It was sent to the Ripon Printing Press, Lahore, for printing sometime in the middle of 1939, after the Sind Muslim League had passed a resolution demanding creation of Pakistan openly, against Jinnah's wishes, it is said.*
>
> *"A manuscript of the book was sent to Mr Jinnah in Bombay also for approval. But Jinnah sent a telegram that he did not want the book to be named Pakistan. So, the printing of the book was hurriedly stopped as per Jinnah's wishes. Its contents were changed to show that the League did not want clean Partition but only a confederation of five federal states. The name was changed from Pakistan to Hindustan. It was meant to give the impression that Muslims were no foreigners in Hindustan.*

"Explaining the change, Mian Kifait Ali changed the name of the book to Confederacy of India and wrote in the new introduction, "the foreign element amongst us is quite negligible and we are as much sons of the soil as the Hindus are. Ultimately our destiny lies within India and not out of it. And it is for this reason that we have abstained from using the word 'Pakistan' and have instead used the word Hindustan to denote the North-Western Muslim block of provinces. Pakistan is a term which has somehow or other gathered round itself some unwholesome and alien associations which are far from our mind."

Evidently, these were the detailed remarks conveyed by Jinnah after sending the telegram. In fact, Jinnah was still considering the pros and cons of his demand and watching the reactions after the passage of the Sind Resolution. He did not use the word Pakistan till early 1941 even when the Lahore Resolution had been passed more than 20 months earlier. But then after that accepted it with a bang on the pretext that the Hindu Press and the Hindu leaders had made it popular and thrust the word on him and so he started openly advocating it. He forgot that it gave the impression of ethnic cleansing of Non-Muslims which the Pakistani Muslims actively engaged in with full help of the Army and the Police in 1947.

In fact, the word Pakistan had been in active circulation since 1933 when the Cambridge student Rahmat Ali first coined it and explained the ideology behind it-"to save the Soul of Islam from Hindu imperialism". He had sent his four-page pamphlet entitled NOW OR NEVER to the Joint Parliamentary Committee of the Third Round Table Conference so that some Englishman had made references to it in its proceedings. But Muslim members ridiculed it. Jinnah had heard of it as he was in London at that time then but kept quiet over it.

Since then, it had been a matter of active discussion in newspaper columns, especially in Punjab. The British-owned Civil and Military Gazette of Lahore had carried a discussion on it in its Readers' column for nearly two years 1933-35 when it was discussed threadbare by Muslims and Hindus alike. But in 1940, Jinnah pretended that Rahmat Ali's scheme did not exist and got the Lahore Resolution passed. The cat was thus, soon out of the bag as soon as he came out with its use in January 1941 for the first time. (Based on Rahmat Ali-A Biography by K.K. Aziz, Vanguard Books, The Mall, Lahore, pp. 375-79.)

One curious thing about the situation at Partition time was that the common people outside West Punjab knew more about the dire danger to Hindus and Sikhs there that those inside. People in West Punjab naturally did not want to leave their hearths and homes and take a leap in the dark. Moreover, they depended on the sermons and assurances of the Congress leaders to stick to their homes. Everybody thought they would be protected by the Indian Government. Very few thought it would be like leaving one's own country to the Paki enemy for ever.

So, I remember my cousins in Ludhiana who were in cloth business, constantly writing to us to come out at least by the end of July and to take out as many household goods, baggage etc. as possible. In response to this, my mother went to our ancestral place in Pind Dadan Khan, a four hour's journey from Jhelum, to bring out as much clothes and precious goods stored there as possible. There she met two influential family friends, friends of my deceased father, Dr. Nanak Chand and Lala Tara Chand the later being living in a glass palace like haveli. The son of late Dhere Shah, richest rais of the town, Tara Chand was known as Tare Shah. They advised her strongly to come to P.D. Khan with her three children, as they thought it was safer place than Jhelum. Raja Ghazanfar Ali had assured the people, no harm would come to anyone. But despite their best efforts, mercifully they failed to change her mind.

So, she brought two big steel trunks, full of precious clothes, and household goods to Jhelum and I was asked to take them to deposit them with my cousins in Ludhiana. It was third week of July. Trains were already running full to capacity. My maternal uncle who was railway guard helped them carry in luggage van while I sat in his cabin. Ultimately I did reach Ludhiana where my cousins took charge of the things. My cousins told me that there was common talk among Muslims there, that the Muslims of West Punjab would not to allow any Hindu or Sikh to come out alive. Fire arms and daggers were being sent to the goondas on the other side on large-scale.

Anyway, coming back to Pind Dadan Khan, its people were the target of two holocausts, not in the town itself but in the two trains that were detailed to carry them to India. The reason, Ghazanfar Ali Khan insisted that Hindu-Sikhs should not leave for Indian. He made it a matter of prestige as he had assured Jinnah and Gandhi to create a Hindu island in Pakistan. But after the usual charade of a few stabbing cases and the burning up of a row of Hindu shops, people became adamant to leave. Meanwhile, they shifted to a relief camp which had come up in the local temple.

Ghazanfar Ali had special grudge against the Dhere Shah family to whom he was heavily indebted. One of my childhood friends, Shri C.P. Nanda who retired as Chief Public Prosecutor at the District Courts of Delhi and was my class fellow upto 5th class when I studied in Pind Dadan Khan before shifting to Jhelum in 1940, tells me that Ghazanfar Ali was quite broke. Nanda knew this because the Raja's wife was a T.B. patient under the treatment of Nanda's father, a doctor. To cut the story short, when people led by the Dhere Shah family insisted on leaving, two trains were arranged. But one was attacked and looted at the very next station. Almost all passengers excepting those of the last compartment containing Dhere Shah family were killed. They were the real target as the attackers called their names, challenging them to come out. But they cronched under the seats and were saved.

Ghazanfar Ali Khan's terrible vengeance on Hindus of his native place for not staying on there. The other train was similarly treated at the notorious Kamoke railway station. Where out of 3000, only 300 survived in a totally shattered condition. They were looted and killed jointly by the mob, the army and the police. I have met only two of my old school fellows, who gave me these accounts. So this was Ghazanfar Ali's vengeance for not being obliged to create a Hindu museum in his estate. One can be sure that they too would also have been killed in due course if they had stayed on. Why were the Hindus and Sikhs of West Punjab unable to put up a powerful resistance against the Muslim marauders in 1947 except in a few pockets where the RSS was strong? The answer lies in the heavy imbalance of numbers. Rawalpindi division had only 15 per cent Hindus and Sikhs. In 11th and 12th centuries almost all Hindus had been finished in West Punjab. However, after peace was established, some came back there and settled as traders and shopkeepers. This was the pattern upto Central Asia. Only traders could survive. Moreover, as the noted historian, Prof. Gulshan Rai of S.D. College Lahore wrote in one of his articles in the Tribune, the Hindu society had lost its artisan class, the real fighting class. Because of Muslim conquests over the centuries, the conquerors set up new zamindars of their ethnic class. As a natural corrolary, the old artisan class and the peasantry (tenants) of the countryside shifted their loyalty to the new ruling classes for livelihood. The discriminatory religious policy made them change their religion for courtly favours. As a result we find, all the Kamins (menias) farm labourers and artisans like carpenters, tailors, cartmen daily wage earners, and even bakers becoming Muslims, in fact the entire riff raff and floating work force became Muslim as it gave them chance to loot the Hindus. There were group conversions. As it was a tribal society, one Chaudhuri bringing his whole caste or tribal brotherhood into Islamic fold to increase his class support. Thus lure of economic favours were a major factor in conversion.

JINNAH AFTER 1920

The year 1920 proved to be a turning point in the life of Jinnah, at that of India. It was the year when Gandhi promised swaraj in one year and got his noncooperative resolution passed by the Congress. When Jinnah stood up to oppose 'Mr. Gandhi's resolution' at the Nagpi session of the Congress he was "howled down with cries of shame shame. "Not 'Mr.' but say 'Mahatma'," the unwieldy crowd yelled. Jinnah taken aback, tried to argue but was shouted down. He left the stage disgust and the Congress for good, "the searing memory of his defeat at Nagpur permanently emblazoned on his mind". He waited for revenge. The importance of Jinnah remained outside the Congress. In 1923 and 1926, he was elected to the Central Legislature from Muslim constituencies His community still believed in him, and he decided to serve the

Mush: community with renewed vigour, as president of the Muslim League.

In 1924, he was appointed a member of the Maddiman Committee, which was to examine the working of India Act of 1919. He was also nominated a member of the Skeen Committee, along with Motilal Nehru which was to examine the problem of Indianisation of army officers. It was evident that the government considered him as one of the most important members of the Central Assembly. When in 1928, the All White Simon Commission visited India, the Jinnah faction of the Muslim League Joined the Congress in boycotting the commission which we appointed to assess the working of the 1919 Act and to propose further, legislation leading towards self-government. Simultaneously, the Al Parties Conference appointed a committee headed by Motilal Nehru in February 1928 "to report on the principle of a constitution for independent India". The committee submitted its report (later called Nehru Report) at the Lucknow meeting in August 1928. The main recommendation were: dominion status; joint electorates; weightage to minorities etc. The parties agreed to the proposals. But the agreement did not last long and when the conference met on 22 December 1928, Muslims under the leadership of Jinnah, made four new demands in the form of amendment These were thirty-three and a half percent representation for the Muslin in the Central Legislature; reservation of seats on population basis; Punjab and Bengal; residuary powers with the provincial government and separation of Sind from Bombay.

The amendments were turndown and Jinnah left the Conference disappointed calling it `parting of ways'. From Calcutta after wrecking the All-Parties Convention, he reached Delhi, to attend the All-Parties Muslim Conference. Aga Khan, who presided over the meeting, welcomed the prodigal to the Islamic fold. Jinnah's four points in Calcutta swelled to fourteen by the time he reached Delhi. The elaborate demands put forward in Jinnah's famous `fourteen points' were not yet Pakistan, "but almost its early embryo, within a weak federal womb." He threw away his nationalist and secular mask which he was wearing since the Lucknow Pact days. "I have no future in any Hindu dominated body," he declared. The Muslim League elected him lifelong president.

Jinnah sailed for England on 4 October 1930, along with his sister Fatima and daughter Dina, to attend the Round Table Conference as a Muslim nominee. There he put forward a wide range of demands of special Muslim interests contained in his fourteen points adding a few more to it.

The vision of Pakistan was getting clearer in his mind. It will remain a mystery why Jinnah was not invited to attend the Second and Third Round Table Conferences. But according to his own admission, "I was not invited to the later sittings of the Conference because I was the strongest opponent of the Federal Scheme". Disappointed, Jinnah decided to stay on in England to practice before the Privy Council but without much success. However, when the Communal Award was announced in 1932, all his fourteen points had been conceded by the British government and actually more concessions to the Muslims were given than what they had asked for.

At the request of several Muslim friends and well-wishers like Iqbal and Liaqat All, Jinnah returned to India in 1934 to lead the Muslim community. Muslims were in need of a dynamic and cunning leader. Between 1928 and 1936 many Muslim leaders of national stature died: Ajmal Khan, Muhammad All, M.A. Ansari, Shafi and Fazli Hussain. Sikandar Hyat Khan in Punjab and Fazlul Haq in Bengal were busy in provincial politics. The burden of rejuvenating the moribund Muslim League fell on Jinnah's shoulders and he seemed to like the role assigned to him. The Communal Award had given a new orientation to the communal politics in the country and Jinnah emerged as the saviour of the Muslim community In the Bombay session of the Muslim League (April 1936), a resolution was adopted rejecting the Federal Scheme c the 1935 Act while recommending the Provincial Scheme to be tried 'for what it is worth'. Elections to the provincial legislatures were held in 193 under the 1935 Act. The results of the elections were extremely disappointing from Jinnah's point of view. Of the 485 Muslim seats, the League could win only 108 seats in all the eleven provinces; the remaining Muslim seats went to other Muslim groups. Congress won almost all the 'general seats' and formed ministries in seven out of eleven province: The defeated Jinnah started vicious propaganda against the Congress ministries charging that inequities and injustices were being inflicted of the Muslims in the 'Hindu Raj'.

To add weight to the accusations, committee headed by Raja of Pirpur was formed to "look into the grievance of Muslims under Congress rule". Another committee was formed in Bihar to go into the details of Muslim suffering under Congress rule which was even more intemperate. "At this distance of time their truth or untruth matters little. What was important is the technique adopted by Jinnah to incite the Muslim masses by making them believe that 'Islam was in danger.'" The Muslim masses flocked to the League, the membership jumping from a few thousand to over hundred thousand in United Provinces alone.

Jinnah had become a mass leader, tens thousands of people greeting him with cries of Allah-o-Akbar and Quaid-e-Azam Zindabad. To Jinnah's delight, the Congress ministries decide to resign in November, 1939, after the War broke out. This, not a vet wise act of Congress, left the political field entirely to be exploited l; the Muslim League. Under Jinnah's orders the Muslims observed 2 December 1939 as the 'Day of Deliverance'.

Only a few months late Jinnah was bold enough to demand a separate area of the country for the 'Muslim nation' in the Lahore session of the Muslim League (Marc 1940). Pakistan had arrived. Henceforth, Pakistan became a passion an a mania with Jinnah. He evolved a strategy to deal with the Congress which puzzled and bewildered the Congress leaders and to a lesser degree the government. Every Congress error was irreversibly exploited Jinnah and the Congress led by Gandhi managed to commit many such errors during 1940-1947. "Never was the Gandhian leadership less relevant to practical politics; never did the Congress need more to recognise its own shortcoming".' Gandhi's launching the Quit India campaign (1942) without proper planning and the government, putting almost all the Congress leaders behind the bars, left the political arena open for Jinnah to exploit to achieve his end. The repeated contradictory announcements by Gandhi that Muslims have a right to ask for the division did help Jinnah to be adamant in demanding division of the country. The worst thing Gandhi did was to go to Jinnah's house in Bombay daily for eighteen days in September 1944 with the offer of Pakistan contained in the Rajaji Formula.

Jinnah, the superb tactician, humbled Gandhi on the last day of their meeting by pointing out that he (Gandhi) did not represent any political organization. Jinnah emerged as the most important leader to decide the destiny of the country. Even before Gandhi's disastrous journey to Jinnah's residence in 1944, several Congress leaders including Jawaharlal Nehru, Rajendra Prasad and Subhash Chandra Bose had tried to convince Jinnah about his unreasonable attitude, through correspondence and personal meetings. But Jinnah was adamant and wanted that the Congress recognize Muslim League as the sole representative of the Muslims.

Congress could not accept that because it claimed to represent all Indians irrespective of caste and creed. Jinnah's technique of getting the other man to make an offer so that he could turn it down and ask for more was difficult to counter and paid him rich dividends. His intransigence became a rewarding strategy and his obstinacy his great asset.

Through these tactics he almost got the Hindu majority reduced to a minority in legislature and services during the Simla Conference (1945) and Cabinet mission (1946) discussions. His greatest triumph came during the December 1945 elections for the Central Assembly in which Muslim League won all the Muslim seats in the Central Assembly securing eighty-seven percent of Muslim votes. There was a chance for India to remain united when the Congress and the Muslim League agreed to the proposals of the Cabinet Mission (March June, 1946). There was some dispute about the 'grouping' of provinces but that was almost resolved. However, a statement by Nehru on 10 July 1946 immediately after taking over as president of the Congress, that Constituent Assembly was a sovereign body and was capable of changing

The accepted plan, gave Jinnah an excuse to reject the Cabinet Mission proposals. Sensing that the vast majority of Muslims were with him he changed his strategy. In the last week of July, the

Muslim League Council met at Bombay and passed a resolution, the significant sentence of which was, "the time has come for the Muslim nation to resort to Direct Action to achieve Pakistan". When a correspondent asked Jinnah if the Direct Action would be violent or nonviolent, Jinnah retorted: "I am not going to discuss ethics." Direct Action was launched in Calcutta on 16 August 1946 as planned.

An orgy of violence, killings, stabbing, looting, arson and rape continued for three days, leaving five thousand dead. Gandhi's reaction to the Calcutta carnage was typical of him: "If through deliberate courage the Hindus had died to a man that would have been deliverance of Hinduism and India and purification of Islam in this land." The riots spread to East Bengal and then to several parts of India. When Hindus retaliated in Bihar, Jinnah was unnerved and on 20 November 1946 he pleaded for complete exchange of population. But the Congress leadership ignored his proposal. Though the Cabinet Mission proposals were rejected, formation of an Interim government and the Constituent Assembly were implemented by the Government. After initial reluctance, the Muslim League joined the Interim Government headed by Nehru but with more Muslim members than the Hindus. The League never participated in the Constituent Assembly of united India. While the Bihar riots were ruthlessly suppressed under Nehru's guidance, riots in other parts of the country continued and Jinnah looked the other way. The worst affected area was now Punjab. By March 1947, the riots became more serious and Hindus and Sikhs started leaving many parts of Panjab. Gandhi and his creed of nonviolence had made the task of Muslim League easier. Jinnah was speaking the language of Hitler. "The riots were a sufficient indication that gangsterism had become a settled part of their strategy in politics.

They seem to be consciously and deliberately imitating the Sudetan, Germans in the means employed by them against the Czecks". Congress leaders were utterly shaken and on 8 March 1947 they passed a resolution asking for the partition of Punjab and Bengal. This was virtually accepting partition of the country. At the same time the British were in a hurry to leave the country as after the War they were in no position to hold on to India. Things moved fast after that. The British Prime Minister, Attlee, announced in Parliament that the British will be leaving India by June 1948. They sent Lord Mountbatten as viceroy in March 1947 to wind up. He advanced the date to 14/15 August 1947. The country was divided on that day and two dominions, Bharat and Pakistan emerged, Jinnah accepting the 'mutilated and motheaten' Pakistan.

The last meeting of, the Muslim League was held in Delhi on 9-10 June 1947 in which Jinnah had a difficult time for the first time. He was accused of 'betrayal' for accepting partition of Punjab and Bengal. Khaksars tried to lynch him; the Muslim League National Guards coming to his rescue. But the most intriguing aspect about the creation of Pakistan is: How Jinnah could delude his co-religionists in Hindu majority provinces into believing that Pakistan was good for them.

Jinnah flew to Karachi along with his sister Fatima on 7 August 1947. His daughter Dina refused to accompany him as she had married a Parsi converted to Christianity, Neville Wadia owner of commercial and textile empire Bombay Dyeing. According to M.C. Chagla, when Jinnah learnt about his daughter's intention to marry a non-Muslim, he was furious said: "There are thousands of Muslim boys to choose from. Why you want to marry a non-Muslim?" The girl retorted, "Father: there were thousands of Muslim girls who would have liked to marry you, why did you marry a Parsi girl?" Jinnah had no answer to that. But he disowned his daughter and left most of his property to his sister Fatima. In poetic exuberance Sarojini Naidu had described Jinnah as an ambassador of Hindu-Muslim unity during the earlier decades of the last century but the label deserves scrutiny. Jinnah's actions and his concern for Muslim interests from the very beginning of his political career cast a doubt about his ever being a nationalist or a secularist.

Jinnah had appointed himself as governor-general of Pakistan. But he was a dying man and he knew that. Doctors had told him some years earlier that tuberculosis had devoured his lungs, and he did not have many years to live. During his thirteen months as Pakistan's governor general, he was fighting ill-health most of the time. He died on 11 September 1948 at Karachi. What kind of man was Jinnah? People who came to know him have assessed him in different ways. In July 1946, when Gandhi's biographer

Louis Fischer asked Gandhi, "What did you learn from your eighteen days with Jinnah?" (in September 1944). Gandhi replied, "I learned that he was a maniac. I could not make any headway with Jinnah because he is a maniac." Mountbatten, after a series of meetings with Jinnah reported to his staff that he considered, "Mr. Jinnah was a psychopathic case." And later added that "Until he had met Mr. Jinnah, he had not thought it possible that a man with such a complete lack of sense of responsibility could hold the power which he did". The reaction of Lord Ismay, Mountbatten's chief of staff, was, "the dominating feature in Mr. Jinnah's mental structure was his loathing and contempt of the Hindus. He apparently thought that all Hindus were sub-human creatures with whom it was impossible for the Muslims to live". Paying a left-handed compliment to Jinnah, VD. Savarkar said in one of his speeches, "Jinnah is a true representative and custodian of Muslim rights. Hindus needed a leader like Jinnah." B.R. Ambedkar gave a detailed assessment of Jinnah, "He (Jinnah) may be too self-opinionated, an egotist without the mask and has perhaps a degree of arrogance which is not compensated by any extraordinary intellect or equipment. It may be on that account he is unable to reconcile himself to a second place and work with others in that capacity for a public cause. He may not be overflowing with ideas although he is not, as his critics make him out to be, an empty headed dandy living upon the ideas of others. It may be that his fame is built up more upon art and less on substance. At the same time, it is doubtful if there is a politician in India to whom the adjective incorruptible can be more fittingly applied. No one can buy him". Jinnah was single-handedly pitted against Indian leaders whom we call 'great' like Gandhi, Nehru, Patel and Rajaji. All of them felt defeated against him.

JINNAH'S VISION OF PAKISTAN

For some years now, Quaid-e-Azam Jinnah's vision of Pakistan has been a source of controversy and conflict. Much of this has however tried to cut Jinnah to fit a predetermined image. A close look at Jinnah's long and chequered public life, encompassing some forty-four years (1904-48), helps determine the core values he was committed to throughout his political career. This chapter examines how Jinnah's politics evolved through main phases, which, though distinct, yet merged into the next, without sudden shifts. It analyses how his liberalism underwent an apparent paradigmatic shift from 1937 onwards, and led to him advocating the charismatic goal of Pakistan, and to elucidate it primarily in Islamic terms. Finally, the Islamic strain in his post independence pronouncements and his 11 August 1947 address is discussed, and an attempt made to reconcile it with his other pronouncements.

Jinnah as Liberal

In the first phase of his public life (1904-20) three main influences shaped Jinnah's personality and politics:

i. nineteenth century British liberalism, first absorbed during his four-years' (1892-96) stay in England as a student of law,
ii. the cosmopolitan atmosphere and mercantile background of metropolitan Bombay where he had established himself as an extremely successful barrister since the turn of the century, and
iii. his close professional and personal contact with the Parsis, who, though only a tiny community provided an example of how initiative, enterprise and hard work could overcome numerical inferiority, racial prejudice and communal barriers.

These formative influences seem to have prompted Jinnah to join the Indian National Congress. Fashioned after liberal principles and cast in their mould, the Congress was at that time pledged to take India on the road to self-government through constitutional means. Soon enough, he rose high in its echelons, high enough to be its 'spokesman' for its representation to the Secretary of State on the reform of the India Council in May 1914. Jinnah believed in moderation, gradualism, ordered progress, evolutionary politics, democratic norms, and above all, in constitutionalism. When the Congress sought to abandon these liberal principles in 1920 and opted for revolution and extra constitutional methods, he walked out of the Congress for good.

The constitutionalist in Jinnah led to him having a similar experience with the Home Rule League (HRL). He had collaborated with it since it was founded by Annie Besant, and joined it in a show of solidarity when Besant was interned in 1917. In October 1920 Mohandas Karamchand Gandhi, upon being elected HRL President on Jinnah's proposals, went about changing its constitution and its aims and objects and renaming it Swarajya Sabha rather unilaterally. Gandhi ruled out Jinnah's objections that the constitution could not be changed unless supported by a three-fourths majority, and without proper notice. Jinnah, along with nineteen other members resigned, charging that the "changes in the constitution were made by adopting a procedure contrary to the rules and regulations of the (HR) League."

Throughout this period, in fact since 1897, Jinnah was active in Anjuman-I-Islam, Muslim Bombay's foremost religio-political body. In 1906 Jinnah opposed the demand for separate electorates, but before long his opposition thawed when he realized that the demand had "the mandate of the community". In 1910 he was elected to the Imperial Council on a reserved Muslim seat. From then on, he came in close contact with Nadwah, Aligarh and the All India Muslim League (AIML), and he was chosen by the AIML to sponsor a bill on Waqf alal Aulad, a problem of deep concern to Muslims since the time of Syed Ahmad Khan. Though not yet a formal member of the League, Jinnah was yet able to get the League committed to the twin ideals of self-government and Hindu-Muslim unity during the next three years, thus bringing the AIML on par with the Congress in terms of its objectives.

He joined the AIML formally in October 1913 and became its President in 1916. He utilized his pivotal position to get the Congress and the League act in concert, and work out common solutions to problems confronting the country. One result of his efforts was the Congress-League, Lucknow Pact of 1916, which settled the controversial electorate issue, at least for the time being, and paved the way towards a entente cordiale between Hindus and Muslims. Another result was the holding of Congress and

League annual sessions at the same time and at the same place for seven years (1915-21).

It can be seen that there were three dominant strands in the first phase (1904-1920) of Jinnah's political career. These were a firm belief in a united Indian nationhood, with Hindus and Muslim sharing in the future Indian dispensation; a sense that Indian freedom could come through Hindu-Muslim unity, and a need for unity in Muslim ranks through strengthening the Muslim League. These strands continued in the second phase (1920-37) as well; but with the years their position came to be reversed in his scale of priorities, as the Congress's ultimate objectives underwent a radical change under the influence of Hindu extremists. Jinnah's efforts for Muslim unity became increasingly pronounced with the years, becoming a passion with him towards the closing of the second phase.

For Jinnah, while national freedom for both Hindus and Muslims continued to be the supreme goal, the means adopted to achieve it underwent a dramatic change. If it could not be achieved through Hindu Muslim unity, it must be done through Hindu-Muslim separation; if it could not be secured through a composite Hindu-Muslim nationalism, it must be done through separate Hindu and Muslim nationalisms; if not through a united India, it must be through partition. In either case, the ultimate objective was to ensure political power for Muslims.

Jinnah's Transformation

The period after 1937 marked a paradigmatic shift. Jinnah became identified in the Muslim mind with the concept of the charismatic community, the concept which answered their psychic need for endowing and sanctifying their sense of community with a sense of power. Increasingly he became the embodiment of a Muslim national consensus, which explains why and how he had become their Quaid-i-Azam, even before the launching of the Pakistan demand in March 1940.

This shift was squarely reflected in his thinking, his posture, his platform, and in his political discourse. And of course his appearance—for his public rallies Jinnah replaced his finely creased

English Saville Row suits with achkan, tight pyjamas and, to boot, a karakuli cap. He still believed in democracy, but now felt parliamentary democracy of the Westminster type was unsuitable for India because of the existence of a permanent majority and a permanent minority, which he defined in specific terms: Minorities means a combination of things. It may be that a minority has a different religion from the other citizens of a country. Their language may be different, their race may be different, their culture may be different, and the combination of all these various elements-religion, culture, race, language, arts, music and so forth makes the minority a separate entity in the State, and that separate entity as an entity wants safeguards.

Extending this elucidation, he occasionally called Muslims 'a nation', stressing their distinct religion, culture, language and civilization, and calling on them to "live or die as a nation". He even called the League flag 'the flag of Islam', arguing that "you cannot separate the Muslim League from Islam.

Jinnah also travelled across the other end of the political and ideological spectrum in other ways. Previously he had disdained mass politics, now he opted for mass politics. Previously he had objected to Gandhi's injection of religion into politics, now he was not averse to couch his appeals in Islamic terms and galvanising the Muslim masses by appealing to them in a cultural matrix they were familiar with. Previously he had called himself an Indian first and last, now he opted for an Islamic identity. Previously he had strived long and hard for a national consensus; now all his efforts were directed towards a Muslim consensus. Jinnah, the erstwhile "ambassador of Hindu-Muslim unity" became the fiercest advocate of Hindu-Muslim separation.

Jinnah had a political basis for this paradigmatic shift, through which Muslims and Islam came to occupy the centre of his discourse. For one thing, how else could Muslims, scattered as they were unevenly throughout the subcontinent, sharing with their non-Muslim neighbours local customs, ethos, languages, and problems and subjected to local conditions (whether political, social or economic) become a 'nation' except through their affiliation with Islam? For another, since Pakistan was to be established in the Muslim majority provinces, why else should the Muslims in the minority provinces struggle for Pakistan, except for their deep concern for the fate and future of Islam in India? Above all, what linked them irretrievably with their fellow Muslims in the majority areas except this concern?

In an address to Gaya Muslim League Conference in January 1938, Jinnah begun mapping out his new world view. He said: When we say 'This flag is the flag of Islam' they think we are introducing religion into politics-a fact of which we are proud. Islam gives us a complete code. It is not only religion but it contains laws, philosophy and politics, In fact, it contains everything that matters to a man from morning to night. When we talk of Islam we take it as an all embracing word. We do not mean any ill. The foundation of our Islamic code is that we stand for liberty, equality and fraternity.

Jinnah then used this to argue the case for Pakistan at two levels. First, he invoked the universally recognized principle of self-determination. But it was invoked not on the familiar territorial basis, but for the Muslim nation alone. As he stipulated in his marathon talks with Gandhi in September 1944, the constituency for the plebiscite to decide upon the Pakistan demand would comprise only the Muslims, and not the entire population of the areas concerned. Second, he spelled out his reasons for reaching out towards the 'Pakistan' goal in his Lahore (1940) address in more or less ideological terms, arguing that "Islam and Hinduism... are not religions in the strict sense of the word, but are... different and distinct social orders", that "the Hindus and Muslims belong to two different religious philosophies, social customs, literature", "to two different civilizations", that they "derive their inspiration from different sources of history"... (with) different epics, different heroes and different episodes." "We wish our people", he declared, "to develop to the fullest our spiritual, cultural, economic, social and political life in a way that we think best and in consonance with our own ideals and according to the genius of our people."

Jinnah developed this into a definition of Muslim nationhood that was most cogent, the most closely argued, and the most firmly based in international law since the time of Sir Syed Ahmad Khan.

"We are a nation," he wrote to Gandhi on 17 September 1944, "with our distinctive culture and civilization, language and literature, art and architecture, names and nomenclature, sense of values and proportion, legal laws and moral code, customs and calendar, history and traditions, aptitude and ambitions; in short, we have our own distinctive outlook on life and of life."

He returned to this more extensively in his Id message in September 1945, saying: "Everyone, except those who are ignorant, knows that the Quran is the general code of the Muslims. A religious, social, civil, commercial, military, judicial, criminal, penal code, it regulates everything from the ceremonies of religion to those of daily life; from the salvation of the soul to the health of the body; from the rights of all to those of each individual; from morality to crime, from punishment here to that in the life to come, and our Prophet has enjoined on us that every Musalman should possess a copy of the Quran and be his own priest. Therefore Islam is not merely confined to the spiritual tenets and doctrines or rituals and ceremonies. It is a complete code regulating the whole Muslim society, every department of life, collective [ly] and individually."

2

Jinnah: Reorganization of All India Muslim League

While in England, the Quaid had been watching the events that were happening in India and was saddened to see how Muslim interests were being sacrificed by the chaotic situation within the Muslim League. The Muslim League was in the hands of rich landlords or some middle class intellectuals with limited horizons, while the All India Congress was emerging as the leading party for Indian independence. In 1933, the "Now or Never" pamphlet by Choudhry Rehmat Ali was published in which the concept of a separate Muslim state was not only highlighted but the name "Pakistan" was also proposed for it. This motivated the young intellectuals of Aligarh and other universities to accelerate the growth of Muslim political consciousness throughout India.

Jinnah realized that organizing the Muslims of India into one powerful and dynamic organization was badly needed and that he would face enormous difficulties in that task. On March 4, 1934, in a combined meeting of various factions of the Muslim League, Delhi, the formation of one Muslim League was decided and Jinnah was elected as president of that Muslim League. He was given an enthusiastic welcome on his arrival in Delhi in April 1934.

He called a meeting of the All India Muslim League Council in Delhi in October 1934 and decisions were taken to prepare grounds for the radical transformation of the Muslim League into a mass party representative of all sections of the Muslim community.

After two trips to England in that year, Jinnah finally returned for good in December 1934. This was the start of a new era in India's struggle for independence. The All India Congress was not willing to acknowledge the Muslim cause and insisted on portraying only two parties in this regard, the Congress and the British. Jinnah emphasized the fact that the Congress could not win the battle of freedom until it gained the support of all the communities and assurance was not given to the minorities about their rights and protection of interest in an independent India.

On February 5, 1935 at a meeting of the Muslim Union at Aligarh, Jinnah said, "I am convinced and you will agree with me that the Congress policy is to divide the Muslims among themselves. It is the same old tactics of the British Government. They follow the policy of their masters. Don't fall into the trap. This is a moment of life and death for the Muslims...The Muslim League is determined to win freedom, but it should be a freedom not only for the strong and the dominant but equally for the weak and the suppressed." He performed two important tasks after his return from England; the first was to unite and activate the Muslim League as the sole representative body of the Muslims of India. The second was to continue the struggle for freedom of India on constitutional lines.

The reorganization of the Muslim League was a difficult task and he was faced with enormous difficulties including opposition from petty politicians with local interests, the propaganda of the Congress-paid nationalist Muslims and open hostility of leaders from different provinces of Muslim majority. He set an example of political and moral rectitude that was unparalleled in India. He meant what he said and was extremely honest in his dealings with friends and foes alike. He followed certain well-defined principles and nothing could persuade him to deviate from this path. He exercised his powers as president with due regard to democratic principles, acted according to the constitution of the Muslim League and never exceeded his powers as president.

1935-1939

The Quaid toured the whole country, visiting every corner of India, addressing meetings, meeting Muslim students, arguing with double-minded local leaders, exposing the policies of the Hindu Congress and slowly creating political consciousness among his people. Meanwhile, the Act of 1935 was passed that was a clear attempt to crush the forces working for democracy and freedom. Therefore, the Muslim League rejected it.

The provincial part of the constitution was however, accepted "for what it was worth". Jinnah concentrated on the constitutional struggle within the Legislative Assembly and advocated his point of view with great strength and skill. "I believe that it (the proposed federation) means nothing but absolute sacrifice of all that British India has stood for and developed during the last 50 years, in the matter of progress in the representative form of the Government. No province was consulted as such. No consent of the provinces has been obtained whether they are willing to federate as federating units on the terms which are laid down... by the British Government. My next objection is that it is not workable."

In order to strengthen the League, bolster its bargaining position, and help prepare it for contesting elections, Jinnah appointed and presided over a new Central Parliamentary Board and affiliated provincial parliamentary boards. These boards, similar to those earlier established by the Congress, were to become Jinnah's organizational arms in extending his power over the entire Muslim community.

In the 1937 elections, the Muslim League did not do well and won only 109 seats out of 482 it contested. The Muslim League failed to win majority in any of the Muslim provinces, where regional non-communal parties like the Unionists in the Punjab won majorities and formed ministries. The results of the elections demoralized many of the League leader. The only redeeming feature was that the Congress had miserably failed to gain any Muslim seat and it had only succeeded in gaining Hindu and Sikh seats in the Muslim provinces. The Congress had failed because it had made no effort to contact the Muslim masses, and was certain that politics based on economic issues would prevail in India. However, the conditions on which the Congress wanted to cooperate with the Muslim League were so humiliating that no self-respecting party could accept them.

The Congress was prepared to accept Muslims only if they ceased to have a separate political entity and were merged in the Hindu-dominated Congress. The Muslim League, of course, refused to do that for the sake of a few cabinet posts. The attitude of the Congress towards other parties opened the eyes of all sections of politically conscious people. The Unionists and other small parties who had been cold towards the Muslim League also changed their attitude within a year of the Congress taking control of power in the provinces. Fear of the dictatorial attitude of the Congress and the pressure of Muslim public opinion soon influenced local Muslim parties and one by one they came into the fold of the League or at least allied themselves with it.

THE ALL INDIA MUSLIM LEAGUE

The year 1906 was extremely important and eventful in the history of Indian nationalism. On 1st October, 1906, a deputation comprising of 35 Muslim leaders from all parts of India gathered in Simla to meet the new viceroy and place forth their appeal for help against the unconcerned attitude of the Hindus towards the needs and status of the Muslim majority in future political setup. They informed the viceroy about their hopes for the representation of Muslims in every branch of government. They further elaborated that the Muslims should not be regarded merely as a minority but a distinct community with strong historical and political background. The Viceroy was sympathetic to the demands of the group and applauded their loyal and articulate address. As a result of this meeting, the Muslims were promised separate electorates, which was a recognition of separate Muslim identity and proved a historical milestone in the making of Pakistan.

In the year 1906, a leading landlord of Dacca, Nawab Salimullah Khan invited the annual Mohammedan Educational Conference to be held in Dacca. The founding meeting of the All India Muslim League was held in Dacca's Shahbagh on December 30th, 1906. It was presided over by Nawab Viqar-ul-Mulk. The resolution was moved by the Nawab of Dacca, and was seconded by Hakim Ajmal Khan. Nawab Viqar-ul-mulk, who was the first president of the infant Muslim League, declared: "The musalmans are only a fifth in number as compared with the total population of the country, and it is manifest that if at any remote period the British government ceases to exist in India, then the rule of India would pass into the hands of that community which is nearly four times as large as ourselves ...our life, our property, our honour, and our faith will all be in great danger, when even now that a powerful British administration is protecting its subjects, we the Musalmans have to face most serious difficulties in safeguarding our interests from the grasping hands of our neighbours."

The main cause for the formation of the Muslim League was to safeguard and advance the rights and the welfare of the Muslim community and to convey their needs and problems to the government. The Muslims had realized that it was important for them to have a platform to voice their demands; their meeting with the Viceroy at Simla had already proved productive and fruitful. Another reason for the formation of the Muslim League was to prevent the rise of any kind of hostility among the Muslims towards other communities. Aga Khan was appointed the first honorary president of the Muslim League. The London branch of the League was also founded by Syed Ameer Ali.

The Realists and the Idealists

The Muslims at that point were divided into two groups. Firstly, there were the Idealists who believed that the Hindus and the Muslims could still work together to achieve their goals. These Idealists joined the Congress. The other group was that of the Realists who were convinced that the Congress was a biased platform which protected only the interests of the Hindus, which will ultimately lead to the Hindus ruling the Muslims. Jinnah attended the annual session of the Congress at Calcutta in 1906 along with other similar minded Muslims, Hindus, Parsis and the Christians. This meeting was presided over by Dadabhai Naoroji and M.A Jinnah acted as his secretary. Dadabhai claimed that by partitioning Bengal, the British had made a grave mistake, which must be remedied for the sake of the people of the subcontinent. Talking about the issue of the mounting distance between the Hindu and the Muslim communities, he said, "Once self-government is attained, then there will be prosperity enough for all, but not till then. The thorough union, therefore, of all the people for their emancipation is an absolute necessity." At that point Jinnah was a firm believer of this ideology and strongly advocated it. He therefore came to be known as the 'Ambassador of Hindu-Muslim unity'. With this stance in mind, he set out to accomplish the Congress's mission of uniting the two communities, which would ultimately help the Indians to achieve swaraj (self rule).

There was a split in the Congress led by the Maharashtra's Lokmanya, Bal Gangadhar Tilak, in the session held at Surat in 1907. Tilak had no confidence in the reforms promised by Morley and in protest his followers first rejected British-made goods and later boycotted their institutions too. They started protesting fervently for swaraj and became popular with the masses. The British government in an attempt to gain control over the situation arrested the prominent leaders of that movement which included Tilak. Tilak chose Jinnah to his case in the High Court and although the British government refused to hear anything on Tilak's behalf, Jinnah's exceptional skills as a barrister and orator were obvious in the way he presented his case. Also the depth of his character can be seen in the fact that he was willing to fight, to the best of his ability, for the leader of an oponent party. This earned him the respect and esteem of one of the most conformist leaders of the subcontinent at that time.

Jinnah was one of the few members to participate in the Viceroy's sixty-man Central Legislative Council in 1910. He represent Bombay. He was 35 at that time and was amongst the youngest members to join this high level council, again verifying his brilliance and standing. This was three years before when he actually joined the Muslim League. King George V annulled the partition of Bengal, in December 1911, leaving the Muslims of India with a feeling of betrayal as the highest officials of the government had assured them of its permanence.

MUSLIM LEAGUE REORGANIZED

Thus, the task that awaited Jinnah was anything but easy. The Muslim League was dormant: primary branches it had none; even its provincial organizations were, for the most part, ineffective and only nominally under the control of the central organization. Nor did the central body have any coherent policy of its own till the Bombay session **(1936)**, which Jinnah organized. To make matters worse, the provincial scene presented a sort of a jigsaw puzzle: in the Punjab, Bengal, Sindh, the North West Frontier, Assam, Bihar and the United Provinces, various Muslim leaders had set up their own provincial parties to serve their personal ends. Extremely frustrating as the situation was, the only consultation Jinnah had at this juncture was in Allama Iqbal **(1877-1938)**, the poet-philosopher, who stood steadfast by him and helped to charter the course of Indian politics from behind the scene.

Undismayed by this bleak situation, Jinnah devoted himself with singleness of purpose to organizing the Muslims on one platform. He embarked upon countrywide tours. He pleaded with provincial Muslim leaders to sink their differences and make common cause with the League. He exhorted the Muslim masses to organize themselves and join the League. He gave coherence and direction to Muslim sentiments on the Government of India Act, **1935**. He advocated that the Federal Scheme should be scrapped as it was subversive of India's cherished goal of complete responsible Government, while the provincial scheme, which conceded provincial autonomy for the first time, should be worked for what it was worth, despite its certain objectionable features. He also formulated a viable League manifesto for the election scheduled for early **1937**. He was, it seemed, struggling against time to make Muslim India a power to be reckoned with.

Despite all the manifold odds stacked against it, the Muslim League won some 108 (about 23 per cent) seats out of a total of 485 Muslim seats in the various legislature. Though not very impressive in itself, the League's partial success assumed added significance in view of the fact that the League won the largest number of Muslim seats and that it was the only all-India party of the Muslims in the country. Thus, the elections represented the first milestone on the long road to putting Muslim India on the map of the subcontinent. Congress in Power With the year **1937** opened the most mementoes decade in modern Indian history. In that year came into force the provincial part of the Government of India Act, 1935, granting autonomy to Indians for the first time, in the provinces.

The Congress, having become the dominant party in Indian politics, came to power in seven provinces exclusively, spurning the League's offer of cooperation, turning its back finally on the coalition idea and excluding Muslims as a political entity from the portals of power. In that year, also, the Muslim League, under Jinnah's dynamic leadership, was reorganized de novo, transformed into a mass organization, and made the spokesman of Indian Muslims as never before. Above all, in that momentous year were initiated certain trends in Indian politics, the crystallization of which in subsequent years made the partition of the subcontinent inevitable. The practical manifestation of the policy of the Congress which took office in **July, 1937**, in seven out of eleven provinces, convinced Muslims that, in the Congress scheme of things, they could live only on sufferance of Hindus and as "*second class*" citizens. The Congress provincial governments, it may be remembered, had embarked upon a policy and launched a PROGRAMME in which Muslims felt that their religion, language and culture were not safe. This blatantly aggressive Congress policy was seized upon by Jinnah to awaken the Muslims to a new consciousness, organize them on all-India platform, and make them a power to be reckoned with. He also gave coherence, direction and articulation to their innermost, yet vague, urges and aspirations. Above all, the filled them with his indomitable will, his own unflinching faith in their destiny.

The New Awakening

As a result of Jinnah's ceaseless efforts, the Muslims awakened from what Professor Baker calls (their) "*unreflective silence*" (in which they had so complacently basked for long decades), and to "*the spiritual essence of nationality*" that had existed among them for a pretty long time. Roused by the impact of successive Congress hammerings, the Muslims, as Ambedkar (principal author of independent India's Constitution) says, "*searched their social consciousness in a desperate attempt to find coherent and meaningful articulation to their cherished yearnings. To their great relief, they discovered that their sentiments of nationality had flamed into nationalism". In addition, not only had they developed*" the will to live as a "*nation*", had also endowed them with a territory which they could occupy and make a State as well as a cultural home for the newly discovered nation. These two prerequisites, as laid down by Renan, provided the Muslims with the intellectual justification for claiming a distinct nationalism (apart from Indian or Hindu nationalism) for themselves. So that when, after their long pause, the Muslims gave expression to their innermost yearnings, these turned out to be in favour of a separate Muslim nationhood and of a separate Muslim state.

LUCKNOW SESSION 1937

Jinnah utilized all his energies on revitalizing the League. With the assistance of the Raja of Mahmudabad, a dedicated adherent of the Muslim League, the Lucknow Session was a grand demonstration of the will of the Muslims of India to stand up to the Congress challenge.

Jinnah travelled by rail from Bombay, and as his train steamed into Kanpur Central Station "a vast crowd of Muslims mobbed his compartment," Jamil-ud-din Ahmad recalled: 'So exuberant was their enthusiasm and so fiery their determination to resist Hindu aggression that Mr. Jinnah, otherwise calm and imperturbable was visibly moved...His face wore a look of grim determination coupled with satisfaction that his people were aroused at last. He spoke a few soothing words to pacify their inflamed passions. Many Muslims, overcome by emotion, wept tears of joy to see their leader who, they felt sure, would deliver them from their bondage'.

He arrived in Lucknow on October 3, 1937, where twenty years before he had acted as a true Ambassador of Hindu-Muslim unity, heralding a bright era of Hindu-Muslim unity that lasted a little longer than World War I. Jinnah's speech at that historic session gave a resounding reply to the Congress policies and exposed the anti-Muslim acts of the Congress ministries.

Jinnah began, addressing the estimated 5,000 Muslims from every province of India: "This Session of the All-India Muslim League is one of the most critical that has ever taken place during its existence. The present leadership of the Congress, especially during the last 10 years, has been responsible for alienating the Muslims of India more and more, by pursuing a policy which is exclusively Hindu; they are in a majority, they have by their words, deeds and programme shown, more and more, the Muslims cannot expect any justice or fair play at their hands. Wherever they were in a majority and wherever it suited them, they refused to cooperate with the Muslim League parties and demanded unconditional surrender and signing of their pledges.

To the Muslims of India in every province, in every district, in every tehsil, in every town, I say: your foremost duty is to formulate a constructive and ameliorative programme of work for the people's welfare, and to devise ways and means for the social, economic and political uplift of the Muslims...Organize yourselves, establish your solidarity and complete unity. Equip yourselves as trained and disciplined soldiers. Create the feeling of an esprit de corps, and the cause of your people and your country. No individual or people can achieve anything without industry, suffering and sacrifice. There are forces that may bully you, tyrannize over you and intimidate you, and you may even have to suffer. But it is going through this crucible of the fire of persecution which may be levelled against you, the tyranny that may be exercised, the threats and intimidations that may unnerve you-it is by resisting, by overcoming, by facing these disadvantages, hardships and suffering, and maintaining your true glory and history, and will live to make its future history greater and glorious not only in India, but in the annals of the world. Eighty millions of Muslims in India have nothing to fear. They have their destiny in their hands, and as a well-knit, solid, organized, united force can face any danger, and withstand any opposition to its united front and wishes. There is a magic power in your hands. Take your vital decisions-they may be grave and momentous and far-reaching in their consequences. Think a hundred times before you take any decision, but once a decision is taken, stand by it as one man."

It was at the Lucknow Session that Jinnah persuaded Sir Sikander Hayat Khan to join the Muslim League along with his Muslim colleagues. That development later became famous as the Jinnah-Sikander Pact. This Session marked a dramatic change not only in the League's platform and political position, but also in Jinnah's personal commitment and final goal. He changed his attire, shedding the Seville Row suit in which he had arrived for a black Punjabi *sherwani* long coat. It was for the first time he put on the compact cap, which would soon be known throughout the world as "Jinnah cap". It was at that session that the title of Quaid-i-Azam (the great leader) was used for Jinnah and which soon gained such currency and popularity that it almost became a substitute for his name.

The great success was achieved the organization front of the Muslim league. Within three months of the Lucknow session over 170 new branches of the League had been formed, 90 of them in the United Provinces, and it claimed to have enlisted 100,000 new members in the province alone.

Allama Iqbal in last years of his life was a pillar of strength to Jinnah. He was an influential man and his poetry had made a place for itself in the hearts and minds of the people of India and abroad and had a special appeal for the Muslims. He was not an active, practical politician, but he could not remain indifferent to the Muslim majority provinces. In his letter of 28 May, 1937 he wrote to Jinnah to concentrate on Muslim majority provinces. He recognized in Jinnah the man chosen to lead the Muslims. "You are the only Muslim in India today to whom the community has a right to look up for safe guidance through the storm which is coming to North-West India, and perhaps the whole of India."

JINNAH'S 1940 ADDRESS TO THE MUSLIM LEAGUE

Ladies and Gentlemen: We are meeting today in our session after fifteen months. The last session of the All-India Muslim League took place at Patna in December 1938. Since then many developments have taken place. I shall first shortly tell you what the All-India Muslim League had to face after the Patna session of 1938. You remember that one of the tasks, which was imposed on us and which is far from completed yet, was to organise Muslim Leagues all over India. We have made enormous progress during the last fifteen months in this direction. I am glad to inform you that we have established provincial leagues in every province. The next point is that in every bye-election to the Legislative Assemblies we had to fight with powerful opponents. I congratulate the Musalmans for having shown enormous grit and spirit throughout our trials. There was not a single bye-election in which our opponents won against Muslim League candidates. In the last election to the U.P. Council, that is the Upper Chamber, the Muslim League's success was cent per cent. I do not want to weary you with details of what we have been able to do in the way of forging ahead in the direction of organising the Muslim League. But I may tell you that it is going up by leaps and bounds.

Next, you may remember that we appointed a committee of ladies at the Patna session. It is of very great importance to us, because I believe that it is absolutely essential for us to give every opportunity to our women to participate in our struggle of life and death. Women can do a great deal within their homes, even under purdah. We appointed this committee with a view to enable them to participate in the work of the League. The objects of this central committee were: (1) to organise provincial and district women's sub-committees under the provincial and district Muslim Leagues: (2) to enlist a larger number of women to the membership of the Muslim League: (3) to carryon an intensive propaganda amongst Muslim women throughout India in order to create in them a sense of a greater political consciousness—because if political consciousness is awakened amongst our women, remember your children will not have much to worry about: (4) to advise and guide them in all such matters as mainly rest on them for the uplift of Muslim society. This central committee, I am glad to say, started its work seriously and earnestly. It has done a great deal of useful work. I have no doubt that when we come to deal with their report of work done we shall really feel grateful to them for all the services that they have rendered to the Muslim League.

We had many difficulties to face from January 1939 right up to the declaration of war. We had to face the Vidya Mandir in Nagpur. We had to face the Wardha Scheme all over India. We had to face ill-treatment and oppression to Muslims in the Congress-governed provinces. We had to face the treatment meted out to Muslims in some of the Indian States such as Jaipur and Bhavnagar.

We had to face a vital issue that arose in that little state of Rajkot. Rajkot was the acid test made by the Congress which would have affected one-third of India. Thus the Muslim League had all along to face various issues from January 1939 up to the time of the declaration of war. Before the war was declared the grratcst danger to the Muslims of India was the possible inauguration of the federal scheme in the central Government. We know what machinations were going on. But the Muslim League was stoutly resisting them in every direction.

We felt that we could never accept the dangerous scheme of the central federal Government embodied in the Government of India Act, 1935. I am sure that we have made no small contribution towards persuading the British Government to abandon the scheme of central federal government. In creating that [state of] mind in the British Government, the Muslim League, I have no doubt, played no small part. You know that the British people are very obdurate people. They are also very conservative; and although they are very clever, they are slow in understanding. After the war was declared, the Viceroy naturally wanted help from the Muslim League. It was only then that he realised that the Muslim League was a power. For it will be remembered that up to the time of the declaration of war, the Viceroy never thought of me but of Gandhi and Gandhi alone. I have been the leader of an important party in the Legislature for a considerable time, larger than the one I have the honour to lead at present, the present Muslim League Party in the Central Legislature. Yet the Viceroy never thought of me. Therefore, when I got this invitation from the Viceroy along with Mr. Gandhi, I wondered within myself why I was so suddenly promoted, and then I concluded that the answer was the 'All-India Muslim League' whose President I happen to be. I believe that was the worst shock that the Congress High Command received, because it challenged their sole authority to speak on behalf of India. And it is quite clear from the attitude of Mr. Gandhi and the High Command that they have not yet recovered from that shock. My point is that I want you to realise the value, the importance, the significance of organising ourselves. I will not say anything more on the subject.

But a great deal yet remains to be done. I am sure from what I can see and hear that the Muslim India is now conscious, is now awake, and the Muslim League has by now grown into such a strong institution that it cannot be destroyed by anybody, whoever he may happen to be. Men may come and men may go, but the League will live for ever.

Now, coming to the period after the declaration of war, our position was that we were between the devil and the deep sea. But I do not think that the devil or the deep sea is going to get away with it. Anyhow our position is this. We stand unequivocally for the freedom of India. But it must be freedom of all India and not freedom of one section or, worse still, of the Congress caucus—and slavery of Musalmans and other minorities.

Situated in India as we are, we naturally have our past experiences and particularly the experiences of the past 2 1/2 years of provincial constitution in the Congress-governed provinces. We have learnt many lessons. We are now, therefore, very apprehensive and can trust nobody. I think it is a wise rule for every one not to trust anybody too much. Sometimes we are led to trust people, but when we find in actual experience that our trust has been betrayed, surely that ought to be sufficient lesson for any man not to continue his trust in those who have betrayed him. Ladies and gentlemen, we never thought that the Congress High Command would have acted in the manner in which they actually did in the Congress-governed provinces. I never dreamt that they would ever come down so low as that. I never could believe that there would be a gentleman's agreement between the Congress and the Government to such an extent that although we cried [ourselves] hoarse, week in and week out, the Governors were supine and the Governor-General was helpless. We reminded them of their special responsibilities to us and to other minorities, and the solemn pledges they had given to us. But all that had become a dead letter. Fortunately, Providence came to our help, and that gentleman's, agreement was broken to pieces and the Congress, thank Heaven, went out of office. I think they are regretting their resignations very much. Their bluff was called off [=was called]. So far so good. I therefore appeal to you, in all [the] seriousness that I can command, to organise yourselves in such a way that you may depend upon none except your own inherent strength. That is your only safeguard, and the best safeguard. Depend upon yourselves. That does not mean that we should have ill-will or malice towards others. In order to safeguard your rights and interests you must create that strength in yourselves [such] that you may be able to defend yourselves, That is all that I want to urge.

Now, what is our position with regard to [a] future constitution? It is that as soon as circumstances permit, or immediately after the war at the latest, the whole problem of India's future constitution must be examined *de novo* and the Act of 1935 must go once for all. We do not believe in asking the British Government to make declarations. These declarations are really of no use. You cannot possibly succeed in getting the British Government out of this country by asking them to make declarations. However, the Congress asked the Viceroy to make a declaration. The Viceroy said, 'I have made the declaration'. The Congress said, 'No, no. We want another kind of declaration. You must declare now and at once that India is free and independent with the right to frame its own constitution by a Constituent Assembly to be elected on the basis of adult franchise or as low a franchise as possible.

This Assembly will of course satisfy the minorities' legitimate interests." Mr. Gandhi says that if the minorities are not satisfied then he is willing that some tribunal of the highest character and most impartial should decide the dispute. Now, apart from the impracticable character of this proposal and quite apart from the fact that it is historically and constitutionally absurd to ask [a] ruling power to abdicate in favour of a Constituent Assembly. Apart from all that, suppose we do not agree as to the franchise according to which the Central Assembly is to be elected, or suppose the solid body of Muslim representatives do not agree with the non-Muslim majority in the Constituent Assembly, what will happen? It is said that we have no right to disagree with regard to anything that this Assembly may do in framing a national constitution of this huge subcontinent except those matters which may be germane to the safeguards for the minorities. So we are given the privilege to disagree only with regard to what may be called strictly safeguards of the rights and interests of minorities. We are also given the privilege to send our own representatives by separate electorates. Now, this proposal is based on the assumption that as soon as this constitution comes into operation the British hand will disappear. Otherwise there will be no meaning in it. Of course, Mr. Gandhi says that the constitution will decide whether the British will disappear, and if so to what extent. In other words, his proposal comes to this: First, give me the declaration that we are a free and independent nation, then I will decide what I should give you back.

Does Mr. Gandhi really want the complete independence of India when he talks like this? But whether the British disappear or not, it follows that extensive powers must be transferred to the people. In the event of there being a disagreement between the majority of the Constituent Assembly and the Musalmans, in the first instance, who will appoint the tribunal? And suppose an agreed tribunal is possible and the award is made and the decision given, who will, may I know, be there to see that this award is implemented or carried out in accordance with the terms of that award? And who will see that it is honoured in practice, because, we are told, the British will have parted with their power mainly or completely? Then what will be the sanction behind the award which will enforce it? We come back to the same answer, the Hindu majority would do it; and will it be with the help of the British bayonet or the Gandhi's "Ahimsa"? Can we trust them any more? Besides, ladies and gentlemen, can you imagine that a question of this character, of social contract upon which the future constitution of India would be based, affecting 90 million of Musalmans, can be decided by means of a judicial tribunal? Still, that is the proposal of the Congress.

Before I deal with what Mr. Gandhi said a few days ago I shall deal with the pronouncements of some of the other Congress leaders—each one speaking with a different voice. Mr. Rajagopalacharya, the ex-Prime Minister of Madras, says that the only panacea for Hindu-Muslim unity is the joint electorates. That is his prescription as one of the great doctors of the Congress organisation. (*Laughter.*) Babu Rajendra Prasad, on the other hand, only a few days ago said, "Oh, what more do the Musalmans want?" I will read to you his words. Referring to the minority question, he says: "If Britain would concede our right of self-determination, surely all these differences would disappear." How will our differences disappear? He does not explain or enlighten us about it.

"But so long as Britain remains and holds power, the differences would continue to exist. The Congress has made it clear that the future constitution would be framed not by the Congress alone but by representatives of all political parties and religious groups. The Congress has gone further and declared that the minorities can have their representatives elected for this purpose by separate electorates, though the Congress regards separate electorates as an evil. It will be representative of all the peoples of this country, irrespective of their religion and political affiliations, who will be deciding the future constitution of India, and not this or that party. What better guarantees can the minorities have?"

So according to Babu Rajendra Prasad, the moment we enter the Assembly we shall shed all our political affiliations, and religions, and everything else. This is what Babu Rajendra Prasad said as late as 18th March, 1940. And this is now what Mr. Gandhi said on the 20th of March, 1940. He says: "To me, Hindus, Muslims, Parsis, Harijans, are all alike. I cannot be frivolous"—but I think he is frivolous—"I cannot be frivolous when I talk of Quaid-i-Azam Jinnah.

He is my brother." The only difference is this that brother Gandhi has three votes and I have only one vote. (*Laughter.*) "I would be happy indeed if he could keep me in his pocket." I do not know really what to say of this latest offer of his. "There was a time when I could say that there was no Muslim whose confidence I did not enjoy. It is my misfortune that it is not so today." Why has he lost the confidence of the Muslims today? May I ask, ladies and gentlemen? "I do not read all that appears in the Urdu Press, but perhaps I get a lot of abuse there. I am not sorry for it. I still believe that without Hindu-Muslim settlement there can be no Swaraj." Mr. Gandhi has been saying this now for the last 20 years.

"You will perhaps ask in that case why do I talk of a fight. I do so because it is to be a fight for a Constituent Assembly."

[He is fighting the British. But may I point out to Mr. Gandhi and the Congress that you are fighting for a Constituent Assembly which the Muslims say they cannot accept; which, the Muslims say, means three to one; about which the Musalmans say that they will never be able, in that way by the counting of head, to come to any agreement which will be real agreement from the hearts, which will enable us to work as friends; and therefore this idea of a Constituent Assembly is objectionable, apart from other objections. But he is fighting for the Constituent Assembly, not fighting the Musalmans at all! He says, "I do so because it is to be a fight for a Constituent Assembly. If Muslims who come to the Constituent Assembly"—mark the words, "who come to the Constituent Assembly through Muslim votes"—he is first forcing us to come to that Assembly, and then says—"declare that there is nothing common between Hindus and Muslims, then alone I would give up all hope, but even then I would agree with them because they read the Quran and I have also studied something of that holy Book." (*Laughter.*)

So he wants the Constituent Assembly for the purpose of ascertaining the views of the Musalmans; and if they do not agree then he will give up all hopes, but even then he will agree with us. (*Laughter.*) Well, I ask you. Ladies and gentlemen, is this the way to show any real genuine desire, if there existed any, to come to a settlement with the Musalmans? (*Voices of no, no.*) Why does not Mr. Gandhi agree, and I have suggested to him more than once and I repeat it again from this platform, why does not Mr. Gandhi honestly now acknowledge that the Congress is a Hindu Congress, that he does not represent anybody except the solid body of Hindu people? Why should not Mr. Gandhi be proud to say. "I am a Hindu. Congress has solid Hindu backing"? I am not ashamed of saying that I am a Musalman. (*Hear, hear and applause.*) I am right and I hope and I think even a blind man must have been convinced by now that the Muslim League has the solid backing of the Musalmans of India (*Hear, hear.*) Why then all this camouflage? Why all these machinations? Why all these methods to coerce the

British to overthrow the Musalmans? Why this declaration of noncooperation? Why this threat of civil disobedience? And why fight for a Constituent Assembly for the sake of ascertaining whether the Musalmans agree or they do not agree? (*Hear, hear.*) Why not come as a Hindu leader proudly representing your people, and let me meet you proudly representing the Musalmans? (*Hear, hear and applause.*) This all that I have to say so far as the Congress is concerned.

So far as the British Government is concerned, our negotiations are not concluded yet, as you know. We had asked for assurances on several points. At any rate, we have made some advance with regard to one point and that is this. You remember our demand was that the entire problem of [the] future constitution of India should be examined *de novo*, apart from the Government of India Act of 1935. To that the Viceroy's reply, with the authority of His Majesty's Government, was—I had better quote that—I will not put it in my own words: This is the reply that was sent to us on the 23rd of December. "My answer to your first question is that the declaration I made with the approval of His Majesty's Government on October the 13th last does not exclude—Mark the words— "does not exclude examination of any part either of the Act of 1935 or of the policy and plans on which it is based." (*Hear, hear.*)

As regards other matters, we are still negotiating and the most important points are: (1) that no declaration should be made by His Majesty's Government with regard to the future constitution of India without our approval and consent (*Hear, hear, and applause*) and that no settlement of any question should be made with any party behind our back (*Hear, hear*) unless our approval and consent is given to it. Well, ladies and gentlemen, whether the British Government in their wisdom agree to give us that assurance or not, but. I trust that they will still see that it is a fair and just demand when we say that we cannot leave the future fate and the destiny of 90 million of people in the hands of any other judge.— We and we alone wish to be the final arbiter. Surely that is a just demand. We do not want that the British Government should thrust upon the Musalmans a constitution which they do not approve of and to which they do not agree. Therefore the British Government will be well advised to give that assurance and give the Musalmans complete peace and confidence in this matter and win their friendship. But whether they do that or not, after all, as I told you before, we must depend on our own inherent strength; and I make it plain from this platform, that if any declaration is made, if any interim settlement is made without our approval and without our consent, the Musalmans of India will resist it. (*Hear, hear and applause.*) And no mistake should be made on that score.

Then the next point was with regard to Palestine. We are told that endeavours, earnest endeavours, are being made to meet the reasonable, national demands, of the Arabs. Well, we cannot be satisfied by earnest endeavours, sincere endeavours, best endeavours. (*Laughter.*) We want that the British Government should in fact and actually meet the demands of the Arabs in Palestine. (*Hear, hear.*)

Then the next point was with regard to the sending of the troops. Here there is some misunderstanding. But anyhow we have made our position clear that we never intended, and in fact language does not justify it if there is any misapprehension or apprehension, that the Indian troops should not be used to the fullest in the defence of our own country. What we wanted the British Government to give us assurance of was that Indian troops should not be sent against any Muslim country or any Muslim power. (*Hear, hear.*) Let us hope that we may yet be able to get the British Government to clarify the position further.

This, then, is the position with regard to the British Government. The last meeting of the Working Committee had asked the Viceroy to reconsider his letter of the 23rd of December, having regard to what has been explained to him in pursuance of the resolution of the Working Committee dated the 3rd of February; and we are informed that the matter is receiving his careful consideration. Ladies and Gentlemen, that is where we stand after the War and up to the 3rd of February.

As far as our internal position is concerned, we have also been examining it, and you know. There are several schemes which have been sent by various well-informed constitutionalists and others who take interest with [=are interested in the] problem of India's future Constitution; and we have also appointed a sub-committee to examine the details of the schemes that have come in so far. But one thing is quite clear: it has always been taken for granted mistakenly that the Musalmans are a minority, and of course we have got used to it for such a long time that these settled notions sometimes are very difficult to remove. The Musalmans are not a minority. The Musalmans are a nation by any definition. The British and particularly the Congress proceed on the basis, "Well, you are a minority after all, what do you want!" "What else do the minorities want?" just as Babu Rajendra Prasad said. But surely the Musalmans are not a minority. We find that even according to the British map of India we occupy large parts of this country where the Musalmans are in a majority, such as Bengal, Punjab, N.W.F.P., Sind, and Balochistan.

Now the question is, what is the solution of this problem between the Hindus and the Musalmans? We have been considering, and as I have already said, a committee has been appointed to consider the various proposals. But whatever the final scheme of constitution, I will present to you my views, and I will just read to you in confirmation of what I am going to put before you, a letter from Lala Lajpat Rai to Mr. C. R. Das. It was written, I believe, about 12 or 15 years ago, and that letter has been produced in a book recently published by one Indra Prakash, and that is how this letter has come to light. This is what Lala Lajpat Rai, a very astute politician and a staunch Hindu Mahasabite, said. But before I read his letter it is plain from [it] that you cannot get away from being a Hindu if you are a Hindu. (*Laughter.*) The word 'nationalist' has now become the play of conjurers in politics. This is what he says: "There is one point more which has been troubling me very much of late and one [about] which I want you to think carefully and that is the question of Hindu-Muhammadan unity. I have devoted most of my time during the last six months to the study of Muslim history and Muslim law and I am inclined to think it is neither possible nor practicable. Assuming and admitting the sincerity of Muhammadan leaders in the noncooperation movement I think their religion provides an effective bar to anything of the kind.

"You remember the conversation I reported to you in Calcutta which I had with Hakim Ajmal Khan and Dr. Kitchlew. There is no finer Muhammadan in Hindustan than Hakim Ajmal Khan, but can any Muslim leader over-ride the Quran? I can only hope that my reading of Islamic law is incorrect.

I think his reading is quite incorrect. "And nothing would relieve me more than to be convinced that it is so. But if it is right then it comes to this, that although we can unite against the British we cannot do so to rule Hindustan on British lines. We cannot do so to rule Hindustan on democratic lines."

Ladies and gentlemen, when Lala Lajpat Rai said that we cannot rule this country on democratic lines it was all right; but when I had the temerity to speak the same truth about eighteen months ago, there was a shower of attacks and criticism. But Lala Lajpat Rai said fifteen years ago that we cannot do so—*viz.*, rule Hindustan on democratic lines. What is the remedy? The remedy, according to Congress, is to keep us in the minority and under the majority rule. Lala Lajpat Rai proceeds further:

"What is then the remedy? I am not afraid of the seven crores [=70 million] of Musalmans. But I think the seven crores in Hindustan plus the armed hordes of Afghanistan, Central Asia, Arabia, Mesopotamia and Turkey, will be irresistible." (*Laughter.*)

"I do honestly and sincerely believe in the necessity or desirability of Hindu-Muslim unity. I am also fully prepared to trust the Muslim leaders. But what about the injunctions of the Koran and Hadis? The leaders cannot over-ride them. Are we then doomed? I hope not. I hope your learned mind and wise head will find some way out of this difficulty."

Now, ladies and gentlemen, that is merely a letter written by one great Hindu leader to another great Hindu leader fifteen years ago. Now, I should like to put before you my views on the subject as it strikes me, taking everything into consideration at the present moment. The British Government and Parliament, and more so the British nation, have been for many decades past brought up and nurtured with settled notions about India's future, based on developments in their own country which has built up the British constitution, functioning now through the Houses of Parliament and the system of [the] cabinet. Their concept of party government functioning on political planes has become the ideal with them as the best form of government for every country, and the one-sided and powerful propaganda, which naturally appeals to the British, has led them into a serious blunder, in producing a constitution envisaged in the Government of India Act of 1935. We find that the most leading statesmen of Great Britain, saturated with these notions, have in their pronouncements seriously asserted and expressed a hope that the passage of time will harmonise the inconsistent elements in India.

A leading journal like the *London Times*, commenting on the Government of India Act of 1935, wrote that "Undoubtedly the difference between the Hindus and Muslims is not of religion in the strict sense of the word but also of law and culture, that they may be said indeed to represent two entirely distinct and separate civilisations. However, in the course of time the superstitions will die out and India will be moulded into a single nation." (So according to the *London Times* the only difficulties are superstitions). These fundamental and deep-rooted differences, spiritual, economic, cultural, social, and political have been euphemised as mere "superstitions." But surely it is a flagrant disregard of the past history of the subcontinent of India, as well as the fundamental Islamic conception of society vis-a-vis that of Hinduism, to characterise them as mere "superstitions." Notwithstanding [a] thousand years of close contact, nationalities which are as divergent today as ever, cannot at any time be expected to transform themselves into one nation merely by means of subjecting them to a democratic constitution and holding them forcibly together by unnatural and artificial methods of British Parliamentary statutes. What the unitary government of India for one hundred fifty years had failed to achieve cannot be realised by the imposition of a central federal government. It is inconceivable that the fiat or the writ of a government so constituted can ever command a willing and loyal obedience throughout the subcontinent by various nationalities, except by means of armed force behind it.

The problem in India is not of an inter-communal character, but manifestly of an international one, and it must be treated as such. So long as this basic and fundamental truth is not realised, any constitution that may be built will result in disaster and will prove destructive and harmful not only to the Musalmans, but to the British and Hindus also. If the British Government are really in earnest and sincere to secure [the] peace and happiness of the people of this subcontinent, the only course open to us all is to allow the major nations separate homelands by dividing India into "autonomous national states." There is no reason why these states should be antagonistic to each other. On the other hand, the rivalry, and the natural desire and efforts on the part of one to dominate the social order and establish political supremacy over the other in the government of the country, will disappear. It will lead more towards natural goodwill by international pacts between them, and they can live in complete harmony with their neighbours. This will lead further to a friendly settlement all the more easily with regard to minorities, by reciprocal arrangements and adjustments between Muslim India and Hindu India, which will far more adequately and effectively safeguard the rights and interests of Muslim and various other minorities.

It is extremely difficult to appreciate why our Hindu friends fail to understand the real nature of Islam and Hinduism. They are not religions in the strict sense of the word, but are, in fact, different and distinct social orders; and it is a dream that the Hindus and Muslims can ever evolve a common nationality; and this misconception of one Indian nation has gone far beyond the limits and is the cause of more of our troubles and will lead India to destruction if we fail to revise our notions in time. The Hindus and Muslims belong to two different religious philosophies, social customs, and literature[s]. They neither intermarry nor interdine together, and indeed they belong to two different civilisations which are based mainly on conflicting ideas and conceptions. Their aspects [=perspectives?] on life, and of life, are different. It is quite clear that Hindus and Musalmans derive their inspiration from different sources of history. They have different epics, their heroes are different, and different episode[s]. Very often the hero of one is a foe of the other, and likewise their victories and defeats overlap. To yoke together two such nations under a single state, one as a numerical minority and the other as a majority, must lead to growing discontent, and final destruction of any fabric that may be so built up for the government of such a state.

History has presented to us many examples, such as the Union of Great Britain and Ireland, Czechoslovakia, and Poland. History has also shown to us many geographical tracts, much smaller than the subcontinent of India, which otherwise might have been called one country, but which have been divided into as many states as there are nations inhabiting them. [The] Balkan Peninsula comprises as many as seven or eight sovereign states. Likewise, the Portuguese and the Spanish stand divided in the Iberian Peninsula. Whereas under the plea of unity of India and one nation which does not exist, it is sought to pursue here the line of one central government, when we know that the history of the last twelve hundred years has failed to achieve unity and has witnessed, during these ages, India always divided into Hindu India and Muslim India. The present artificial unity of India dates back only to the British conquest and is maintained by the British bayonet, but the termination of the British regime, which is implicit in the recent declaration of His Majesty's Government, will be the herald of the entire break-up, with worse disaster than has ever taken place during the last one thousand years under the Muslims. Surely that is not the legacy which Britain would bequeath to India after one hundred fifty years of her rule, nor would Hindu and Muslim India risk such a sure catastrophe.

Muslim India cannot accept any constitution which must necessarily result in a Hindu majority government. Hindus and Muslims brought together under a democratic system forced upon the minorities can only mean Hindu Raj. Democracy of the kind with which the Congress High Command is enamoured would mean the complete destruction of what is most precious in Islam. We have had ample experience of the working of the provincial constitutions during the last two and a half years, and any repetition of such a government must lead to civil war and [the] raising of private armies, as recommended by Mr. Gandhi to [the] Hindus of Sukkur when he said that they must defend themselves violently or nonviolently, blow for blow, and if they could not they must emigrate.

Musalmans are not a minority as it is commonly known and understood. One has only got to look round. Even today, according to the British map of India, out of eleven provinces, four provinces where the Muslims dominate more or less, are functioning notwithstanding the decision of the Hindu Congress High Command to non-cooperate and prepare for civil disobedience. Musalmans are a nation according to any defamation of a nation, and they must have their homelands, their territory, and their state. We wish to live in peace and harmony with our neighbours as a free and independent people. We wish our people to develop to the fullest our spiritual, cultural, economic, social, and political life, in a way that we think best and in consonance with our own ideals and according to the genius of our people. Honesty demands [that we find], and [the] vital interest[s] of millions of our people impose a sacred duty upon us to find, an honourable and peaceful solution, which would be just and fair to all. But at the same time we cannot be moved or diverted from our purpose and objective by threats or intimidations. We must be prepared to face all difficulties and consequences, make all the sacrifices that may be required of us, to achieve the goal we have set in front of us.

Ladies and gentlemen, that is the task before us. I fear I have gone beyond my time limit. There are many things that I should like to tell you, but I have already published a little pamphlet containing most of the things that I have said and I have been saying, and I think you can easily get that publication both in English and in Urdu from the League Office. It might give you a clearer idea of our aims. It contains very important resolutions of the Muslim League and various other statements. Anyhow, I have placed before you the task that lies ahead of us. Do you realise how big and stupendous it is? Do you realise that you cannot get freedom or independence by mere arguments? I should appeal to the intelligentsia. The intelligentsia in all countries in the world have been the pioneers of any movements for freedom. What does the Muslim intelligentsia propose to do? I may tell you that unless you get this into your blood, unless you are prepared to take off your coats and are willing to sacrifice all that you can and work selflessly, earnestly, and sincerely for your people, you will never realise your aim. Friends, I therefore want you to make up your mind definitely, and then think of devices and organise your people, strengthen your organisation, and consolidate the Musalmans all over India. I think that the masses are wide awake. They only want your guidance and your lead. Come forward as servants of Islam. organise the people economically, socially, educationally, and politically, and I am sure that you will be a power that will be accepted by everybody.

Lessons from Constitutional History

Acts/facts occupy specific political contextual frames of time and space. With the passage of time facts are interpreted differently at different times and under different circumstances, depending on the ever-changing lenses of various social political and economic schools of thought. As a student of law, and particularly of constitutional law and history of Pakistan, I wish to make certain factual observations. One can go deep into dialectical debates about reactions to certain actions, though unconstitutional and illegal but needed and required at a specific time in the 'Supreme National Interest', now more popularly known as the 'Law of Necessity'. But the historical facts indelibly remain that they occurred.

[Mr. Anwar Syed's letter appeared in your paper as response to comments made by Mr. A.R.Siddiqui regarding Mr. Jinnah's role as Governor General vis-vis than Prime Minister Liaqat Ali Khan. He made these comments on article "Constitutional History of Pakistan" by Mr.S.M.Zafar published earlier and subsequently certain observation were made by some other foreign based writer. This provoked me as well to comment on this historical issue. As a student of law and particularly of constitutional law and history of Pakistan, I am afraid that I could not agree more with the observation of Mr. A.R.Siddiqui for unveiling a very important fact. Political scientists may view such acts/facts in a specific political contextual frame of time and space and one can also go deep in the dialectical debates about reaction to certain actions, though unconstitutional and illegal but needed and required at a specific time in the "Supreme national interest" which is popularly called the "Law of necessity". But historical facts remain as they occurred and that remain as it is. With passage of time facts are interpreted differently at different times in different circumstances by various social, political and economic schools of thoughts.]

The constitutional history of Pakistan is as chequered and shameful as it is relatively short. One need not travel very far in the past to find its roots in the year 1861. This was the year when the Indian Councils Act was enacted. This was the first ever push for self government and of representative government which was not quite substantive democracy, but rather its obverse. Under this Act some Indians were nominated in the Viceroy's advisory, and a lower level, council. The proportion of British nominated non-official Indians in the councils was increased by another Act in 1892. In 1909, the Minto-Morley reforms extended the links between higher and lower councils. "Thus building bridges which local men with power and pelf...", as Pakistani scholar Ayesha Jalal writes, the lower casts and Muslims were the main construct.

This Act not only survived but was extended under 1919 Montague-Chelmsford reforms and later on all these were incorporated into the Government of India Act of 1935. This Act in its character was the largest Bill ever passed by the mother Parliament—the British House of Commons. It was aptly commented upon, "the overriding character of an imperial power which set apart its subjects in block with interests fundamentally antagonistic to rulers". This Act was primarily designed to exert effective central control on a colony through the offices of Viceroys and later on, through Governor Generals. These offices were meant to exercise the real despotic power while the physical centre was at six months distance from Indian shores. The government of India Act of 1935 was the lengthiest piece of legislation ever debated and passed by the House of Commons. It took around eleven years to make, pass and enact. It was declared to be the most monstrous legislation by opposition MP's in the House of Commons, and not fit for a civil society. Treasury benches had to exert protracted effort to convince the House that the legislation was not for the civil society of England but to spread Pax-Britannica to the colony of India, the jewel in the crown of the British Empire. And this is the same Act—the Government of India Act 1935—was adopted as the Constitution of India and Pakistan on the eve of transfer of power (not independence, as is wrongly held till to date).

The so-called constitutionalist, Mr. Muhammad Ali Jinnah, stepped into the shoes of the Representative of Her Majesty the Queen of England, as Governor General, the chief executive of the newly born dominion of Pakistan. He was also elected President of the Constituent and Legislative Assembly. This Assembly in its own blend was elected indirectly on the basis of limited franchise. In addition, Mr. Jinnah was also the president of the ruling party, the Muslim League. With regard to his status as a great constitutionalist, an opinion may aptly be quote: "There cannot be any constitutionalist in pre partition days as there was no constitution as such. A lawyer well versed in Anglo-Saxon law has a different connotation". Another fact remains that the British of transfer of power deleted the clause in the Act of 1935 which gave the Viceroy the power to dismiss the provincial government or legislative council. This truncated Act then became the Constitution of Pakistan. An early clause remained wherein the Viceroy, in his own discretion, had power to take any actions in the pursuance of maintenance of law and order and the policies of her Majesty the Queen of England. Another fact is that no viceroy ever invoked the said clause, in spite of the fact that period between 1935 to 1947—from the British point of view—was the most turbulent period in British colonial history, but Mr. Jinnah invoked that very clause and dismissed the elected ministry (not the assembly) in N.W.F.P. It took quite long period of time to launch Muslim League government in that province, in which period no elections were held. Such actions by Mr. Jinnah may well be seen as being very much desired and nationalistic, but it must also be seen as the invocation of the 'Law of Necessity' for the first time in Pakistan as well.

Facts remain that Mr. Jinnah also presided over cabinet meetings, took most decisions unilaterally and, under the 1935 Act, acted as the representative of the Queen. The role of the Prime Minister remained ceremonial. The facts also say that after Mr. Jinnah's unfortunate demise, Mr. Liaqat Ali Khan got incorporated a clause in 1935 Act which empowered the dismissal of governments and assemblies and continued to use viceregal powers by dismissing the Punjab and Sindh governments. The final scene witnessed that Governor General Ghulam Muhammad, invoked the same clause in 1954 to dismiss Prime Minister Nazimuddin which was earlier used by Mr. Jinnah to dismiss the N.W.F.P. government. And then the Governor General gave the death blow to the Constituent and Legislative Assembly by putting a lock on the gates and surrounding the building with police when its members came to attend the session. And for doing so the same clause of the same monstrous Act was invoked which had been invoked earlier. The legitimization of such acts by courts and by public opinion is also a sad and shameful fact of history.

Mr. Jinnah's actions may be brimmed with acute desire of nation building but definitely his viceroyal attitude and acts vis-vis other institution of states are factual and will remain the facts of the constitutional history of Pakistan. A student of history of constitution will have to oversee the successive chain of events to learn from the past and prepare to prevent such events antagonistic to polity and society do not occur in future. We must all learn from history and shun prejudice towards individual personalities. Seeing Mr. Jinnah historically and objectively might call for a partial revision in the dominant perspective which regards him a constitutional lawyer. One must not avoid those facts which may be unfortunately responsible for the dismal political and constitutional scenario at present on the screen of the country called Pakistan.

3

Freedom Fighter Jinnah as a Divided Legacy

Jinnah's father Jinnahbhai Poonja (born 1850) was the youngest of three sons. He married a girl Mithibai with the consent of his parents and moved to the growing port of Karachi. There, the young couple rented an apartment on the second floor of a three-storey house, Wazir Mansion.

The Wazir Mansion has since been rebuilt and made into a national monument and museum owing to the fact that the founder of the nation, and one of the greatest leaders of all times was born within its walls. On December 25, 1876, Mithibai gave birth to a son, the first of seven children. The fragile infant who appeared so weak that it 'weighed a few pounds less than normal'. But Mithibai was unusually fond of her little boy, insisting he would grow up to be an achiever.

Officially named Mahomedali Jinnahbhai, his father enrolled him in school when he was six—the Sindh Madrasatul-Islam; Jinnah was indifferent to his studies and loathed arithmetic, preferring to play outdoors with his friends. His father was especially keen towards his studying arithmetic as it was vital in his business. By the early 1880s' Jinnahbhai Poonja's trade business had prospered greatly. He handled all sorts of goods: cotton, wool, hides, oil-seeds, and grain for export. Whereas Manchester manufactured piece of goods, metals, refined sugar and used to import into the busy port. Business was good and profits were soaring high.

In 1887, Jinnahbhai's only sister came to visit from Bombay. Jinnah was very fond of his Aunt and vice versa. She offered to take her nephew back with her in order to give him a chance of better education at the metropolitan city Bombay, that was much to his mother's dismay who could not bear the thought of being separated from her undisputedly favourite child. Jinnah joined Gokal Das Tej Primary School in Bombay. His spirited brain rebelled inside the typical Indian primary school which relied mostly on the method of learning by rote. He remained in Bombay for only six months, returned to Karachi upon his mother's insistence and joined the Sind Madrassa. But his name was struck off as he frequently cut classes in order to ride his father's horses. He was fascinated by the horses and lured towards them. He also enjoyed reading poetry at his own leisure. As a child Jinnah was never intimidated by the authority and was not easy to control.

He then joined the Christian Missionary Society High School where his parents thought his restless mind could be focused. Karachi proved more prosperous for young Jinnah than Bombay had been. His father's business had prospered so much by this time that he had his own stables and carriages. Jinnahbhai Poonja's firm was closely associated with the leading British managing agency in Karachi, Douglas Graham and Company. Sir Frederick Leigh Croft, the general manager of the company, had a great influence over young Jinnah, which possibly lasted his entire life.

Jinnah looked up to the handsome, well dressed and a successful man. Sir Frederick liked Mamad, recognizing his extreme potential, he offered him an apprenticeship at his office in London. That kind of opportunity was the dream of all young boys of India, but the privilege went to only one in a million. Sir Frederick had truly picked one in a million when he chose Jinnah.

JINNAH: A LIFE

Mohammed Ali Jinnah was born to an ordinary if comfortable household in Karachi, not far from where Islam first came to the Indian subcontinent in AD 711 in the person of the young Arab general Muhammad bin Qasim. However, Jinnah's date of birth—25 December 1876—and place of birth are presently under academic dispute. Just before Jinnah's birth his father, Jinnahbhai Poonja, had moved from Gujarat to Karachi. Significantly, Jinnah's father was born in 1857—at the end of one kind of Muslim history, with the failed uprisings in Delhi—and died in 1901 (F. Jinnah 1987: vii).

Jinnah's family traced its descent from Iran and reflected Shia, Sunni and Ismaili influences; some of the family names—Valji, Manbai and Nathoo—were even 'akin to Hindu names' (F. Jinnah 1987: 50). Such things mattered in a Muslim society conscious of underlining its non-Indian origins, a society where people gained status through family names such as Sayyed and Qureshi (suggesting Arab descent), Ispahani (Iran) and Durrani (Afghanistan). Another source has a different explanation of Jinnah's origins. Mr Jinnah, according to a Pakistani author, said that his male ancestor was a Rajput from Sahiwal in the Punjab who had married into the Ismaili Khojas and settled in Kathiawar (Beg 1986: 888). Although born into a Khoja (from khwaja or 'noble') family who were disciples of the Ismaili Aga Khan, Jinnah moved towards the Sunni sect early in life. There is evidence later, given by his relatives and associates in court, to establish that he was firmly a Sunni Muslim by the end of his life (Merchant 1990).

One of eight children, young Jinnah was educated in the Sind Madrasatul Islam and the Christian Missionary Society High School in Karachi. Shortly before he was sent to London in 1893 to join Graham's Shipping and Trading Company, which did business with Jinnah's father in Karachi, he was married to Emibai, a distant relative (F. Jinnah 1987: 61). It could be described as a traditional Asian marriage—the groom barely 16 years old and the bride a mere child. Emibai died shortly after Jinnah left for London; Jinnah barely knew her. But another death, that of his beloved mother, devastated him (ibid.).

Jinnah asserted his independence by making two important personal decisions. Within months of his arrival he left the business firm to join Lincoln's Inn and study law. In 1894 he changed his name by deed poll, dropping the 'bhai' from his surname. Not yet 20 years old, in 1896 he became the youngest Indian to pass. As a barrister, in his bearing, dress and delivery Jinnah cultivated a sense of theatre which would stand him in good stead in the future.

It has been said that Jinnah chose Lincoln's Inn because he saw the Prophet's name at the entrance. I went to Lincoln's Inn looking for the name on the gate, but there is no such gate nor any names. There is, however, a gigantic mural covering one entire wall in the main dining hall of Lincoln's Inn. Painted on it are some of the most influential lawgivers of history, like Moses and, indeed, the holy Prophet of Islam, who is shown in a green turban and green robes. A key at the bottom of the painting matches the names to the persons in the picture. Jinnah, I suspect, was not deliberately concealing the memory of his youth but recalling an association with the Inn of Court half a century after it had taken place. He had remembered there was a link, a genuine appreciation of Islam. Had those who have written about Jinnah's recollection bothered to visit Lincoln's Inn the mystery would have been solved. However, knowledge of the pictorial depiction of the holy Prophet would certainly spark protests; demands from the active British Muslim community for the removal of the painting would be heard in the UK.

In London Jinnah had discovered a passion for nationalist politics and had assisted Dadabhai Naoroji, the first Indian Member of Parliament. During the campaign he became acutely aware of racial prejudice, but he returned to India to practise law at the Bombay Bar in 1896 after a brief stopover in Karachi. He was then the only Muslim barrister in Bombay. Jinnah was a typical Indian nationalist at the turn of the century, aiming to get rid of the British from the subcontinent as fast as possible. He adopted two strategies: one was to try to operate within the British system; the other was to work for a united front of Hindus, Muslims, Christians and Parsees against the British. He succeeded to an extent in both.

Jinnah's conduct reflected the prickly Indian expression of independence. On one occasion in Bombay, when Jinnah was arguing a case in court, the British presiding judge interrupted him several times, exclaiming, 'Rubbish.' Jinnah responded: 'Your honour, nothing but rubbish has passed your mouth all morning.' Sir Charles Ollivant, judicial member of the Bombay provincial government, was so impressed by Jinnah that in 1901 he offered him permanent employment at 1,500 rupees a month. Jinnah declined, saying he would soon earn that amount in a day. Not too long afterwards he proved himself correct.

Stories like these added to Jinnah's reputation as an arrogant nationalist. His attitude towards the British may be explained culturally as well as temperamentally. He was not part of the cultural tradition of the United Provinces (UP) which had revolved around the imperial Mughal court based in Delhi and which smoothly transferred to the British after they moved up from Calcutta. Exaggerated courtesy, hyperbole, dissimulation, long and low bows, salaams that touched the forehead repeatedly—these marked the deference of courtiers to imperial authority. Even Sir Sayyed Ahmad Khan, one of the most illustrious champions of the Muslim renaissance in the late nineteenth century, came from a family that had served the Mughals, but had readily transferred his loyalties to the British.

Jinnah often antagonized his British superiors. Yet he was clever enough consciously to remain within the boundaries, pushing as far as he could but not allowing his opponents to penalize him on a point of law. In short he learned to use British law skilfully against the British.

At several points in his long career, Jinnah was threatened by the British with imprisonment on sedition charges for speaking in favour of Indian home rule or rights. He was frozen out by those British officials who wished their natives to be more deferential. For example, Lord Willingdon, Viceroy of India in 1931-6, did not take to him, and even the gruff but kindly Lord Wavell, Viceroy in 1943-7, was made to feel uncomfortable by Jinnah's clear-minded advocacy of the Muslims, even though he recognized the justice of Jinnah's arguments. The last Viceroy, however, Lord Mountbatten, could not cope with what he regarded as Jinnah's arrogance and haughtiness, preferring the natives to be more friendly and pliant.

The Wedding

When Jinnah's mother heard of his plans of going to London

for at least two years, she objected strongly to such a move. For her, the separation for six months while her dear son had been in Bombay was testing, she said that she could not bear this long never ending stretch of two to three years. Maybe the intuition told her that separation would be permanent for her and that she would never see her son again.

After much persuasion by adamant Jinnah, she consented, but with the condition that Jinnah would marry before he went to England. 'England', she said 'was a dangerous country to send an unmarried and handsome young man like her son. Some English girl might lure him into marriage and that would be a tragedy for the Jinnah Poonja family.' Realizing the importance of his mother's demand, Jinnah conceded to it. Mithibai arranged his marriage with a fourteen-year-old girl named Emibai from the Paneli village. The parents made all wedding arrangements. The young couple quietly accepted the arranged marriage including all other decisions regarding the wedding like most youngsters in India at that time.

'Muhammad was hardly sixteen and had never seen the girl he was to marry.' Jinnah's sister Fatima reports. 'Decked from head to foot in long flowing garlands of flowers, he walked in a procession from his grandfather's house to that of his father-in-law, where his fourteen year old bride, Emi Bai, sat in an expensive bridal dress, wearing glittering ornaments, her hands spotted with henna, her face spotted with gold dust and redolent with the fragrance of attar.'

The ceremony took place in February 1892; it was a grand affair celebrated by the whole village. Huge lunch and dinner parties were arranged and all were invited. It was the wedding of Jinnahbhai Poonja and Mithibai's first son and the entire village was lured into the festivity. During their prolonged stay in Paneli, Jinnahbhai's business began to suffer. It was needed for him to return but he wished to take his family and his son's new bride along with him. The bride's father however, was adamant that Jinnah should stay for the customary period of one and a half month after marriage. The two families, newly bonded in marriage, were about to break into a quarrel until the intervention of young Jinnah. He spoke to his father-in-law in privacy and informed him that it was necessary for his father to return immediately along with his family. He gave the option of either sending the young bride back with him or sending her later when he would go to England for two or three years. Jinnah's persuasive power, coupled with extreme politeness was evident even at that age. Emi Bai's father consented to send his daughter, and the wedding party returned to Karachi.

How Jinnah felt about that marriage and his new bride was uncertain, he had little time to adjust since he sailed off to England soon after his return. Upon their return to Karachi, his young bride observed the custom of covering her face with her headscarf in front of her father-in-law. But the progressive Jinnah soon encouraged her to discard this practice. He studied in the Christian Mission School until the end of October in order to improve his English before his voyage that was planned by November 1892, though some argue that he sailed in January 1893. He was not to see his young bride ever again as she died soon after he sailed from India.

A Journey to London

Jinnah barely sixteen sailed for London in the midst of winter. When he was saying goodbye to his mother her eyes were heavy with tears. He told her not to cry and said: 'I will return a great man from England and not only you and the family but the whole country will be proud of me. Would you not be happy then?' This was the last time he saw his mother, for she, like his wife, died during his three and a half year stay in England. The youngest passenger on his own, was befriended by a kind Englishman who engaged in conversations with him and gave tips about life in England. He also gave Jinnah his address in London and later invited to dine with his family as often as he could.

His father had deposited enough money in his son's account to last him the three years of the intended stay. Jinnah used that money wisely and was able to have a small amount left over at the end of his three and a half year tenure. When he arrived in London he rented a modest room in a hotel. He lived in different places before he moved into the house of Mrs. F. E. Page-Drake as a houseguest at 35 Russell Road in Kensington. This house now displays a blue and white ceramic oval saying that the 'founder of Pakistan stayed here in 1895'.

Mrs. Page-Drake, a widow, took an instant liking to the impeccably dressed well-mannered young man. Her daughter however, had a more keen interest in the handsome Jinnah, who was of the same age of Jinnah. She hinted her intentions but did not get a favourable response. As Fatima reflects, "...he was not the flirtatious type and she could not break through his reserve."

On March 30, 1895 Jinnah applied to Lincoln's Inn Council for the alteration of his name the Books of Society from Mahomedalli Jinnahbhai to Muhammad Ali Jinnah, which he anglicized to M.A. Jinnah. This was granted to him in April 1895. Though he found life in London dreary at first and was unable to accept the cold winters and gray skies, he soon adjusted to those surroundings, quite the opposite of what he was accustomed to in India.

After joining Lincoln's Inn in June 1893, he developed further interest in politics. He thought the world of politics was 'glamorous' and often went to the House of Commons and marvelled at the speeches he heard there. Although his father was furious when he learnt of Jinnah's change in plan regarding his career, there was little he could do to alter what his son had made his mind up for. At that point in life Jinnah was totally alone in his decisions, with no moral support from his father or any help from Sir Frederick. He was left with his chosen course of action without a pillar of support to fall back upon. It would not be the only time in his life when he would be isolated in a difficult position. But without hesitation he set off on his chosen task and managed to succeed.

The Theatre

During his stay in London, Jinnah frequently visited the theatre. He was mesmerized by the acting, especially those of the Shakespearean actors. His dream was to 'play the role of Romeo at the Old Vic.' It is unclear when his passion for theatre was unfurled, perhaps it occurred while watching the performances of barristers, 'the greatest of whom were often spellbinding thespians'. This was no passing phase in life, but an obsession which continued even in his later years. Fatima reminiscences, " Even in the days of his most active political life, when he returned home tired and late, he would read Shakespeare, his voice...resonant."

With a theatrical prop, his monocle, always in place in court, he performed like an actor on stage in front of the judge and jury. With dramatic interrogations and imperious asides, he was regarded as a born actor.

After being enrolled to the Bar he went with his friends to the Manager of a theatrical company who asked him to read out pieces of Shakespeare. On doing so, he was immediately offered a job. He was exultant and wrote to his parents about his newfound passion. He said: 'I wrote to them that law was a lingering profession where success was uncertain; a stage career was much better, and it gave me a good start, and that I would now be independent and not bother them with grants of money at all. My father wrote a long letter to me strongly disapproving of my project; but there was one sentence in his letter that touched me most and which influenced a change in my decision: "Do not be a traitor to the family." I went to my employers and conveyed to them that I no longer looked forward to a stage career. They were surprised, and they tried to persuade me, but my mind was made up. According to the terms of the contract I had signed with them, I was to have given them three months notice before I quitting. But you know, they were Englishmen, and so they said: "Well when you have no interest in the stage, why should we keep you, against your wishes?"'

The signed contract is proof that how important the stage career was for Jinnah at that time, it was possibly his first love. His father's letter had dissuaded him for the time being, disheartened and dejected, he had consented to his wish. But it was probably the last time he changed his mind after seriously devoting it to something.

Ruttie Jinnah

After his return to India Jinnah chose Bombay for his residence since he no longer had any interest in Karachi after the demise of his mother and his wife. His father joined him there and died in Bombay on the 17th of April 1902, soon after Jinnah had started his political career.

In the next two decades after his return from London, Jinnah established himself first as a lawyer and then as a politician. Devoted completely to his work he sailed between England and India and from one stage of his political career to the next.

Jinnah vacationed in the north in Darjeeling in 1916, staying at the summer home of his friend Sir Dinshaw Manockjee Petit, the son of one of the richest and most devoutly orthodox Parsi of the nineteenth century. It was in that summer that he met Dinshaw's only daughter Ratanbai. Born on February 20, 1900, Ratanbai, or Rutti as she used to be called, was a charming child. '*...Precociously bright, gifted in every art, beautiful in everyway. As she matured, all of her talents, gifts and beauty were magnified in so delightful and unaffected a manner that she seemed a fairy princess*'-Stanley Wolpert, *Jinnah of Pakistan.*

She was sixteen at that time and Jinnah was about forty. He was enamoured by her beauty and charm and she was awe struck by Jay, as she called him. Jinnah spoke to Sir Dinshaw about inter-communal marriages, to which his friend had replied that he was not opposed to them. When Jinnah put forth his offer of a marriage proposal for his daughter Ruttie, Sir Dinshaw was taken aback. He refused bluntly and said there was no chance of his ever agreeing to such a thing. That was the end of their friendship as Sir Dinshaw never gave in. He forbade Ruttie to meet Jinnah while she lived in his house. The couple patiently waited for two years required for Ruttie to come of age. In February 1918 Ruttie turned 18 and was free to marry. On April 18, 1918 Ruttie converted to Islam at Calcutta's Jamia Mosque. On April 19, 1918 Jinnah and Ruttie married at a quiet ceremony at Jinnah's house in Bombay. The Raja Sahib of Muhamdabad and a few friends attended the wedding. The wedding ring that Jinnah presented to Ruttie was a gift from the Raja. Nobody from Ruttie's family attended the wedding.

The first few years of their marriage were a dream for both of them. They were a head-turning couple; he in his elegant suits, stitched in London, she with her long, flowing hair decked in flowers. There was no limit to their joy and satisfaction at that time. Their only woe was Ruttie's complete isolation and ostracism from her family. Jinnah's political life began to take its toll on his time in 1922. His heavy work schedule did not allow him to spend enough time with his young and vibrant wife. Though she was supportive of his work, the element of his lack of time was taxing for her. She could not lure him away from his work. She was engulfed with feelings of desolation. By September of 1922 she packed her bags and took their only daughter Dina with her to London.

Though her heart was still set on life with Jinnah, she could not accommodate herself to his busy schedule. From London she wrote a letter to her friend Kanji in India in which she said: 'And just one thing more-go and see Jinnah and tell me how he is-he has a habit of overworking himself and now that I am not there to tease and bother him, he will be worse than ever.'

When she returned from England, the couple tried to give their marriage another chance, but Jinnah was involved in campaigning for elections as an independent Muslim for the general Bombay seat. Jinnah was to undergo a five-month tour to Europe and North America. He decided to take Ruttie along as an attempt to save their failing marriage. But in this trip the rift grew. There was no chance of reconciliation and in January 1928 the couple separated.

Ruttie lived at the Taj Mahal Hotel in Bombay, almost as a recluse, her health failing drastically. On February 20, 1929, Ruttie Jinnah died. It was her 29th birthday. She was buried two days later in Bombay according to Muslim rites. Jinnah sat like a stone statue throughout the funeral. But when asked to be the first to throw earth on the grave as the closest relative, Jinnah broke down and wept uncontrollably. Later Justice Chagla said, 'That was the only time when I found Jinnah betraying any shadow of human weakness.' Jinnah had been good to his wife. He had been a doting husband, fulfilling the demands of his young and enthusiastic wife. She also, had played her part justly, had supported him and encouraged him in his career. But the lack of time fatefully pulled them so far apart that eventually no reconciliation was possible. The time of their separation was a trying one for Jinnah, in the photographs of this period he is never seen smiling.

THE TWO NATIONS THEORY

Events in the late 1920s and 1930s led Muslims to begin to think that their destiny might be in a separate state, a concept that developed into the demand for partition. Motilal Nehru convinced an "all-party" conference in 1929 to suggest changes that would lead to independence when British took up the report of Simon Commission. The majority of delegates demands the end of the system of separate electorates. Jinnah, in turn, put forward fifteen points that would satisfy Muslim interests-in particular, the retention of separate electorates or the creation of "safeguards" to prevent a Hindu-controlled legislature. Jinnah's proposals were rejected, and from then on cooperation between Hindus and Muslims in the independence movement was rare.

In his presidential address to the Muslim League session at Allahabad in 1930, the leading modern Muslim philosopher in South Asia, Sir Muhammad Iqbal (1877-1938), described India as Asia in miniature, in which a unitary form of government was inconceivable and religious community rather than territory was the basis for identification. To him, communalism in the highest sense was the key to formation of a harmonious whole in India. Therefore, he demanded the establishment of a confederation India to include a Muslim state consisting of Punjab, N.W.F.P, Sindh, and Balochistan. In subsequent speeches and writings, Iqbal reiterated the claims of Muslims to be considered a nation "based on unity of language, race, history, religion, and identity of economic interests".

Iqbal gave no name to his projected state. That was done by a group of students at Cambridge in Britain who issued a pamphlet in 1933 entitled Now or Never (by Ch. Rehmat Ali). They opposed the idea of federation, denied that India was a single country, and demanded partition into regions, the Northwest receiving national status as a "Pakistan". They explained the terms follows: "Pakistan...is...composed of letters taken from the names of our homelands: that is Punjab, Afghani, [N.W.F.P.], Kashmir, Sindh, Tukharistan, Afghanistan, and Balochistan. It means the land of the Paks, the spiritually pure and clean."

In 1934, Jinnah returned to the leadership of the Muslim League after a period of residence in London, but found it divided and without a sense of mission. He set about restoring a sense of purpose to Muslims, and he emphasised the Two Nations Theory.

The 1937-40 period was critical in the growth of the Two Nations Theory. Under the 1935 Government of India Act, elections to the provincial legislative assemblies were held in 1937. Congress gained majorities in seven of the eleven provinces. Congress took a strictly legalistic stand on the formation of provincial ministries and refused to form coalition government with the Muslim League, even in the United Provinces, which had substantial Muslim minority, provinces such as Punjab and the N.W.F.P. The conduct of Congress governments in Muslim-minority provinces permanently alienated the Muslim League.

By the late 1930s, Jinnah was convinced of the need for a unifying issue among Muslims, and Pakistan was the obvious answer. At its annual session in Lahore on March 23, 1940, the Muslim League resolved that the areas of Muslim Majority in Northwestern and Eastern India should be grouped together to constitute independence plan without this provision was unacceptable to Muslims. Federation was rejected. The Lahore Resolution (forward by Sher-e-Bengal Mr. A. K. Fazal-e-Haq) was often referred to as the "Pakistan Resolution"; however, the word Pakistan did not appear in it.

An interesting aspect of the Pakistan movement was that it received its greatest support from area in which Muslims were a minority. In those areas, the main issue was finding an alternative to replacing British rule with Congress, that is, Hindu Rule.

TOWARD PARTITION

Congress predictable opposed all proposals for partition and advocated a united India with a strong centre and a fully responsible parliament. To many, notable to Jawaharlal Nehru, the idea of a sovereign state based on a common religion seemed a historical anachronism and a denial of democracy. From 1940 on, reconciliation between Congress and the Muslim League became increasingly difficult, if not impossible.

During World War II, the Muslim League and Congress adopted different attitudes toward British priorities were driven by the expediencies of defence, and war was declared abruptly without any prior consultation with Indian politicians. Congress ministries in the provinces resigned in protest. As a consequence, Congress, with most of its leaders in jail opposition of the Rule, lost its political leverage over the cooperation, gaining time to consolidate. The British appreciated the loyalty and valour of the British India Army, many of whose members were Punjabi Muslims. The Muslims League's success could be gauged from its sweep of 90 percent of the Muslim seats in the 1946 elections, compared with only 4.5 percent in the 1937 elections. The 1946 election was, in effect, a plebiscite among Muslims on Pakistan. In London it became clear that there were three parties in any discussion on the future if India: the British, Congress and the Muslim League.

Spurred by Japanese advance in Asia and forceful persuasion from Washington, British prime minister Winston Churchill's coalition war government in 1942 had dispatched Sir Stafford Cripps to India with a proposal for settlement. He plan provided for dominion status after the war for and Indian union if British Indian provinces and princely states wishing to accede to, a separate dominion for those who did not, and firm defence link between Britain and an Indian union. Cripps himself was sympathetic to Indian nationalism. However, his mission failed, and Gandhi described it as "a postdated cheque on a crashing bank."

In August 1942, Gandhi launched the "Quit India Movement" against the British. Jinnah condemned the movement. The government retaliated by arresting about 60,000 individuals and outlawing Congress. Communal riots increased. Talks between Jinnah and Gandhi in 1944 proved as futile as negations between Gandhi and the viceroy.

New elections to provincial and central legislatures were ordered, and a three-man team came to India from Britain to discuss plans for self-government. The cabinet Mission Plan, proposed by Cripps, represented Britain's last, desperate attempt to transfer the power it retained over India to a single union. The mission put forward a three-tier federal form of government in which the central government would be limited to power over defence, foreign relations, currency and communication; significant over powers would be delegated to the provinces. The plan also prescribed the zones that would be created: northwest Bengal and Assam would be joined to form a zone with a slight Muslim majority; in northwest, Punjab, Sindh, N.W.F.P., and Balochistan would be joined for a clear Muslim majority; and the remainder of the country would be third zone, with a clear Hindu majority. The approximation of the boundaries of a new Pakistan was clear from the delineation of the zones. The mission also suggested the right of veto on legislation by communities that saw their interests adversely affected. Finally, the mission proposed that an interim government be established immediately and that new elections be held.

Congress and the Muslim League emerged from the 1946 elections as the two dominant parties, although the Muslim League again was unable to capture a majority of the Muslim seats in the N.W.F.P. At first, both parties seemed to accept Cabinet Mission Plan, despite many reservations, but the subsequent behaviour of the leaders soon led to bitterness and mistrust. Nehru effectively quashed any prospect of the plan's success when he announced that Congress would not be "fettered" by agreements with the British, thereby making it clear that Congress would be its majority in the newly created Constituent Assembly to write a constitution that conformed to its ideas. The formation of an interim government was also controversial. Jinnah demanded equality between the Muslim League and Congress, a proposal rejected by the viceroy. The Muslim League boycotted the interim government, and each party disputed the right of the other appoint Muslim ministers, a prerogative Jinnah claimed belonged solely to the Muslim League.

When the viceroy proceeded to form an interim government without the Muslim League, Jinnah called for demonstrations, or "Direct Action", on August 16, 1946. Communal rioting broke out on an unprecedented scale, especially in Bengal and Bihar. The massacre of Muslims in Calcutta brought Gandhi to the scene, where he worked with the Muslim League provincial chief minister, Hussain Shaheed Suhrawardy. Gandhi's and Suharwardy's efforts clamed fears in Bengal, but rioting quickly spread elsewhere and continued well into 19476. Jinnah permitted the Muslim League to inter the interim government in an effort to stem further communal violence. Disagreements among the ministers paralysed the government, already haunted by the spectre of civil war.

In February 1947, Lord Mountbatten was appointed viceroy with specific instructions to arrange for a transfer of bower by June 1948. Mountbatten assessed the situation and became convinced that Congress was willing to accept partition as the price for independence, that Jinnah would accept a smaller Pakistan than one he demanded (that is, all of Punjab and Bengal), and Sikhs would learn to accept a division of Punjab. Mountbatten was convinced by the rising temperature of too distant and persuaded most Indian leaders that immediate acceptance of his plan was imperative.

On June 3, 1947, British prime minister Clement Attlee introduced a bill in the House of Commons called for the Independence and Partition of India. On July 14, the House of Commons passed the India Independence Act, by which two independent dominions were created on the subcontinent; the princely states were left to accede to either. The partition plan stated that contiguous Muslim-majority districts in Punjab and Bengal would go to Pakistan, provided that the legislatures of the two provinces agreed that the provinces should be partitioned-they did. Sindh's legislature and Balochistan's jirga (council of tribal leaders) agreed to join Pakistan. A plebiscite was held in Sylhet District of Assam, and as a result, part of the district was transferred to Pakistan. A plebiscite was also held in N.W.F.P. Despite a boycott by Congress, the province was deemed to have chosen Pakistan. The princely states, however, presented a more difficult problem. All but three of the more than 500 states quickly acceded to Pakistan or India under guidelines established with the aid of Mountbatten. The states made their decision after giving consideration to the geographic location of their respective area and to their religious majority. Two states hesitated but were quickly absorbed into India: Hyderabad, the most populated of the princely states, whose Muslim ruler desired independence; Junagadh, a small state with a Muslim prince that tried to accede to Pakistan despite's majority Hindu population. The accession of the third state, Jammu and Kashmir, also could not be resolved peacefully, and its indeterminate status has poisoned relations between Pakistan and India ever since.

Throughout the summer of 1947, as communal violence mounted, preparations for partition proceeded in Delhi. Assets were divided, boundary commission were set up to demarcate frontiers, and British troops were evacuated. The military was restructured into two forces. Law and order broke down in different parts of the country. Civil servants were given choice of joining either country; British officers could retire with compensation if not invited to stay on. Jinnah and Nehru tried unsuccessfully to quell the passions of communal fury that neither fully understood. On August 14, 1947, Pakistan and India achieved independence. Jinnah became the first governor general of Dominion of Pakistan.

JINNAH'S SHADOW OVER CONTEMPORARY POLITICS IN INDIA

The question whether Jinnah was secular is meaningless unless one defines the term 'Secular'. If to be secular means to be anti-religious or pro-religious, to have no religious inhibitions, to deny, ignore and not to practise religious duties, then Gandhi or Azad was not secular, Jinnah, in that sense was secular until he donned the Shervani and the Jinnah cap and became the Quaid-e-Azam. Nehru was but he professed to be a sceptic and not religious. But since Hinduism is impossible to define, he considered himself, and was considered by his followers, to be a Hindu.

If secularism is defined as non-discrimination on ground of religion, then the term is lifted from the common way of life to the lofty heights of power. Indeed Secularism is an attribute of the State which treats its citizens equally irrespective of religion. As an individual, any person is ever free to choose his friends, his spouse, the religion of his children, but as the law-giver, as a person in power, as a representative of the State he serves, he cannot import religion into his official life, in dealing with the people at large or his subordinates. So a religious or even orthodox person may well be secular as the holder of a public office. Conversely, an irreligious person may be anti-secular or communal in his public life.

Let us take a look at the problem from the conceptual angle of nationalism. Jinnah's name is synonymous with the Two-Nations Theory; the theory covers Hindus and Muslims only but they are not the whole of India. It has followers of at least 4, if not 6 or 7, recognized religions: Hindus, Muslims, Sikhs, Christians, Buddhists and Jains, and the Parsis, and many 'other religions'. The question was and is: if Muslims and Hindus constitute nations, then why should not the other religious groups also be regarded as 'nations'.

So Jinnah should have logically espoused the Many Nations Theory, all based on religion. What, in fact, he conceptually propounded after 1937 may be called the theory of Religion-based Nationalism or Religious Nationalism, in contrast to Territorial Nationalism which implies that all persons who inhabit a common territory constitute one nation. Territorial Nationalism tends to break down with the size of the territory as in a particular part, a minority group may command a majority. It also tends to break down with historically determined relations among distinct peoples inhabiting the territory. Territorial Nationalism implies a relationship of friendly intercourse between different peoples inhabiting the territory, participating in its governance, sharing the responsibility for development and defence, facing common perils and sharing joys and sorrows. But Territorial Nationalism whatever the size of the territory has to be secular nationalism if inhabited by more than one religious groups. On the other hand, Religious Nationalism which recognizes followers of a particular religion as nationals or citizens and the followers of other religions, living in the same territory, as the 'others' and discriminates among them is anti-secular and leads to a theocratic State. The anti-thesis of Secularism is Communalism, to place the interest of the religious group above the national interest or the common good.

Territorial Nationalism is essential for the liberation of a territory from foreign yoke or occupation because it has the potential to mobilize all the people for a common cause. So the Indian Freedom Movement was above all based on Territorial Nationalism promising freedom for the people of India of all religions, languages, races and castes. However, it is also a fact that, whatever the historical or political reasons, the Freedom Movement failed to accommodate the urges and aspirations, fears and hopes of several social groups. Above all, it could not resolve the communal problem which was essentially a Hindu-Muslim problem because Hindus and Muslims, the two biggest religious groups, meant 90% of the people of India.

But Communalism, a pejorative term in Indian politics, needs also to be adopted. In the age of social justice and of identity politics every community has its right to an equitable share of national assets and resources. In the age of democracy, every social group has a right to demand and struggle peacefully for its rights, for its share of the cake, for its place in the sun, for its finger on the levers of power. Indeed it is in the national interest to have contented minorities, rather than to deny them their due and push them to the wall. Of course, the minorities, religious or otherwise, have to function within the bounds of democratic and constitutional legitimacy. In the long road, the nationalist movement traversed from the Lucknow Pact of 1916 to the Partition of 1947, it is impossible to absolve anyone totally and equally unfair to tar anyone wholly.

Separatism, leading to the Partition, a very imperfect and even irrational solution, emerged to fill the vacuum. Jinnah championed it, particularly after 1937 and it became his formal objective after 1940. In this sense Jinnah can be called a 'separatist'. But on this ground alone he cannot be called anti-secular because till the very end he wanted a united India with constitutional safeguards in terms of federalism and minority rights because he knew that the two States of India and Pakistan, had the Partition not used blood to draw the new boundaries, would both be multi-religious, not mono-religious, States and in that sense, both would have no option but to adopt Territorial Nationalism and Secularism as their ideology. This is the dilemma that was given expression to by Jinnah in his 11 August, 1947 speech, which Advani quoted, as if he had discovered it! In any case, Savarkar coined the Two-Nation Theory 16 years before Jinnah used it. Lajpat Rai spoke of Partition at least 15 years before the Pakistan Resolution of 1940.

No doubt Jinnah held the brief for Pakistan, but did he believe in it? A lawyer does not have to believe in his brief. Yet after the failure of the All Parties Congress in 1928, followed by the rejection of a consensus on the Hindu-Muslim Question at the Round Table Conference, he retired from active politics, living in exile in London. The bitter experience of formation of provincial government after the 1937 elections under the 1935 Act, the rising Muslim fear of cultural submergence and religious assimilation and consequent loss of religious identity, Nehru's philosophy of economic determinism, the slow but steady exit of Muslims from the Congress platform, the artificial, egoistic claim of the Congress to represent all Indians while it had few Muslims of eminence left and an array of leaders who believed in Hindu Nationalism and who were opposed to any constitutional safeguards for or political concessions to the Muslims gave Jinnah an opportunity to re-enter national politics as a Man with a Mission – to secure equality, if not parity with the Hindus for the Muslims. He used all available arguments – religious and pseudo-religious, realistic and sentimental, rational and irrational, historical and pseudo-historical, rational and irrational, to promote and plead his case. Denied negotiations, on equal terms as in 1916, in the late 30's and 40's, he forced himself and his party into all negotiations between the Freedom Movement and the Imperial power, at least cast his shadow over it.

Yet it is doubtful whether Pakistan had become inevitable before the announcement of the Partition on 3 June, 1947. There could have been an agreement on a federal structure, with Centre limited to specific subjects like defence, external affairs, communication and finance and with autonomous provinces also enjoying specified powers plus all residual powers, a multi-level democratic system with a charter of fundamental rights and a uniform code for the treatment of religious and linguistic minorities everywhere. Perhaps the British wanted to weaken the successive

State. Perhaps those who believed in united India had lost patience; even Gandhi had secluded himself from the march of events, the separatist had his way but the anti-separatists had their pound of flesh in the form of religious partition of Bengal and Punjab. And Jinnah had to bow to the logic of Partition and lump it and accept what he called and motheaten Pakistan.

Jinnah's speech of 11 August, 1947 expresses his realization of the irrationality of the Pakistan idea and he could not refuse it when it was presented to him on platter. But he did not foresee the mass exodus and the bloodshed, nor could he stop it when it began.

His speech was his last effort to stem the tide and he saw the theoretical foundation he had envisaged for the welfare of half the Muslims who remained in India though what has been inhumanly called 'balance of hostages', crumbling before his own eyes. This is, indeed, an irony of fate that those Muslims of the Subcontinent who needed no protection got protection and those who needed it more, were left unprotected!

Jinnah's speech of 11 August, 1947 could not and did not abate the religious pressure for the transformation of Pakistan into a modern laboratory for Islam, an Islamic State. The Islamists of Pakistan accused Jinnah, the Father of Pakistan, of having strangled his baby at its birth! But the speech does not mean a reversal of course for Jinnah. He had gone too far. But, it is said that on his death bed, he regretted what he had done and wished to go to Delhi to plead with Nehru for annulling Partition.

It would be an injustice to Jinnah to give him the full blame, or whole credit depending upon how one looks at it, for the creation of Pakistan. Political developments beyond his control, since the late 20's, the Hindu dominance of the nationalist movement through penetration of the forces of Hindu nationalism, majoritarianism or secular follies of his contemporaries, support by the British when it suited them, the sheer sentimentalism of the Muslim masses, the sidelining of the Muslim Ulema, all contributed to the Partition. A historic event is the culmination of a process and never the handiwork of such individual. So was it Jinnah? Or was it like the culmination of a Greek tragedy?

While Advani was wrong in attributing secularism to Jinnah, he was absolutely right and realistic in accepting the fact that Pakistan exists and Partition cannot be undone and, logically, supporting the cause of friendly and peaceful coexistence in the larger and common interest of all the peoples of the Subcontinent, perhaps, with 'Muslim Pakistan' and cooperating with 'Muslim Indian'.

The RSS mindset, nourished on the concept of Akhand Bharat cannot accept Pakistan as a permanent reality; it cannot accept the assertion of religious identity by the Muslim Indians; it cannot accept Territorial Nationalism; it understands and accepts Hindu Nationalism, redefined cleverly by Advani who gave it a modern nomenclature as 'Cultural Nationalism'.

What is interesting is to see the contrast when the RSS did not object when Prime Minister Vajpayee visited the Minar-e-Pakistan in Lahore or when he played the Muslim card as a part of his electoral strategy to restore the Sangh Parivar to power. Today, out of power, it is up against Advani for the sin of visiting Jinnah's Mazar in Karachi and eulogizing him as secular for his speech of 11 August, 1947. We can understand the RSS reaction particularly in the context of the on-going war of succession within the BJP and the continuing war of ideological supremacy between the RSS and the BJP. RSS wants to purge leaders of national eminence and place the BJP in the hands of dependable and obedient youngman who cannot take one step, win one seat, without the RSS support.

But what about Advani's motives in going to Pakistan and saying what he said. Surely as an astute politician with 50 years of experience, he should have anticipated the reaction of his open and hidden adversaries. Did he wish to soften his image, emerge as the only possible successor of Vajpayee in the BJP, acceptable to the other members of the NDA as the Leader? Did he wish to play his own Muslim card? But he could have done both without visiting Pakistan and paying tribute to Jinnah. Did he think his gesture would impress the Muslims and the secular-liberal crowd? Didn't he learn anything from the flop that Vajpayee's Muslim Card proved itself to be in May, 2004? Doesn't he realize that the Rath Yatra, the Demolition and the Gujarat Massacre have left deep scars on the Muslim mind? That no Muslim Indian regards Pakistan as a protector or as a guardian or accept it as its advocate, the defunct Nehru-Liaquat Pact of 1950 notwithstanding, that the Muslim Indians and the secular liberal Hindu shall judge the BJP (and Advani) not by token gestures but only by a clear change in its divisive and exclusive ideology, in its anti-Muslim policies, in its reduction of national politics to a zero-sum game between the Hindus and the Muslims, even when the Hindus form 82% and Muslims only 13% of the national population. A Muslim Indian does not imagine, as Mr. Advani does, that a Ziarat of 'Pakistan Sharif' climaxed by respectful homage to the Dargah of its patron-saint will wash away all the sins of omission and commission, like a dip in the Ganges does for an orthodox Hindu! But the RSS mindset which identifies Muslim Indians with Pakistan is convinced that the path to a Muslim Indian's heart or mind passes through Pakistan.

The visit and the statements are bound to create a lingering controversy. These controversies will echo and re-echo. One hopes and prays that they do not reopen the wounds of Partition and regenerate the hatred, ill-will and hostility – the communal environment – that we have nearly overcome over the last 50 years. It would be a sad day if Hindu mobs begin reenacting Gujarat all over the country, calling the Muslim Indians 'Jinnah ki Aulad' and holding them responsible for Partition and begin hunting them.

But what was the motive of Pakistan in inviting Advani, the iron man, when, out of power, known for his opposition to Indo-Pakistan reconciliation, for his hard line on Kashmir and for his antipathy to the Muslim Indians? Until the other day Advani was held responsible for the fiasco at Agra. Today he is given a red carpet treatment. What did Pakistan hope to achieve from this show of hospitality and by raising his stature in his Hindu constituency for getting him to inaugurate the rebuilding of an ancient Hindu temple in Pakistan, associated with the Mahabharat. Pakistan establishment has publicly confessed to its disappointment at BJP's defeat. Does Pakistan calculate that the UPA Government may fall and the BJP, with Advani as its head, may resume power?

Or did Pakistan wish to soften the opposition of the Hindu Right to any deal with India which may mean a concession to Pakistan. Come to think of it, both the RSS and the Pakistan establishment are ready for yet another partition – of J&K – more or less on the same basis *i.e.* religion. Do they have a common objective? Yet Pakistan should know that the Hindu Right will oppose even the slightest concession by the UPA to Pakistan, though it may swallow bigger concessions, if the BJP was in power. In any case, for Pakistan, the Advani episode is an insurance, a gamble for the future.

Time Now to Recall Quaid's Warning to Muslim World

The "*Quaid-e-Azam*" says Frank Moraes, formerly editor, *Times of India* (Mumbai), "is assured of a place among the great Muslims of our times. Kamal Ataturk revived the ramshackle state which was Turkey. But Jinnah's achievement was in a sense more considerable. Out of next to nothing, he willed a state into being." To most observers, as to Moraes, Jinnah's achievement tests on his founding a state. But what is significant about it is that it was not just another state when several existing ones were disappearing in the wake of political turmoil and convulsion: it was Pakistan. And it represented the political expression of a religious community.

Actually, the Pakistan movement was launched as part of a worldwide movement for Muslim revival and renaissance. More important, it was done on the basis of a transcendent ideal-the Islamic ideology. Theoretically speaking, Pakistan was not meant to be a mere territorial expression of the cherished yearnings of the hundred million Muslims of undivided India; it was meant to found a home in pursuit of this transcendent ideal.

And in taking up the cause of Pakistan, the primary aim was to gain power for Muslims in a particular region with a view to keeping the faith uncorrupted-that is, to enable the Muslims to live Islamically. Pakistan was thus visualised in terms of "free Islam in free India". Power was sought not merely for material gains, but primarily to enable the Muslims to live as Muslims, both in their individual and collective sphere. In incorporating the Islamic ideal within its concept, the Pakistan movement was, to a certain extent, pan-Islamic. But the concept was restricted to those areas in the subcontinent where the Muslims constitute a majority, in order to make it politically realisable.

Clearly, in this nationalist-oriented world and at the present juncture, it would be futile to strive towards pan-Islamism of an earlier age. What, however, would promote the cause of Islam was to subscribe to the ideology of Islamic or Muslim nationalism as a via media between pure pan-Islamism and unalloyed nationalism. A blend of the two concepts, Muslim nationalism, while recognising the multiplicity of nation within Islam, strives to promote the solidarity, identity of outlook and close cooperation between the various Muslim nations on the basis of their religious urges and cultural coherence. Thus, while Indian Muslim nationhood was largely constructed on the basis of Islam and of an Islamic *weltanschauung*, besides certain allied factors, the Indian Muslims were yet pronounced a distinct nation not only in the Subcontinent, but in the world of Islam as well.

In a sense, this represented a translation in mundane terms of what Iqbal, the ideologue of Pakistan, had laid down earlier. After diagnosing the malaise of the Muslim world in his famous Lectures, he had come to the conclusion that "for the present every Muslim nation must sank into her own deeper self, temporarily focus her vision on herself alone, until all are strong and powerful to form a living family of nations."

Likewise, in one the darkest hours of their history, Jinnah told Indian Muslims: "only on thing can save the *Musalmans* and energise them to regain their lost ground. They must first recapture their own soul and stand by their lofty position and principles which form the basis of their unity, and which bind them in one body-politic." Conceived, thus, as a movement to "energise" Muslims into a dynamic people with a view to making them a self-contained unit in what Iqbal calls a "living family of Muslim nations", Pakistan represented a significant contribution towards Muslim renaissance in modern times.

Nor was the achievement of Pakistan as conceived by its founders, an end in itself. Rather, it was meant to be the beginning of an end, the supreme goal being the emancipation of all Muslim peoples wherever they may be, and the re-birth of the Muslim world as a powerful force in the counsels of the world.

Apart from what Pakistan has done for the emancipation of the various Muslim peoples during the fifty years of her existence, Pakistan, by the very act of carving out important territories in the northwest and northeast of the Subcontinent as a separate political entity, had checkmated the rise of a giant Hindu state in the Subcontinent. Thus by her very creation, Pakistan had, as it were, constricted the tentacles of the Hindu "octopus" in India, which would otherwise have spread to the countries both to east and west of the Subcontinent. And but the Pakistan the successor Hindu regional power in India would have been too stupendous for the neighbouring small countries to resist: as a successor state to the British Indian Empire, it might as well have tried to fill in the vacuum created by the exit of the British. It would, moreover, have laid serious claim to those tacitly recognised spheres of influence which the British had enjoyed by virtue of their occupation of India.

Corroboration of this viewpoint is contained in the writings, among others, of Sardar Pannikar, former Indian Ambassador to China and Egypt, and the chief theoretician of India's foreign policy. "The Indian security policy in South East Asia sphere," he wrote in 1945, "covers the entire Indian Ocean area, India's interest in the security of the Persian Gulf, the integrity and stability of Persia and Afghanistan, the neutralisation of Sinkiang and Tibet and the security of Burma, Siam and Indo-Chinese coastline, apart of course from Malaya and Singapore, is obvious enough to all." "The strategic area in Indian warfare" Pannikar explained on another occasion, "was not so much the Burmese frontier, as Malaya, Singapore and the neglected Andaman Islands. What was of utmost importance in safeguarding India's communication with Europe was not Bombay or Colombo, but Diego Suarez and Aden."

Other Indian leaders have put forward the same idea, couched in more diplomatic terms, if only in order not to arouse the suspicions of India's neighbours. Both before and after independence, *Pandit* Nehru, India's first Prime Minister (1947-64), had often talked of the "compelling factors of "geography" and "history" and of "the force of circumstances", goading India "to play a very important part in Asia. If you have to consider any question affecting Middle East, India inevitably comes in the picture. If you have to consider any question concerning South East Asia, you cannot do so without India. So also with the Far East." Shorn of its sophistry and euphemism, it meant that India even in her constricted form, has inherited certain "inevitable" spheres of influence.

In the light of this Indian world-view, how significant was Jinnah's warning in December 1946. During his sojourn, in Cairo, he told his Egyptian audience: "It is only when Pakistan is established that we (Indian Muslims and the Egyptians) should be really free, otherwise there will be the menace of a Hindu imperialist *Raj* spreading its tentacles right across the Middle East." "If India will be ruled by a Hindu imperialist power," he added, "it will be as great a menace for the future, if not greater, as the British imperialist power has been in the past. Therefore, I think the whole of the Middle East will fall from frying pan into the fire. The Middle East countries want to be free and self-governing and not subject to spheres of influence."

Seen in the context, could not the Pakistan movement be described as part of a larger movement for Islamic re-birth and revival? If today India is seeking the friendship of the Middle Eastern countries it is because of existence of Pakistan; otherwise, it would have well claimed spheres of influence. Viewed in this perspective, had not the architect of Pakistan, in some respects, a profound influence on the present pattern of the Muslim world?

Once Pakistan was created, Jinnah stressed the need for cohesion among Muslims all over the world and a broad-based policy of cooperation inspired by Islamic identity. In his last *Eid-ul-Fitr* message, he warned the Muslim world: "We are all passing through perilous times. The drama of power-politics that is being waged in Palestine, Indonesia and Kashmir should serve as an eye-opener to us. It is only by putting up a united front that we can make our voice felt in the `counsels of the world." Even prior to independence, the Indian Muslim that taken an active interest in the affairs of the Muslim countries, especially, Palestine. On their behalf, Jinnah had demanded in November, 1939, the fulfilment of all reasonable national demands of the Arabs in Palestine as one of the pre-requisites for Muslim League's cooperation in the British was effort in India; he threatened "to call out the Muslim ministries in the Provinces" on the issue of British injustice to Palestinian Arabs; he extracted assurance from the Viceroy about the stoppage of Jewish immigration into Palestine after the quota stipulated in the White Paper of Palestine (1939) had been exhausted.

Thus the movement that Jinnah headed was neither out and out pan-Islamic nor thoroughly nationalist. With Jamal al-Din al-Afghani's movement in late 19th century, it had points of contact, it was striving for the transcendent ideal of Islam and for Muslim unity. Even so, the Pakistan movement was couched in modern political terminology, and employed terms like "nation", "the right of self-determination", "plebiscite", etc. and took resort to the modern techniques of *hartals*, slogans, boycott, and the passing of resolutions to build up pressure incrementally upon both the British government and the Hindu-dominated Congress party.

The Pakistan movement, thus, grows out of a blending of the concepts of pan-Islamism and nationalism, and approximates largely to what Lothrop Stoddard defines as "Islamic Nationalism ". And Jinnah had the vision and foresight to recognise the dictates of these two concepts while laying the foundation of the

A NATION DIVIDED

The freedom struggle from the British Raj commenced in 1947 by Gandhi and the independence of India was declared, however there was a heavy price to pay. Jinnah, the leader of the Muslim League, demanded that a separate state for the Muslim minority was now necessary. In 1937 there had been an election in India. Jinnah's Muslim League could not obtain enough majority to get into power and so he needed alternative strategy to obtain a significant political opinion on behalf of the Muslims in India. He had previously supported Hindu-Muslim unity, but after the election his thinking changed and he started to be in favour of a separate Muslim state. In March 1940, he declared to the All-Indian Muslim League: ".....If the British Government are really earnest and sincere to secure peace and happiness of the people of this subcontinent, the only course open to us all is to allow the major nations separate homelands by dividing India into autonomous national states".

This meant the division of India which deeply distressed Gandhi. The Lahore Resolution stated that if any province of India had a Muslim majority, that province would be declared Muslim land. This was the reason why Sindhis left Sind. Sind had a Muslim majority and so was taken over completely by Muslims. Gandhi's response was: "My whole soul rebels against the idea that Hinduism and Islam represent two antagonistic cultures and doctrines. To assent to such a doctrine is for me a denial of God."

In 1942, Cripps, who was sent by Sir Winston Churchill to act as a mediator for the dispute, agreed with the statement of the Lahore Resolution and Jinnah that Muslims should have their own country which would be made up of the whole of Sind, half of Bengal and half of Punjab. In 1942, both Jinnah and Gandhi were locked into their respective positions. Gandhi initially desired that the British leave India before they were to go any further with the creation of Pakistan. Churchill imprisoned Gandhi and the Congress Party as a result of them opposing the Raj and desiring that India should become a free state not under British Rule. This imprisonment meant that they were unable to express themselves politically. Jinnah collaborated with the British in order to aid them to win the Second World War, after which they were promised by the British to give them a homeland of their own, Pakistan.

After this war had ended, the Congress members were released. The expectations of the people in India towards the new socialist Labour government in Britain were high, it was believed that the new government was going to result in the ending of the Raj. However, this did not happen immediately. In Sind, as the majority of the population were Muslims, the priority was not concerned with the method of taking over Sind. Nevertheless, it was believed that it would be a complicated matter to decide what other provinces would also make up Pakistan. Jinnah made a major flaw in his plans while deciding on which provinces would be claimed as Pakistan, he decided that the provinces would be on the East and West of India which would mean that Pakistan would not be united by land. Much of the predominantly Muslim areas were swampland and therefore would not be of benefit agriculturally to the Muslims. He also resolved to go further and claim more land on the opposite side of India.

Wavell, the Viceroy of India, made two recommendations: Muslims should be allowed to govern themselves in Muslim-majority areas and non Muslims should not be forced to live in Pakistan against their will. Jinnah was asking for a large amount of land which he expressed as nothing too big, he wanted a sea connection between Karachi and Calcutta to be under the control of Muslims. The Secretary of State, Pethick Lawrence, was not convinced that this plan was practically a good idea for economic reasons. The two states, he thought, would be in poverty and therefore would not be able to support their people with their economy. Jinnah was afraid that after the election, he would not obtain Pakistan and so he organized Direct Action Day in order to make his voice heard by the Government of India. Jinnah accepted a limited Pakistan, but also said that he was prepared for war if it was necessary. The Interim government was formed by the Congress Party, after which there was a lot of bloodshed. Some of Jinnah's party joined the Government of India to attempt to resolve the situation, but this was unsucessful. The violence continued and Jinnah and the Congress were invited to London to negotiate a settlement, but the talks failed.

The state of India in the early part of 1947 caused Congress to again consider Partition. India was in the midst of rioting and bloodshed. Gandhi, a man of nonviolence, could see no other alternative to stop the mass killings and so it was decided that the Partition of India in 1947 was the only solution for a non-violent India. He despised this notion, but in his opinion it was the better of the two evils. In March 1947 the Congress decided on the Partition of Punjab and Bengal. Mountbatten entered the negotiations and talked through logically Jinnah's proposals and their consequences. Mountbatten told Gandhi about the Cabinet Mission Plan, which gave India a weak centre and a lot of smaller regions which would govern themselves and leave major decisions to the central government. Gandhi was in favour of this notion. Mountbatten and Jinnah were in talks, but the leader of the Muslim League was obstinate and did not move from the idea of a new Pakistan. He refused the Cabinet Mission Plan outright. On April 8th, 1947 Mountbatten asked Jinnah what he would do if he were in the Viceroys place, Jinnah replied that he would give the Muslims Pakistan as soon as possible.

Mountbatten used Jinnah's argument against him. He said if India was to divide into India and Pakistan, the same principle would apply to Bengal and Punjab.

Therefore the land of Pakistan would be a lot smaller than the original plan. Mountbatten went on to explain that if we had a lot of small states, such as Bengal, Punjab and Pakistan their power in the world would not be significant enough to influence decisions on a global scale. After two hours of this meeting, Mountbatten felt Jinnah bending under the weight of his arguments and he was pleased with himself.

Mountbatten found it easier to deal with Jinnah than the Congress Party as the Congress were divided in their views and Jinnah was a person who had only one goal. After much negotiation, Jinnah agreed to take half of Punjab and Bengal and the whole of Sind along with the North-West Frontier Province. The partition of Assam was also agreed. Mountbatten was convinced that the people would not blame the British for the division of India, and Pakistan would be safe from the Indian people rebuking the British government. Instead, the responsibility would lie on the Indian government.

In a public announcement by Nehru in April 1947, he said that Jinnah would have Pakistan which would be made up of Sind, half of Punjab and half of Bengal. Mountbatten knew that the Cabinet Mission Plan had failed and was not worth pursuing. Jinnah told Mountbatten: " *In fact the leaders of Congress are so dishonest, so crooked, and so obsessed with the idea of smashing the Muslim League, that there are no lengths to which they will not go to do so; and the only way of giving Pakistan a chance is to make it an independent nation of the British Commonwealth, with its own army, and the right to argue cases at any Central Council on this basis.*"

The Mountbatten Plan was leaked to the newspapers and contained the following statements:

1. Both the Congress and the League consider division of India inevitable.
2. The division will involve district wise partition of the Punjab and Bengal, and the appointment of a boundary commission.
3. Before division is carried out, Members of the Legislative Assemblies of the districts concerned should be given the opportunity to decide whether they would prefer to remain in the Indian Union or have a separate state or their areas.
4. If the M.L.A.s decide in favour of partition then they will be asked to elect new representatives to a Constituent Assembly or Constituent Assemblies for their joint or separate areas on the basis of one representative for each million. The present Constituent Assembly for the Indian Union will remain intact. Only the members representing the partitioned areas will cease to be its members.
5. If partition is to take place, the N.W.F.P. should have fresh elections to decide whether its people would desire to remain in the Indian Union or join Pakistan or become an independent territory.

It was realized that Jinnah wanted to claim 40% of Indian territory. This was not representative of the population of India, (*i.e.* there were not 40% Muslims in India, but 25%). However, it was thought that India would be stronger without the Muslims and their conflicts.

On 10th May, Mountbatten received the approval from the home authorities. However, this plan to divide India was altered by the British Cabinet. The new plan indicated that the British Cabinet wanted to break up India into smaller provinces. Nehru's reaction to this was not positive. He said that the plan was biased towards the Muslim League and would not be acceptable to the people of India. He went on to say that:

"It appears to me that the inevitable and obvious consequences of the proposals and the approach in them are:

(a) to invite the Balkanisation of India,

(b) to provoke certain civil conflict and to add to violence and disorder,

(c) to a further breakdown of the Central Authority which alone can prevent the chaos that is growing,

(d) to demoralize the army, the police, and the central services."

Mountbatten, who respected Nehru, came up with another plan which was to minimize Pakistan and a united India. Jinnah proposed a corridor running through the heart of India to link East Pakistan with West Pakistan. This demand was made on 22nd May 1947 while Mountbatten was briefing the Cabinet in London about his plan.

The plan of the corridor was rejected by Nehru, and the Congress Party thought that Jinnah was trying to use this corridor plan as a bargaining point in the attempt to obtain more land. When Mountbatten returned to India, he said that the matter of partition should be resolved as soon as possible in order not to make the situation more complicated than it already was. He also wanted to speed up the negotiations in order to minimize bloodshed, which took 48 hours to complete.

After Mountbatten negotiated, he thought it would be wise to divide Punjab, as most of the Muslims were in one half of this state in any case. The Sikhs were evenly spread over the province and so the division would affect them in a major way. The British were coming to the end of their Raj. They wanted to hand over power as soon as possible. Jinnah did not approve of the plan and much to the surprise of the Viceroy he said that he wanted to discuss his situation with the Muslim population in a democratic way.

The Plan was approved by all parties by midnight on 2nd June 1947. On 3rd June 1947 Mountbatten and the parties involved began sorting out the practical issues involved in the partition of India. He was convinced that once the decision of partition had been taken, Gandhi would appeal to the nation for nonviolence. However, violence was possible as a lot of Gandhi's ideas would be rejected by the population. On the same day, Nehru, Jinnah and Baldev Singh announced the partition of India on the radio. Mountbatten announced this decision first. Jinnah did not follow the radio script in the announcement, he instead made a political announcement which encouraged people to vote for his party.

The news of the partition was also announced in the House of Commons in the U.K. All this time, Gandhi was silent. He did not show approval or disapproval of the plan. So Mountbatten interpreted his silence as a sign of assent. Mountbatten made out that he had followed Gandhi's advice in the making of the plan. However, Gandhi did not react one way or another.

Discussion took place about the Interim Government which was basically to establish who would govern India while the hand over of power from the British to the Indian and Pakistan governments was taking place. Jinnah had argued that the Congress was made up of too many Hindus and therefore would not have the best interests of Pakistan. In order to do away with confusion and misunderstanding, the Viceroy proposed that:

"My advice therefore is:

(a) that so far as HMG is concerned, India minus Pakistan should inherit the entity of India internationally;

(b) that Hindustan will take over all the international obligations of the present government of India; and (c) that agreement should be reached between the governments of Hindustan and Pakistan as regards division of assets and liabilities on an equitable basis."

On 20th June the Bengal Legislative Assembly voted in favour of partition, on 23rd June the Punjab Legislative Assembly also voted the same way and three days later the Sind Legislative Assembly voted to be completely taken over by the new Pakistan government.

As the time grew nearer to partition, there was an increase in misunderstanding between Gandhi and Mountbatten. Mountbatten was aiming to push the partition through as soon as possible in order that Jinnah would not find any excuse to ridicule him or his procedure and negotiations in public.

The Indian Independence Bill on 4th July went to Parliament, the second reading was on the 10th and on 18th the Royal assent was given. The bill stated that: " As from the fifteenth day of

August, nineteen hundred and forty-seven, two independent Dominions shall be set up in India, to be known respectively as India and Pakistan."

Jinnah, the grandson of a Hindu, left Delhi on 7th August for his new duties in Karachi. His dream of an Islamic state had been realized. This resulted in Gandhi feeling an enormous amount of grief and despair. *Partition and the people of Sindh...*

In 1947 before the creation of Pakistan, Sindhi Hindus were a minority community in their own province of Sindh, having no rights or privileges, unlike their Muslim neighbours who were a majority community. Sindhi Hindus and Muslims had lived side by side for hundreds of years with hardly any animosity between them, with the honouring of each other's religions. Most mosques were decorated during Diwali (a Hindu festival) in Sindh. This harmony between Muslims and Hindus came to an end a few months before the Partition, during which the "Muhajirs", who were a politically extreme Muslim organization, migrated from India and forcibly took over the properties of Sindhi Hindus. So began a long and bitter process in history.

It was declared by the Government of Sindh, that any land owned by Muslims before 1907 would be given back to them, regardless of Hindu ownership. Sindhis were aware of the potential violence after 1947. Places of Hindu worship would be destroyed, and so they wanted to flee before the violence began.

On December 21st, 1947, a raid took place in the houses of Hindus starting with Hyderabad. People were thrown into camps awaiting deportation to India. Similar action was organized by Muslims on January 6th 1948 in Karachi and all the Hindus were gathered at the exit camps, for the forced migration to India by road, rail and sea. Hindu Sindhis did not show resistance for their extration. The eruption of riots and violence in Sind was started by the Muhajirs and encouraged by Punjabi Muslims. Hindu Sindhis were forced to flee with just the clothes that they were wearing and a few personal belongings, often tied up in a bed sheet. Some were fortunate to have the opportunity to sell their belongings on the street. The Sindh government ordered them not to lock their properties before leaving, there was little point in doing so, as the Muslims forced their way in and took possession as ordered by their government. Sindhis fled for their lives to the borders of India to escape get away from the mass killings by the Muslims who were now entering Sind. Some reports even mentioned that women who were at that time in hospital delivering their babies were murdered in cold blood along with their innocent new-borns.

India was now their only hope: A land of freedom and opportunity. On arrival, they found themselves hungry, homeless and unemployed. Employment and food were hard to find and so voluntary support was a necessary part of survival. 11 lakhs (1.1 million) Sindhis migrated to India, aiming to settle down. The government of India set up refugee camps to provide shelter, schooling, medical care, markets, hospitals and other amenities. Some were relieved to be reunited with their families who had been separated in the struggle to leave Sind. It was only despair and bewilderment for those who never found their loved ones. They were unaware of what happened to them and did not know if they were alive or had been killed in Sind. Many refugee families shared the same military camps. In the evening they put up sheets to partition the room into family sections, but for the majority of the day they would cook, eat and wash communally. The conditions were appalling and were unhygienic, many died of tuberculosis, cholera, and of snake and scorpion poisoning.

Those who survived managed to find their own way of feeding their families. They attempted to be employed in any area possible. Soon they started their own businesses and became highly successful business people. Sewing and cooking were the main occupations of Sindhi women in order to earn a living. Food stalls were set up and run by Sindhis. Nevertheless, begging was not considered by Sindhis as a method of making ends meet and they relied on making and selling food and other articles of use.

The survival skills they learned made them into one of India's shrewdest business communities. This tradition still continues. In India the accommodation was too expensive for the common refugee of Sind to buy or rent, so they remained in their military camps for many years. Some time later Bombay housing commissions were set up and run by Sindhis in order to provide affordable accommodation for them to settle down in. Today this community has made the world their home, they have managed to survive the partition and have settled all over the world.

Sind, once the home to Hindu Sindhis, no longer exists, except in the memories, hearts and history books of those who left Sind under desperate circumstances. Sindhis were forced to give up their homeland, where their forefathers lived, for the betterment of the whole nation of India. The people of Sind who survived the trauma of partition, have been scattered all over the world. Many lives were lost and many families were split in two.

The devastation of the partition was so great that up until now, some of those who had lost touch are still without their loved ones in today. It should be remembered that the older members of the Sindhi community, who have witnessed Partition, and who safely and lovingly brought their children through this difficult and dangerous period in history, have learned much from it. There is much to learn from them about how to survive and stay strong.

4

Jinnah and the Simla Conference

As the conditions of war began to turn in favour of the Allies, the Viceroy Wavell felt that the time had come to make proposals for a resolution of the political deadlock in India. His objective, as stated in a letter to Churchill, was to form "a provisional government, of the type suggested in the Cripps Declaration, within the present Constitution, coupled with an earnest but not necessarily simultaneous attempt to devise a means to reach a constitutional settlement."

TALKING TO GANDHI

Wavell had a one-and-a-quarter hour meeting with Churchill on 29 March 1945. The Prime Minister thought that the problem of India, 'could be kept on ice", but Wavell told him quite firmly that the question of India was very urgent and very important. It was on 31 May that Wavell at last got a go-ahead from the Cabinet largely on the lines he had desired. He left London on June 1, and landed at Karachi on June 4.

The British Government's new proposals were publicly disclosed on 14 June 1945, on which date the Viceroy made a broadcast at New Delhi and the Secretary of State made a statement in the House of Commons. In this broadcast, Wavell said the proposals he was making were not an attempt to impose a constitutional settlement, but the hope that the Indian parties would agree on a settlement of the communal issue which had not been fulfilled, and in the meantime great problems had to be solved. He therefore invited the great leaders to a conference in Simla on 25 June to consult with him the formation of the new Executive Council. The Viceroy concluded the broadcast with the announcement that orders had been given for the immediate release of the members of the Congress Working Committee who were in detention.

Wavell separately interviewed Azad, Gandhi and Jinnah on 24 June. Azad appeared to accept the main principles underlying the proposals, including wholehearted support for the war effort. He said that the Congress would accept equality of Caste Hindus and the Muslims but would not compromise on the method of selection. The Congress must have a voice in the selection of non-Hindus and the Muslims in particular must not be selected by an exclusive communal body.

Gandhi said that he would attend the conference if the Viceroy insisted but would "sit in a corner". In the end he did not attend the meeting but remained available at Simla for the duration.

Jinnah expressed the anxiety that the Muslims would be in a minority in the new Executive Council and he claimed that the Muslim League had the right to nominate all the Muslim members to the Council. Wavell said he could not accept this. Jinnah argued that the League had won all the by-elections in the preceding two years and therefore represented all the Muslims of India.

TALKING TO GOVIND VALLAH PANT AT SIMLA

On the very first day of the conference on June 25, it became clear that the real issue was the composition of the Executive Council; all parties would accept the proposal if they could reach an agreement on the method of selection. By June 29 it became clear that the parties would not be able to come up with an agreed list of Executive Councillors and the conference was adjourned till July 14 to enable them to file separate lists.

In a meeting with the Viceroy on June 27, Jinnah had said that he wanted a council of fourteen, including the Viceroy and commander-in-chief with five Hindus, five Muslims, one Sikh and one Scheduled Caste. He said that this was the only council in which the Muslims would stand a chance of not being outvoted on every issue. It was after seeing Jinnah on July 11 that the Viceroy accepted that the conference had failed because he had been unable to accede to Jinnah's demands. After the failure of the conference Jinnah explained: "...if we accept this arrangement, the Pakistan issue will be shelved and out into cold storage indefinitely, whereas the Congress will have secured under this arrangement what they want, namely, a clear road for their advance towards securing Hindu national independence of India, because the future Executive will work as unitary Government of India, and we know that this interim or provisional arrangement will have a way of settling down for an unlimited period, and all the forces in the proposed Executive, plus the known policy of the British Government and Lord Wavell's strong inclination for a united India, would completely jeopardize us."

When the conference met on July 15, Wavell formally announced his failure and sportingly blamed himself for the result. In fact, the Viceroy deserved the greatest praise. With resolution and persistence he had succeeded in winning the consent of Churchill and of others to open the Indian question and give the Indian leaders another chance to install a national government. It was the two principal political parties, the Congress and the Muslim League, that were really responsible for the failure. They had taken up positions that admitted no compromise.

Congress leaders blamed Jinnah for the lost opportunity and said that the Viceroy should have gone ahead without the League. But in fact the entire plan had been based on the idea that the Executive Council would be an all-party body.

Some days after the conference, at a public meeting the Quaid-i-Azam, referred to Gandhi's presence at Simla during the Simla Conference in scathing terms: "The *first question is why did Mr. Gandhi as one of the leaders of the recognized parties go to Simla? Having gone there, why did Mr. Gandhi not attend the conference? The reason is simple. It was to play the role of wire puller."*

He Interim Government

Wavell wrote identical letters to Nehru and Jinnah on July 22,

1946 asking them whether the Congress and the Muslim League would be prepared to enter an interim government on the basis that six members (including one Scheduled Caste representative) would be nominated by the Congress and five by the Muslim League. Three representatives of the minorities would be nominated by the Viceroy. Jinnah replied that the proposal was not acceptable to the Muslim League because it destroyed the principal of parity. At Nehru's invitation, he and Jinnah conferred together on August 15 but could not come to an agreement on the question of the Congress joining the interim government.

The Working Committee of the Muslim League had decided in the meantime that Friday 16 August, 1946 would be marked as the 'Direct Action Day". There was serious trouble in Calcutta and some rioting in Sylhet on that day. The casualty figures in Calcutta during the period of 16-19 August were 4,000 dead and 10,000 injured. In his letter to Pethick-Lawrence, Wavell had reported that appreciably more Muslims than Hindus had been killed. The "Great Calcutta Killing" marked the start of the bloodiest phase of the "war of succession" between the Hindus and the Muslims and it became increasingly difficult for the British to retain control. Now, they had to cope with the Congress civil disobedience movement as well as furious Muslims that had also come out in the streets in thousands.

The negotiations with the League reached a deadlock and the Viceroy decided to form an interim government with the Congress alone, leaving the door open for the League to come in later. A communique was issued on August 24 which announced that the existing members of the Governor General's Executive Council had resigned and that on their places new persons had been appointed. It was stated that the interim government would be installed on September 2.

Jinnah declared two days later that the Viceroy had struck a severe blow to Indian Muslims and had added insult to injury by nominating three Muslims who did not command the confidence of Muslims of India. He reiterated that the only solution to Indian problem was the division of India into Pakistan and Hindustan. The formation of an interim government consisting only of the

Congress nominees added further fuel to the communal fire. The Muslims regarded the formation of the interim government as an unconditional surrender of power to the Hindus, and feared that the Governor General would be unable to prevent the Hindus from using their newly acquired power of suppressing Muslims all over India.

After the Congress had taken the reins at the Centre on September 2, Jinnah faced a desperate situation. The armed forces were predominantly Hindu and Sikh and the Indian members of the other services were also predominantly Hindu. The British were preparing to concede independence to India if they withdrew the Congress was to be in undisputed control, the Congress was to be free to deal with the Muslims as it wished. Wavell too, felt unhappy at the purely Congress interim government. He genuinely desired a Hindu-Muslim settlement and united India, and had worked hard for that end.

Wavell pleaded with Nehru and Gandhi, in separate interviews, that it would help him to persuade Jinnah to cooperate if they could give him an assurance that the Congress would not insist on nominating a Nationalist Muslim. Both of them refused to give way on that issue. Wavell informed Jinnah two days later that he had not succeeded in persuading the Congress leaders to make a gesture by not appointing a Nationalist Muslim. Jinnah realized that the Congress would not give up the right to nominate a Nationalist Muslim and that he would have to accept the position if he did not wish to leave the interim government solely in the hands of the Congress. On October 13, he wrote to Wavell that, though the Muslim League did not agree with much that had happened, "in the interests of the Muslims and other communities it will be fatal to leave the entire field of administration of the Central Government in the hands of the Congress". The League had therefore decided to nominate five members for the interim government. On October 15, he gave the Viceroy the following five names: Liaquat Ali Khan, I.I Chundrigar, Abdur Rab Nishtar, Ghazanfar Ali Khan and Jogindar Nath Mandal. The last name was a Scheduled Caste Hindu and was obviously a tit-for-tat for the Congress insistence upon including a Nationalist Muslim in its own quota.

New Indian Policy and Mountbatten's Appointment as the Viceroy

The Muslim League's refusal to take part in the Constituent Assembly meant that the plan of the Cabinet Mission for the transfer of power in accordance with a Constitution framed cooperatively by the Indian political parties themselves had come to a deadlock. Accordingly, Prime Minister Attlee made the following statement on Indian policy in the House of Commons on February 20, 1947: His Majesty's Government desire to hand over their responsibility to authorities established by a Constitution approved by all parties in India in accordance with the Cabinet Mission's plan, but unfortunately there is at present no clear prospect that such a Constitution and such authorities will emerge. The present state of uncertainty is fraught with danger and cannot be indefinitely prolonged. His Majesty's Government wish to make it clear that it is their definite intention to take the necessary steps to effect the transference of power into responsible Indian hands by a date not later than June 1948...if it should appear that such a Constitution will not have been worked out by a fully representative Assembly before the time mentioned, His Majesty's Government will have to consider to whom the powers of the Central Government in British India should be handed over, on the due date, whether as a whole to some form of Central Government for British India or in some areas to the existing Provincial Governments, or in such other way seem most reasonable and in the best interests of the Indian people.

In regard to the Indian States, as was explicitly stated by the Cabinet Mission, His Majesty's Government do not intend to hand over their powers and obligation under paramountcy to any government of British India. It is not intended to bring paramountcy, as a system, to a conclusion earlier than the date of the final transfer of power, but it is contemplated that for the intervening period the relations of the Crown with individual States may be adjusted by agreement.

It was announced at the same time that Rear-Admiral the Visount Mountbatten would succeed Lord Wavell as the Viceroy in March. Lord and Lady Mountbatten landed at Delhi on March

22, 1947 and he took over as the Viceroy two days later. He could very well have represented to the British Government that both the Congress and the Muslim League had already asked for the partition of India into Muslim-majority and non-Muslim majority areas and sought their permission to embark upon the process of partition straightaway. But he chose to follow the policy that first the attempt to transfer power in accordance with the Cabinet Mission plan must continue. It is to that end, therefore, that he first directed his endeavours.

Mountbatten's relations with the Congress party had a flying start. The foundation of Nehru's friendship with Lord and Lady Mountbatten had been laid in March 1946 when the Indian leader visited Singapore. The political conditions in India too had changed in favour of the Congress. In post-independence India the Congress party was expected to rule the country. Consequently, it was the Congress's friendship that had now to be cultivated. The fact that Mountbatten personally was bitterly opposed to partition, made it much easier for him to court the Congress leaders. All these factors greatly increased the already formidable odds facing the Quaid-i-Azam in his fight for Pakistan. In his meetings with Mountbatten, he refused to budge from the position that Pakistan was the only solution acceptable to the Muslim League.

The Plan of June 3, 1947

The plan for the transfer of power to which all concerned had agreed, was authoritatively announced by the British Government in the form of a statement on June 3, by Prime Minister Attlee in the House of Commons and Secretary of State for India the Earl of Listowel in the House of Lords. The existing Constituent Assembly would continue to function but any constitution framed by it could not apply to those parts of the country which were unwilling to accept it. The procedure outlined in the statement was designed to ascertain the wishes of such unwilling parts on the question whether their constitution was to be framed by the existing Constituent Assembly or by a new and separate Constituent Assembly. After this had been done, it would be possible to determine the authority or authorities to whom power should be transferred.

The final phase of the partition of India (meeting on June 2, 1947). The Provincial Legislative Assemblies of Bengal and the Punjab (excluding the European members) will therefore each be asked to meet in two parts, one representing the Muslim majority districts and the other the rest of the Province.

The members of the two parts of each Legislative Assembly sitting separately will be empowered to vote whether or not the Province should be partitioned.

If a simple majority of either part decides in favour of partition, division will take place and arrangements will be made accordingly. For the immediate purpose of deciding on the issue of partition, the members of the Legislative Assemblies of Bengal and the Punjab will sit in two parts according to Muslim majority districts and non-Muslim majority districts.

This is only a preliminary step of a purely temporary nature as it is evident that for the purposes of final partition of these Provinces a detailed investigation of boundary questions will be needed; and, as soon as a decision involving partition has been taken for either Province, a Boundary Commission will be set up by the Governor General, the membership and terms of reference of which will be settled in consultation with those concerned.

Moreover, it was stated that the Legislative Assembly of Sind was similarly authorized to decide at a special meeting whether the province wished to participate in the existing Constituent Assembly or to join the new one.

If the partition of the Punjab was decided, a referendum would be held in the North-West Frontier Province to ascertain which Constituent Assembly they wished to join. Balochistan would also be given an opportunity to reconsider its position and the Governor General was examining how this could be most appropriately done.

Lord Mountbatten-11 days before the Transfer of Power

In his broadcast, Mountbatten regretted that it had been impossible to obtain the agreement of Indian leaders either on the Cabinet Mission plan or any other plan that would have preserved the unity of India. But there could be no question of coercing any large area in which one community had a majority to live against their will under a government in which another community had a majority.

The only alternative to coercion was partition. On the morning of June 4, the Viceroy held a press conference and said for the first time publically that the transfer of power could take place on "about 15 August" 1947. The Council of the All India Muslim League met in New Delhi on 9th and 10th of June 1947 and stated in its resolution that although it could not agree to the partition of Bengal and the Punjab to give its consent to such partition, it had to consider the plan for the transfer of power as a whole. It gave full authority to the Quaid-i-Azam to accept the fundamental principles of the plan as a compromise and left it to him to work out the details.

The All India Congress Committee passed a resolution on June 15 accepting the 3rd June plan. However, it expressed the hope that India would one day be reunited.

The Radcliffe Boundary Award

Two boundary commissions were set up by the Viceroy, one of them was to deal with the detailed partition of Bengal and separation of Sylhet from Assam and the other to deal similarly with the partition of the Punjab. Each of the commissions would have a chairman and four members, two appointed by the Congress and two by the Muslim League. Sir Cyril Radcliffe, a leading member of the English Bar, was appointed the chairman of both the commissions. Radcliffe had never visited India before and there is no indication that he had any worthwhile knowledge of Indian affairs. He arrived in Delhi on July 8. Mountbatten disclosed the awards to the Indian leaders on August 17.

The awards satisfied no one. The Congress' criticism of the award relating to Bengal mainly related to the allotment of the Chittagong Hill Tracts to Pakistan. The major Pakistani criticism was the allotment of Calcutta to India. With regard to the Ferozepore district, Pakistan pointed out that Muslim majority tahsils of Ferozepore and Zira, contiguous to Pakistan, were first allotted by Radcliffe to Pakistan later on as the result of a last minute intervention by Mountbatten, were alloted to India.

The Quaid-i-Azam could do no more than to console his countrymen, *'we have been squeezed in as much as was possible and the latest blow that we have received is the Award of the Boundary Commission. It is an unjust, incomprehensible and even perverse Award. It may be wrong, unjust and perverse; and it may not be a judicial but a political Award, but we have agreed to abide by it and it is binding upon us. As honourable people we must abide by it. It may be our misfortune but we must bear up this one more blow with fortitude, courage and hope."*

SIMLA CONFERENCE OF 1945

The Simla proposal, popularly known as the Wavell Plan, was the first British move after the abortive Cripps Plan (1942). Like the Cripps proposals, the Wavell Plan was also meant to secure Indian cooperation in the prosecution of the war against the Japanese in the East, and to associate Indians in the administration at the centre.

Hence His Majesty's Government proposed on June 14, 1945 the reconstitution of the Viceroy's Executive Council, whose members, except for the Commander-in-Chief (i.e., the War Member), would be Indians, representing Indian political parties. Improvising upon the Gandhi-blessed Desai-Liaquat formula (1944) of Congress-League parity, the Wavell proposals envisaged Hindu-Muslim parity, each being assigned five places in a cabinet of fourteen. The rest being filled in by the representatives of the scheduled castes, Sikhs, Indian Christians and Parsis. Simultaneously with the announcement of the Wavell Plan, members of the Congress Working Committee, jailed since the launching of the Quit India Movement (August 8, 1942), were released. The Viceroy called the leaders of the various parties to a conference at Simla on June 25, to explore ways and means as how best to reconstitute the Executive Council and to work out a broad consensus on its composition.

But the Simla Conference ended in failure on July 14, chiefly because neither the Congress nor Wavell would concede the League its representative status among Muslims, a fundamental principle which Jinnah had been tirelessly arguing for acceptance in all his parleys with both the Congress and the British since 1938.

The Congress insisted upon implanting two Muslim Congressmen and the Viceroy upon including a (pro-British) Unionist Muslim as a representative of the Punjab in the Muslim quota of seats.

Azad, the Congress President, tried hard to "consolidate the minor parties with the Congress against the Muslim League.... He believed that on this basis Jinnah and the League could be broken." The result, the Congress' "list", reported Wavell, "was disappointing — it displayed a desire to dominate the Executive Council and a tenancy to put forward stooges from smaller minorities out of all proportion to their political capacity and importance". Azad also sent for the Congress-aligned Jamiat leader, Husain Ahmad Madani, and leaders of "nationalist" Muslim parties to Simla, to embarrass Jinnah and erode his position.

On the Unionist representation issue, Governor Glancy (Punjab) and Khizar Hayat Khan Tiwana, the Premier, were initially insistent, the former characterising Jinnah's claim to nominate all the five Muslims 'outrageously unreasonable' and conceding him only three places. VP Menon, Reforms Commissioner, also insisted "that we could not let down the Unionist Party which alone... could speak for the Punjab..." By July 3, both Glancy and Khizar would take a more realistic view: "...it would be inadvisable if Jinnah maintains his present attitude to attempt forming Council without League representation." Some other provincial Governors — those of Bengal, UP, and CP — agreed with Wavell that the Council "would not work" without the League. So did Whitehall.

"Cabinet rather pernickety on point that Jinnah, if you can make him abandon his present attitude and agree to your list of Moslem names, should accept them as his nominations or at least as League ones", reported Amery, Secretary of State for India, after a cabinet meeting. "They are afraid of the whole onus of failure being thrown on Muslims, but that is Jinnah's funeral and you will no doubt rub the point into him as strongly as you can."

"So all our plans have for the moment broken down in face of Jinnah's intransigence," wrote Amery, badly caught up in a frustrating election campaign against R Palme Dutt, that was to unseat him.

But what was Jinnah's 'intransigence'? His refusal to abandon the Muslim League's (AIML)'s 'fundamental' principle that it 'must have the right to nominate the entire block of Muslim members' and that it could not concede the Viceroy, to quote Jinnah, 'the right to nominate Muslims and to include non-League Muslims among them'.

"Their fear that the Congress, by parading its national character and using Muslim dummies will permeate the entire administration of united India," conceded Wavell, "is real, and cannot be dismissed as an obsession of Jinnah and his entourage." Thus, to Jinnah as well, AIML's representative character was the main issue on which "the Conference had failed".

Even so, to quote HV Hodson (The Great Divide), "Jinnah's demonstration of imperious strength at... Simla... was a shot in the arm for the League and a serious blow for its Muslim opponents, especially in the Punjab"; "the immediate effect was greatly to heighten the prestige of the Muslim League..." Clearly, Jinnah's Simla strategy went extremely well with Muslims.

"You have once again saved the community from a serious pitfall and steered the ship of Muslim politics clearly through rough and stormy weather to a safe anchorage," wrote Khaliquzzaman to Jinnah, on July 23, 1945. "I have never seen the like of the enthusiasm that prevails amongst the conscious Muslims of the Punjab today after Simla," reported Mumtaz Daultana from the Punjab. Indeed, Simla gave the League a tremendous psychological boost, perhaps as much as Lucknow (1937) and Lahore (1940).

In any case, the sheer fact that the Viceroy could not go ahead with his plans in the face of Jinnah's opposition meant that Jinnah's 1937 assertion of Muslims being 'a third party' to Nehru's 'two-forces' dictum (1936) had finally become a reality, that the Muslim side of the political triangle in India had now assumed an importance that its consent was considered indispensable in any long or short-term settlement of the Indian problem. In that sense, as Azad points out, "the Simla Conference marks a breakwater in Indian political history."

Asia's most magnificent landscapes... Pakistan displays some of Asia's most magnificent landscapes as it stretches from the Arabian Sea, its southern border, to some of the world's most spectacular mountain ranges in the north. Pakistan is also home to sites that date back to word's earliest settlements rivalling those of ancient Egypt and Mesopotamia.

Located in South Asia, Pakistan shares an eastern border with India and a northeastern border with China. Iran makes up the country's southwest border, and Afghanistan runs along its western and northern edge. The Arabian Sea is Pakistan's southern boundary with 1,064 km of coastline.

5

Pakistan, Birth of a Free Nation

On the morning of June 3, Mountbatten concluded the conference by announcing that an official announcement of the acceptance of the plan would be made by him and by the two leaders, Jinnah and Nehru, that evening in a radio broadcast.

The Delhi Station of All India Radio was agog with excitement. Mounbatten was there to announce, on behalf of His Majesty's Government, what Churchill in his inimitable style had termed, a few years back as the impending liquidation of the British Empire in India. Mountbatten spoke with poise and dignity, and millions that heard him all over India, realized that the end of a long drawn-out struggle for independence was in sight, as he declared in unequivocal terms that power would be definitely transferred by the British to two successive sovereign States. The Viceroy concluded his broadcast with the words, *"I have faith in the future of India and I am proud to be with you all at this momentous time. May your decisions be wisely guided and may they be carried out in the peaceful and friendly spirit of the Gandhi-Jinnah appeal."*

Then Nehru, in a solemn voice announced that the Congress had accepted the plan for India's independence, as set out in His Majesty's Plan announced by the Viceroy. Then it was the Quaid-i-Azam, who was to address the Muslim Nation. His first sentence on that historic occasion was, *"I am glad that I am offered an opportunity to speak to you directly through this Radio from Delhi."* Regarding the Plan for the transfer of power to the peoples of India, he said: had to take momentous decisions and handle grave issues, *"Therefore we must galvanize and concentrate all our energy to see that the transfer of power is affected in a peaceful and orderly manner."* In this, his finest hour, he was meek and humble, *"I pray to God that at this critical moment that He may guide us and enable us to discharge our responsibilities in a wise and statesmanlike manner."* He did not forget to pay his tribute to those that had suffered and sacrificed in the struggle for Pakistan. *"I cannot help but express my appreciation of the sufferings and sacrifices made by all classes of Muslims"*. He gave wholehearted credit for *"the great part the women of the Frontier played in the fight for our civil liberties."* He did not forget those who had died or suffered in the struggle for Pakistan, *"I deeply sympathize with all those who have suffered and those who died or whose properties were subjected to destruction"*.

Quaid-i-Azam ended his memorable speech by saying, extemporaneously, *"Pakistan Zindabad"*. The Quaid-i-Azam and his sister Fatima Jinnah flew from New Delhi to Karachi on August 7, 1947. The Constituent Assembly of Pakistan elected Jinnah as its president at its inaugural session on August 11, 1947. In his presidential address to the Assembly, the Quaid said that the first duty of a government was to maintain law and order so that the life, property and religious beliefs of its subjects are fully protected. If Pakistanis wanted to make their country happy and prosperous they should "wholly and solely concentrate on the well being of the people, and especially of the masses and the poor."

In that historical address he remarked further: "You are free; you are free to go to your temples, you are free to go to your mosques or any other place of worship in this State of Pakistan...You may belong to any religion or caste or creed—that has nothing to do with the business of the State...We are starting in the days when there is no discrimination between one caste or creed or another. We are starting with this fundamental principle that we are all citizens and equal citizens of one State....My guiding principle will be justice and complete impartiality, and I am sure that with your support and cooperation, I can look forward to Pakistan becoming one of the greatest Nations of the world."

On the afternoon of August 13, Lord and Lady Mountbatten flew from Delhi to Karachi. The state procession on August 14 was staged in open cars with Jinnah and Mountbatten in the leading car and Miss Fatima Jinnah and Lady Mountbatten in the next car. Mountbatten addressed the Constituent Assembly of Pakistan followed by Jinnah. Pakistan became constitutionally independent at midnight between the 14th and 15th August 1947. The Quaid assumed charge as Governor General on August 15 and the Cabinet of Pakistan, with Liaquat Ali Khan as Prime Minister, was sworn in on the same day.

BRIEF HISTORY OF PAKISTAN

The first permanent Muslim foothold in the South Asian Subcontinent was achieved with Muhammad Bin Qasim's conquest of Sind in 711 C.E. An autonomous Muslim state was established and Arabic was introduced as official language. At the time of Mahmud of Ghazna's invasion, Muslim rule still existed, though in a weakened form, in Multan and some other regions. The Ghaznavids (976-1148) and their successors, the Ghurids (1148-1206), were central Asian by origin and outlook and they ruled their territories, which covered mostly the regions of present Pakistan, from capitals outside India. It was in early 13th century that the foundations of Muslim rule in India were laid with extended boundaries and Delhi as the capital. From 1206 to 1526 C.E., five different dynasties held sway. Then followed the period of Mughal ascendancy (1526-1707), and their rule continued, though nominally, till 1857.

From the time of Ghaznavids, Persian replaced Arabic as the official language. The economic, political and religious institutions developed by the Muslims bore their unique impression. The law of the state was based on Shariah and in principle the rulers were bound to enforce it. The question of Muslims identity assumed seriousness during the decline of Muslim power in South Asia. The first person to realize its acuteness was the encyclopedic scholar-theologian Shah Waliullah (1703-62). He laid the foundations of Islamic renaissance in the subcontinent and became a source of inspiration for almost all the subsequent social and religious reform movements of the 19th and 20th centuries. His immediate successors, inspired by his teachings, tried to establish a model Islamic state in the northwest of India and they, under the leadership of Sayyid Ahmad (1786-1831), waged an unsuccessful Jihad against the Sikhs.

Meanwhile, the British had emerged as the dominant force in South Asia. Their rise to power was gradual extending over a period of nearly one hundred years. They replaced the Shariah by what they termed as the Anglo-Muhammadan law. English became the official language. These and other developments had great social, economic and political impact especially on the Muslims of South Asia. The failure of the 1857 War of Independence had disastrous consequences for the Muslims. Determined to stop such a recurrence in future, they followed deliberately a repressive policy against the Muslims. Properties and estates of those even remotely associated with the freedom fighters were confiscated and conscious efforts were made to close all avenues of honest living for the Muslims.

The Muslims kept themselves aloof from western education as well as government service. But their compatriots, the Hindus, did not do so. They accepted the new rulers without reservation. They acquired western education, imbibed the new culture and captured positions hitherto filled in by the Muslims. If this situation had prolonged, it would have done the Muslims an irreparable loss. The man to realize the impending peril was Sir Syed Ahmed Khan (1817-1898), a witness to the tragic events of 1857. His assessment was that the Muslims' safety lay in the acquisition of western education and knowledge. He took several positive steps to achieve this objective. He founded a college at Aligarh to impart education on western lines. Of equal importance was the Anglo-Muhammadan Education Conference, which he sponsored in 1886, to provide an intellectual forum to the Muslims for the dissemination of views in support of western education and social reform. Similar were the objectives of the Muhammadan Literary Society, founded by Nawab Abdul Latif (1828-93), but its activities were confined to Bengal.

Sir Syed Ahmed Khan was averse to the idea of Muslims participation in any organized political activity which, he feared, might revive British hostility towards the Muslims. He also disliked Hindu-Muslim collaboration in any joint venture. His disillusionment in this regard primarily stemmed from the Urdu-Hindi controversy of the late 1860s when the Hindu enthusiasts vehemently championed the cause of Hindi in place of Urdu. He, therefore, opposed the Indian National Congress, when it was founded in 1885, and advised his community to abstain from its activities. His contemporary and a great scholar of Islam, Syed Ameer Ali (1849-1928), shared his views about the Congress, but he was not opposed to Muslims organizing themselves politically. In fact, he organized the first significant and purely communal political body, the Central National Muhammadan Association. Although its membership was limited, it had above fifty branches in different parts of the subcontinent and it accomplished some solid work for the educational and political uplift of the Muslims. But its activities waned towards the end of the 19th century.

At the dawn of the 20th century, a number of factors convinced the Muslims of the need to have an effective political organization. One of the factors was the replacement of Urdu by Hindi in the United Provinces. The creation of a Muslim province by partitioning the Province of Bengal and the violent resistance put up the Hindus against this decision was another. But the most important factor was the proposed constitutional reforms. The Muslims apprehended that under such a system they would not get due representation. Therefore, in October 1906, a deputation comprising 35 Muslim leaders met the Viceroy at Simla and demanded separate electorates. Three months later, the All-India Muslim League was founded at Dhaka mainly with the object of looking after the political rights and interests of the Muslims. The British conceded separate electorates in the Government of India Act of 1909 which confirmed League's position as an All-India Party.

The visible trend of the two major communities going in opposite directions caused deep concern to leaders of all-India stature. They struggled to bring the Congress and the Muslim League on one platform. Quaid-i-Azam Muhammad Ali Jinnah (1876-1948) was the leading figure among them. After the annulment of the partition of Bengal and the European powers' aggressive designs against the Ottoman empire and North Africa, the Muslims were receptive to the idea of collaboration with the

Hindus. The Congress-Muslim League rapprochement was achieved at the Lucknow session of the two parties in 1916 and a joint scheme of reforms was adopted. In the Lucknow Pact, the Congress accepted the principle of separate electorates and the Muslims in return for 'weightage' to the Muslims of the Muslim minority provinces agreed to surrender their slim majorities in the Punjab and Bengal. The post-Lucknow Pact period witnessed Hindu-Muslim amity and the two parties came to hold their annual sessions in the same city and passed resolutions of similar content.

The Hindu-Muslim unity reached its climax during the Khilafat and the Noncooperation Movements. The Muslims of South Asia, under the leadership of Ali Brothers, Maulana Muhammad Ali and Maulana Shaukat Ali, launched the historic Khilafat Movement after the First World War to protect the Ottoman empire from dismemberment. Mohandas Karamchand Gandhi (1869-1948) linked the issue of swaraj (or self-government) with the Khilafat issue to associate the Hindus with the Movement. The ensuing Movement was the first countrywide popular movement. Although the movement failed in its objectives, it had far-reaching impact on the Muslims of South Asia. After a long time they forged a united action on a purely Islamic issue which created momentarily solidarity among them. It also produced a class of Muslim leaders experienced in organizing and mobilizing the public. This experience was of immense value to the Muslims during the Pakistan Movement.

The collapse of the Khilafat Movement was followed by the period of bitter Hindu-Muslim antagonism. The Hindus organized two highly anti-Muslim movements, the Shudhi and the Sangathan. The former movement was designed to convert Muslims to Hinduism and the latter was meant to create solidarity among the Hindus in the event of communal conflict. In retaliation, the Muslims sponsored the Tabligh and Tanzim organizations.

In the 1920s the frequency of communal riots was unprecedented. In the light of this situation, the Muslims revised their constitutional demands. They now wanted preservation of their numerical majorities in the Punjab and Bengal; separation of Sind from Bombay; constitution of Balochistan as a separate province and introduction of constitutional reforms in the North-West Frontier Province. It was partly to press these demands that one section of the All-India Muslim League cooperated with the Statutory Commission sent by the British Government, under the chairmanship of Sir John Simon in 1927. The other section of the League boycotted the Simon Commission for its all-white character and cooperated with the Nehru Committee to draft a constitution for India. The Nehru Report had an extremely anti-Muslim bias and the Congress leadership's refusal to amend it disillusioned even the moderate Muslims.

Several leaders and thinkers having insight into the Hindu-Muslim question proposed separation of Muslim India. However, the most lucid exposition of the inner feelings of the Muslim community was given by Allama Muhammad Iqbal (1877-1938) in his presidential address to the All-India Muslim League at Allahabad in 1930. He proposed a separate Muslim state at least in the Muslim majority regions of the northwest. Later on, in his correspondence with Quaid-i-Azam Muhammad Ali Jinnah, he included the Muslim majority areas in the northeast also in his proposed Muslim state. Three years after his Allahabad address, a group of Muslim students at Cambridge, headed by Choudhry Rehmat Ali, issued a pamphlet Now or Never in which, drawing letters from the names of the Muslim majority regions they gave the nomenclature of Pakistan to the proposed state.

Meanwhile, three Round Table Conferences was convened in London during the period 1930-32, to resolve the Indian constitutional problem. The Hindu and Muslim leaders could not draw up an agreed formula and the British Government had to announce a 'Communal Award' which was incorporated in the Government of India Act of 1935. Before the elections under this Act, the All-India Muslin League, which had remained dormant for some time, was reorganized by Muhammad Ali Jinnah, who had returned to India in 1935 after a self imposed exile of nearly five years in England. The Muslim League could not win a majority of Muslims seats since it had not yet been effectively reorganized. However, it had the satisfaction that the performance of the Indian National Congress in the Muslim constituencies was bad. After the elections, the attitude of the Congress leadership was arrogant and domineering. The classic example was its refusal to form a coalition government with the Muslim League in the United Provinces. Instead it asked the League leaders to dissolve their parliamentary party in the Provincial Assembly and join the Congress. Another important Congress move after the 1937 elections was its Muslim mass contact movement to persuade the Muslims to join the Congress and not the Muslim League. One of its leaders, Jawaharlal Nehru, even declared that there were only two forces in India, the British and the Congress. All this did not go unchallenged. Quaid-i-Azam countered that there was a third force in South Asia constituting the Muslims. The All-India Muslim League, under his gifted leadership, gradually and skilfully started to consolidate the Muslims on one platform. It did not miss to exploit even small Congress mistakes in its favour.

The 1930s saw realization among the Muslims of their separate identity and their anxiety to preserve it within separate territorial boundaries. An important element that brought this simmering Muslim nationalism in the open was the charter of the Congress rule in the Muslim minority provinces during 1937-39. The Congress policies in these provinces hurt Muslim susceptibilities. These were calculated aims to obliterate the Muslims as a separate cultural unity. The Muslims now abandoned to think in terms of seeking safeguards and began to consider seriously the demand for a separate Muslim state. During 1937-1939, several Muslim leaders and thinkers inspired by Allama Iqbal's ideas, presented elaborate schemes of partitioning the subcontinent on communal lines. The All-India Muslim League on March 23, 1940, in a resolution at its Lahore session, demanded separate homeland for the Muslims in the Muslim majority regions of the subcontinent. The resolution was commonly referred to as the Pakistan Resolution.

The British Government recognized the genuineness of the Pakistan demand indirectly in the proposals for the transfer of power which, Sir Stafford Cripps brought to India in 1942. Both the Congress and the All-India Muslim League rejected these proposals for different reasons. The principle of secession of Muslim

India as a separate dominion was, however, conceded in these proposals. After the failure, a prominent Congress leader, C. Rajagopalacharya, suggested a formula for a separate Muslim state in the Working Committee of the Indian National Congress, which was rejected at the time but later on, in 1944, formed the basis of the Gandhi-Jinnah talks.

The Pakistan demand was popularized during the Second World War. Every section of the Muslim community - women, students, Ulema and businessmen - was organized under the banner of the All-India Muslim League. Branches of the party were opened in the remote corners on the subcontinent. Literature in the form of pamphlets, books, magazines and newspapers was produced to explain the Pakistan demand and distributed largely.

The support gained by the All-India Muslim League and its demand for Pakistan was tested after the failure of the Simla Conference 1945. Elections were called to determine the respective strength of the political parties. The Muslim League swept all the thirty seats in the central legislature and in the provincial elections also its victory was outstanding. After the elections, on April 8-9, 1946, the All-India Muslim League called a convention of the newly elected League members in the central and provincial legislatures at Delhi. This convention which constituted virtually a representative assembly of the Muslims of South Asia, on a motion by the Chief Minister of Bengal, Hussein Shaheed Suhrawardy, reiterated the Pakistan demand in clearer terms.

In early 1946, the British Government sent a Cabinet Mission to the subcontinent to resolve the constitutional deadlock. The Mission conducted negotiations with various political parties but failed to evolve an agreed formula. Finally, Cabinet Mission announced its own plan which, among other provisions, envisaged three federal groupings, two of them comprising the Muslim majority provinces, linked at the Centre in a loose federation with three subjects. The Muslim League accepted the Plan, as a strategic move, expecting to achieve its objective in a not-too-distant future. The Congress also agreed to the Plan but soon realizing its implications to the Congress, its leaders began to interpret in a way not visualized by the authors of the Plan. This provided the

All-India Muslim League an excuse to withdraw its acceptance of the Plan and the party observed August 16 as a 'Direct Action Day' to show Muslim solidarity in support of the Pakistan demand.

In October 1946, an Interim Government was formed. The Muslim League sent its representatives under the leadership of its General Secretary, Mr. Liaquat Ali Khan, with the aim to fight for the party objective from within the Interim Government. After a short time the situation inside the Interim Government and outside convinced the Congress leadership to accept Pakistan as the only solution of the communal problem. The British Government, after a last attempt to save the Cabinet Mission Plan in December 1946, also moved toward a plan for the partition of India. The last British Viceroy, Lord Louis Mountbatten, came with a clear mandate to draft a plan for the transfer of power. After holding talks with political leaders and parties, he prepared a Partition Plan for the transfer of power which, after its approval by the British Government, was announced on June 3, 1947. Both the Congress and the Muslim League accepted the plan. Two largest Muslim Majority provinces, Bengal and Punjab was partitioned. The assemblies of west Punjab, East Bengal, and Sind; and in Balochistan, the Quetta Municipality and the Shahi Jirga voted for Pakistan. Referenda were held in the North-West Frontier Province and the District of Sylhet in Assam which resulted in an overwhelming vote for Pakistan. On August 14, 1947, the new state of Pakistan came into existence.

THE COMMERCIAL POLICY OF PAKISTAN

It gives me great pleasure, Mr. Chairman, to be here this morning with you all at this you're 88th Annual General Meeting. I presume it is an accident to hold this meeting in the premises of the Karachi Cotton Association, for one can hardly dissociate Karachi from commerce and the commerce of this place from cotton. You have, Mr. Chairman, covered a very wide field in your address, from the founding of the sovereign and independent State of Pakistan to the petty usurpations of power by minor official here and there over this far-flung Dominion, from the intricacies of cotton trade to the common place of delays. You will, however, hardly expect me to follow you in every detail in my reply. I cannot, however, let an opportunity, such as you have presented to me today, pass without calling attention to certain salient points arising out of your address.

Let me, Mr. Chairman first acknowledge the tribute which you have justly paid to my Government and my people for the manner in which they faced up to the tragic events which so closely followed the establishment of Pakistan. It was inevitable that many otherwise sensible people should greet Pakistan as an unwanted and intolerable child whose birth could not long survive their displeasure. You have rightly pointed out how mistaken were the people who, because the idea of Pakistan was new and unfamiliar to them, thought Pakistan would have but only an ephemeral existence. None can now doubt, in your words, Mr. Chairman that a new Power was born among the nations of the world on August 14, 1947. The difficulties and the tribulations through which Pakistan has passed have helped to strengthen and temper the new State into steel, which is now, well and truly set upon the course on the uncharted seas of the future. The people who have made the effort which secured their separate freedom in the face of derision, disbelief and the utmost political opposition will not fail to make the additional effort necessary to consolidate their liberties, and any delusion or elusion from which some people still suffer, let me make it clear, that the sooner they bring their notion—Pakistan surrendering to India or seeking Union with Central Government—the better it will be for peace and prosperity of both the Dominions and will help a great deal to establish goodwill and neighbourly good feelings.

I am glad to note that you are disaffiliating your Chambers from the Associated Chambers of Commerce of India as a necessary corollary of the partition, and intend to form an Association of your Pakistan Chambers of Commerce.

You, Mr. Chairman, have rightly given pride of place to cotton in dealing with trade and commerce. I am glad to know that you have recognised that Pakistan's cotton policy could not have been more liberal or less restrictive than it was until the impact of India's decision to decontrol cloth and refuse it to us except in return for cotton, forced measures of regulation on us. Even so, all contracts made before 23rd January 1948 by traders in Pakistan—national or foreign—were honoured. That the cotton trade should have shown such admirable capacity to adjust itself to changing conditions is a matter for gratification. I would like to express the appreciation of the Government of Pakistan for the manner in which traders have played their part in helping to move cotton to the port and from the port to the markets of the world.

You have also referred at some length to the import policy of the Government of Pakistan and internal controls exercised within the country and have pleaded that, as few handicaps should be placed on trading as possible. Regulation and restriction with their attendant administrative evils will be imposed only where conditions compel, and any expressions of opinion you care to make from time to time will always receive my Ministry's careful thought. I can assure you on behalf of the Government of Pakistan that it is their intention and policy to let the channels of free trading flow as freely as possible. In so far as the internal controls on essential commodities are concerned, my Government have already decided to review them at a conference with the Provinces in an attempt to relax and remove as many of these as circumstances would now permit So far as overseas trade is concerned a considerable sector of imports has been released from licensing by the notification of an Open General Licence for a wide range of goods coming from Commonwealth sterling countries. This list will be kept under constant review with the object of expanding it and the question of including therein imports and other soft currency areas is now receiving the attention of the Ministry for Commerce. The situation in regard to dollar imports and other hard currencies is, of course very difficult and licensing must continue to protect the balance of payments. Even in this field, however, you can assist by bending your energies to directing and increasing our exports to dollar and hard currency countries. This, fortunately, should not be difficult in the case of the major Pakistan raw materials and I shall look forward, Gentlemen to your constant support in this matter. Anything that Government cans do to facilitate exports to these areas by removing as many restrictions as possible will be done. I have little doubt, gentlemen, that your efforts in this direction will bear fruit as we are rich in the commodities which the world so badly requires, like cotton, jute, hides, skins and wool. You have made a plea that in the interests of trade. Government should make an announcement of the import policy in good time. The Government of Pakistan fully appreciates this view and will do all they can to make as early an announcement as circumstances would permit. The uncertain factors, which delayed the announcement of their policy in the past will, Government hopes, not recur in future.

The complete breakdown of the banking and financial mechanism in the West Punjab is a matter which government action alone cannot remedy. We can make the conditions as favourable as possible but bankers alone can repair the machine. It is our unalterable determination to maintain law and order and to secure and retain public confidence in our administration of affairs. In this context and given your goodwill, the reconstruction and restoration of our commerce and trade should proceed apace. This is my appeal to you today, Gentleman, to make a steady and sustained effort to help us to help you.

There is one matter, Mr. Chairman, which you have mentioned only in passing, namely, the statement issued by my Government on the Industrial Policy of Pakistan. The statement is of such far-reaching character that I would ask of you as a business community to examine it with the care and attention which the importance of the subject and the direct bearing it has on your own well-being requires. That my Government should have taken time to consider matters carefully before formulating their policy, which must vitally, effect the future of the country, is a matter that need not cause any sense of frustration. For I am reminded in the connection of an observation of that wiseman, Francis who said—"It is good to commit the beginnings of all great actions to Argos with his hundred eyes and the ends to Briarcus with his hundred hands; first to watch and then to speed" Whilst I do not propose to recapitulate the statement here, I would like to call your particular attention to the keen desire of the Government of Pakistan to associate individual initiative and private enterprise at every stage of industrialisation. The number of industries Government has reserved for management by themselves consists of Arms and Munitions of War, generation of Hydel Power and manufacture of Railway wagons, Telephone, Telegraph and Wireless apparatus. All other industrial activity is left open to private enterprise, which would be given every facility a Government can give for the establishment and development of industry. Government will seek to create conditions in which industry and trade may develop and prosper by undertaking surveys of Pakistan's considerable resources of minerals, schemes for the development of country's water and power resources plans for the improvement of transport services and the establishment of the ports and an Industrial Finance Corporation. Just as Pakistan is agriculturally the most advanced country in the Continent of Asia as mentioned by you, I am confident that if it makes the fullest and the best use of its considerable agricultural wealth in the building up of her industries, it will, with the traditions of craftsmanship for which her people are so well known and with their ability to adjust themselves to new techniques, soon make its mark in the industrial field. I am glad to know that you are favourably impressed with the concessions announced by the Finance Minister to new industrial enterprises in the matter of Income Tax and depreciation that you regard the statement as holding out more encouragement to new industry than the corresponding statement of policy made by the Government of India. If you want any clarification of any aspect of the policy, my Government will be only too willing to furnish the same.

Fortunately, in the port of Karachi, we have adequate facilities to handle not only the trade of Western Pakistan but also such trade as offers for Afghanistan and the adjoining areas of the Indian Dominion. For reasons into which I need not here enter, this trade has suffered a severe setback since partition. I hope that in everybody's interest you will endeavour to restore Karachi's standing in this regard. I have no doubt that the port of Karachi has a very bright future. It is the only port, which serves this side of Pakistan, and the location of the Pakistan Naval Headquarters had added greatly to its importance. I can look with confidence to its rapid development. The scheme for remodelling the East Wharf and the provision of Naval and Commercial Dry Docks is under our active consideration and should, when completed, make Karachi one of the most modern ports. I may assure the business community that I am watching with keen interest the present and future interests of the port.

The end of the period of "Standstill" and the consequent entry of India and Pakistan into normal international relations should advance and give precision to the movement of trade. Bonding facilities are being provided by my Government in Karachi port for this purpose. On the other side of the subcontinent, the Government of India has also agreed to provide bonding facilities in Calcutta so that from now on, the capacity of the port of Chittagong to handle raw jute will be supplemented by transit facilities through the port of Calcutta.

In the field of Civil Aviation, Pakistan is fortunate in having at Karachi, the best-equipped airport in the East. Its position and climate are in its favour and now that Karachi has become the Capital of Pakistan, there is no likelihood of the Airport ever losing its importance. Its pre-eminent position will be maintained, as we are alive to the need of its continued development in accordance with the international standards and to the need of facilitating in every way national and international air transport operations. Karachi will remain one of the main centres of international air traffic as most of the progressive countries of the world have approached us for bilateral air transport agreements and we already have agreements with U.S., France, Netherlands, Iraq and recently negotiated agreement with India and Ceylon. Delegations from U.K and other countries are expected in Karachi soon. For all these Karachi will remain the airport of entry and departure. The use of Bombay as the port of entry for Trans-World Airlines was provided for in Air Transport Agreement between U.S.A. and India before partition and does not indicate a subsequent tendency to transfer operation from Karachi to Bombay. On this service Karachi Airport was used, in the first instance, as a temporary measure pending the provision of health facilities at Santa Cruz. You have referred to the rise in airline operating costs occasioned by the recently increased cost of aviation spirits in Pakistan. This is question, which I have, no doubt will be considered by my Government in the light of your observations.

I am glad to hear that you have appreciated the difficulties which beset Orient Airways in establishing, at a very short notice, vital air communications within Pakistan between Eastern and Western Pakistan and between Karachi and Delhi and between Karachi and Bombay. These agreements had to be made on a temporary basis while a long-term national air transport was being formulated. The Government announced their policy on the 5th of December 1947, limiting air transport operations to two commercial airlines to be selected for the operation of all the scheduled services to be licensed by the Government. The names of these companies will be announced shortly together with the routes to be operated by them subject to finalisation of agreement recently negotiated with the Government of India. To serve these companies and to a large extent, the Royal Pakistan Air Force, it is also proposed to establish, at Karachi a company to carry out major overhaul and repair of aircraft, the training of mechanics and maintenance engineers, and such other common services as the Government and airlines may require. The Government will participate financially in this enterprise and plans for the establishment of this company are now under active consideration of the Government.

You have referred to the difficulties experienced by your members on account of the uncertainty of booking restrictions. As you are aware, booking restrictions have been rendered necessary on account of coal shortage due to spasmodic and insufficient receipt from India. The Northwestern Railway has always endeavoured to move as much traffic as possible with their available resources. The movement of refugees placed a heavy strain on the Railway's capacity at a time when coal receipts were at their lowest, but in spite of these difficulties essential goods, *e.g.* foodstuffs, kept on moving though restrictions had perforce to be imposed on the movement of goods carried under lower priorities. The Railways, however, relaxed restrictions to the extent possible whenever there was even a slight improvement in coal receipts, but whenever the coal position deteriorated restrictions were reimposed.

In spite of the manifold difficulties created by inadequate supplies of coal from India, the refugee traffic, the numerous staff problems created by partition, the Railway administration, as and when the position improved, restored the facilities which had to be curtailed from time to time. I hope that the Chamber would appreciate their efforts in keeping the rail transport going. There was some improvement in the coal position on the Northwestern Railway during February and March and as you are aware, unrestricted booking was resumed with effect from 4th March in local bookings and from 12th April in foreign bookings. Unfortunately, coal supplies from India have been inadequate during April and, although some of the coal ordered from the U.S.A. has been received, stocks are dwindling. Representations have been made to India, and it is hoped that there will be no reimposition of the previous unfortunate restrictions, except those occasionally imposed for operational reasons.

As regards the complaint that the railway staffs at stations are unaware of the restrictions imposed from time to time, I am advised that all restrictions are conveyed to stations immediately on their imposition. It is possible that in the early days after partition, due to large-scale transfers of staffs, there was a certain amount of disorganisation resulting in incorrect information being furnished to merchants. The Northwestern Railway has, however, taken suitable action to ensure that correct information relating to restrictions is conveyed to merchants.

As regards preparation claims, I hope you are aware of the provisions of the Indian Independence (Rights, Property and Liabilities) Order 1947, under which the liabilities and financial obligations of the governor-general in Council, outstanding immediately before 15th August, 1947, devolved on the Dominion of India. The Pakistan Government has already made the position in this respect clear in their press note of the 25th March 1948. The matter is under correspondence with the Government of India and it is hoped that a settlement in regard to this outstanding question will be reached at an early date.

Reference has been made by you to the difficulties and anxieties, which naturally spring, from shortage of residential and office accommodation in this town. The Government of Pakistan has, subject to the approval of the Constituent Assembly, decided to locate the permanent Capital of Pakistan at Karachi. Detailed planning of the layout will take some time but this should not delay construction of some residential accommodation. In this field, as in many others, gentlemen, you have a big contribution to make. There are vast open areas where buildings could, with advantage, be constructed. Building materials such as cement and stone are available in abundance, though steel and timber are rather scarce. All the same, my Government would like to see the business community take up a programme of large-scale building construction in Karachi.

Mr. Chairman, Commerce and Trade are the very lifeblood of the nation. I can no more visualise a Pakistan without traders than I can one without cultivators or civil servants. I have no doubt that in Pakistan, traders and merchants will always be welcome and that they, in building up their own fortunes, will not forget their social responsibility for a fair and square deal to one and all, big and small. Government have for sometime been perturbed over the constantly rising spiral of prices of the necessities of life in Pakistan. They are now engaged in a study of how best the spiral could be broken and prices brought down. I have little doubt that my Government can confidently count on your full support in every measure they may decide to take to achieve this object

Commerce, Gentlemen, is more international than culture and it behaves you to behave in such a way that the power and prestige of Pakistan gain added strength from every act of yours. I have no doubt the Commerce of Pakistan would be an effective instrument in the establishment and maintenance of high standards of business integrity and practice. If Pakistani goods are to establish for themselves a reputation all their own, a beginning must be made now and here. I assure you, Gentlemen, that anything my Government can do to achieve this end, and they shall do. I would like Pakistan to become a synonym and hallmark for standard and quality in the market places of the world.

Let me, Mr. Chairman, thank you once again for the honour you have done me in asking me to be the guest of your Chamber on this occasion. I wish you and your Chamber well in the many years that lie ahead of us and may you as true Pakistanis help to reconstruct and build Pakistan to reach mighty and glorious status amongst the comity of nations of the world and that let us pray that Pakistan will make its contribution for peace, happiness and prosperity of the world.

WHAT DO WE MEAN BY PAKISTAN?

I quote myself: in the February 1947 number of Arafat (p. 166): "The Pakistan movement... can become the starting-point of a new Islamic development if the Muslims realize-and continue realizing it when Pakistan is achieved-that the real, historic justification of this movement does not consist in our dressing or talking or salaaming differently from the other inhabitants of the country, or in the grievances which we may have against other communities, or even in the desire to provide more economic opportunities and more elbowroom for people who-by sheer force of habit-call themselves 'Muslims': But that such a justification is to be found only in the Muslims' desire to establish a truly Islamic polity: in other words, to translate the tenets of Islam into terms of practical life.'

This, in short, is my conception of Pakistan: and I do not think that I am far wrong in assuming that it is the conception of many other Muslims as well. Of many: but not all; and not even of most of them. For, by far the larger part of our intelligentsia do not seem to consider Pakistan in this light. To them, it means no more and no less than a way to freeing the Muslims of India from Hindu domination, and the establishment of a political structured in which the Muslim community would find its 'place in the sun' in the economic sense.

Islam comes into the picture only in so far as it happens to be the religion of the people concerned-just as Catholicism came into the picture in the Irish struggle for independence because it happened to be the religion of most Irishmen. To put it bluntly, many o four brother and sisters do not seem to care for the spiritual, Islamic objectives of Pakistan, and permit themselves to be carried away by sentiments not far removed from nationalism.; and this is especially true of many Muslims educated on western lines. They are unable to think otherwise than in western patterns of though, and so they do not believe in their hearts that the world's social and political problems are capable of being subordinated to purely religious considerations. Hence, their approach to Islam is governed by convention rather than ideology, and amounts, at best, to a faintly 'cultural' interest in their community's historical traditions.

Now this is a very poor view of Pakistan: a view, moreover, which does not do justice to the Islamic enthusiasm at present so markedly-if chaotically-displayed by the overwhelming masses of our common people. While many of our so-called intelligentsia are interested in Islam only in so far as it fits into their struggle for political self-determination, the common people most obviously desire self-determination for the sake of Islam as such.

As far as the Muslim masses are concerned, the Pakistan movement is rooted in their instinctive feeling that they are an ideological community and have as such every right to an autonomous political existence. In other words, they feel and know that their communal existence is not-as with other communities-based on racial affinities or on the consciousness of cultural traditions held in common, but only-exclusively-on the fact of their common adherence to the ideology of Islam: and that, therefore, they must justify their communal existence by erecting a socio-political structure in which that ideology-the Shariah-would become the visible expression of their nationhood.

This, and not a solution of the all-India problem of Muslim minorities, is the real, historic purpose of the Pakistan movement. Insofar as there will always remain non-Muslim minorities in Pakistan as well as Muslim minorities in the rest of India, Pakistan cannot be said to solve the minorities problem in its entirety.

But this is precisely a point which we-and our opponents-would do well to understand: the problem of minorities, however important in all considerations of India's political future, is, in itself, not fundamentally responsible for the Pakistan movement, but is rather an incidental accompaniment to the movement's intrinsic objective-the establishment of an Islamic polity in which our ideology could come to practical fruition. Only thus can we understand why the Muslims in, say, Bombay or Madras-who of course cannot expect that their provinces would become part of Pakistan, are as much interested in its realization as are the Muslims of the Punjab or of Bengal.

They are interested in Pakistan not because they hope to come within its orbit in a territorial sense, but because they feel, as intensely as their brethren in the so-called 'Muslim majority' provinces, that the birth of an Islamic polity in Pakistan would vindicate the claim that Islam is a practical proposition, and that the Muslims-because of their being Muslims-are a nation unto themselves, irrespective of their geographical location.

For, in this respect, the Pakistan movement is truly unique among all the political mass movements now evident anywhere in the Muslim world. No doubt, in the vast territories that go by this name there are many other lovers of Islam besides us, but nowhere in the modern world, except in the Pakistan movement, has a whole Muslim nation set out on the march towards Islam. Some of those states, like Turkey and (the then Shah's) Iran, are explicitly anti-Islamic in their governmental aims, and openly declare that Islam should be eliminated from politics and from the people's social life. But even those Muslim states in which religion is still being valued-in varying degrees-as a spiritual treasure, are 'Islamic' only insofar as Islam is the religion professed by the majority of their inhabitants: while their political aims are not really governed by Islamic considerations but, rather, by what the rulers or ruling classes conceive as 'national' interests in exactly the sense in which national interests are conceived in the West.

In the Pakistan movement, on the other hand, there undoubtedly exists such a direct connection between the people's attachment to Islam and their political aims. Rather, more than that: the practical success of this movement is exclusively due to our people's passionate, if as yet inarticulate, desire to have a state in which the forms and objectives of government would be determined by the ideological imperatives of Islam-a state, that is, in which Islam would not be just a religious and cultural 'label' of the people concerned, but the very goal and purpose of state-formation.

And it goes without saying that an achievement of such an Islamic state-the first in the modern world-would revolutionize Muslim political thought everywhere, and would probably inspire other Muslim peoples to strive towards similar ends; and so it might become a prelude to an Islamic reorientation in many parts of the world.

Thus, the Pakistan movement contains a great promise for an Islamic revival: and it offers almost the only hope of such a revival in a world that is rapidly slipping away from the ideals of Islam. But the hope is justified only so long as our leaders, and the masses with them, keep the true objective of Pakistan in view, and do not yield to the temptation to regard their movement as just another of the many 'national' movements so fashionable in the present-day Muslim world.

There is an acute danger of the Pakistan movement being deflected form its ideological course by laying too much stress on a 'cultural' nationalism-on a community of interests arising not so much from a common ideology as from the desire to preserve certain cultural traits, social habits and customs and, last but not the least, to safeguard the economic development of a group of people who happen to be 'Muslims' only by virtue of their birth. Nobody can doubt that the cultural traditions and the immediate economic requirements of the Muslim community are extremely important in our planning the Muslim fixture on Islamic lines. But this is just the point: they should never be viewed independently of our ideological goal-the building of our fixture on Islamic lines.

It appears, however, that the majority of our intelligentsia are about to commit just this mistake. When they talk of Pakistan, they often convey the impression that the 'actual' interests of the Muslim world could be viewed independently of what is described as the 'purely ideological' interests of Islam; in other words, that it is possible to be a good Pakistani without being primarily interested in Islam as the basic reality in one's own and in the community's life.

[However], such an arbitrary division between 'Muslim' and 'Islamic' interests is sheer nonsense. Islam is not just one among several characteristics of Muslim communal existence, but its only historical cause and justification: and to consider Muslim interests as something apart from Islam is like considering a living being as something apart from the fact of its life.

It should [therefore] be our leaders' duty to tell their followers that they must become better Muslims today in order to be worthy of Pakistan tomorrow: instead of which they merely assure us that we shall become better Muslims 'as soon as Pakistan is achieved'.

This easy assurance will not do. It is self-deceptive in the extreme. If we do not sow the seeds of Islamic life now, when our enthusiasm is at its fighting pitch, there is no earthly reason to expect that we will suddenly be transformed into better Muslims when the struggle is over and our political autonomy secured.

I can almost hear some of our leaders say: 'Brother, you are too pessimistic-or perhaps a little bit too apprehensive. Almost every one of us desires a truly Islamic life. Only, it would be impolitic to insist on this ideal right now. In our ranks there are many people who render the most valuable services to our political cause, but-owing to a wring upbringing-do not care too much for religion; and if we stress the religious side of our struggle from the very beginning, those valuable workers might cool down in their zeal, and so be lost to our cause. We do not want to lose them: we cannot afford to lose them: and so we are obliged to postpone our work for the people's religious uplift until after we have won a state of our own. At present, we must concentrate all our energies on the short-term objective before us-the freeing of the Muslims from non-Muslim domination-and not dissipate them on purely religious considerations. If we insist, at this stage, too loudly on our long-term objective-the deepening of Islamic consciousness in the Muslims and the creation of a truly Islamic polity-we might not only estrange many of our westernized brothers and sisters from our cause, but also increase the apprehensions of the non-Muslim minorities who live in the area of Pakistan.'

The above reasoning is extremely fallacious and intellectually dishonest.

As for the apprehensions which our insistence on an Islamic life might cause among the non-Muslim minorities, I should like you to ask yourselves: What is it that makes non-Muslims so bitterly antagonistic to the idea of Pakistan? Obviously, a fear of what they describe as a 'communal raj' and the probability of the Muslim-dominated areas being cut off from the rest of India. The question as to whether the Muslims truly intend to live according to the principles of Islam or not leaves the non-Muslims cold. They are afraid of Muslim political preponderance in certain areas, and it does not make prima facie the least difference to them whether the Muslims are inspired in their endeavours by Islamic or any other considerations. Hence, they will oppose Muslim endeavours in any case, and with all strength at their disposal.

With all this, the attitude of our opponents might-though I do not say that it definitely will-be to some extent influenced by the thought that what we Muslims really aim at is justice for all: provided that we succeed in convincing them that we are really moved by moral convictions and not by a wish to exploit non-Muslims for the benefit of Muslims. It is, therefore, our duty to prove to the whole world that we really mean to live up the standard laid down in these words of the Holy Quran: 'You are the best of community that has been sent forth unto mankind: for you enjoin the Right and forbid the Wrong, and have faith in God' (Al-I-'Imran 3:110).

Our being a worthy ummah in the sight of God depends on our being prepared to struggle, always and under all circumstances, for the upholding of justice and the abolition of injustice and this should preclude the possibility of a truly Islamic community being unjust to non-Muslims. I can well imagine that a non-Muslim feels apprehensive about his fixture in a state which, in his opinion, would aim at giving economic preference to the Muslim community at the expense of non-Muslims: but he will have less reason to feel such an apprehension if he becomes convinced that the Muslims are determined to ensure justice to Muslim and non-Muslim alike.

And we cannot convince our opponents of our bona fides unless we prove, firstly, that an Islamic polity connotes justice for all, and secondly, that we Muslims are really serious in our avowals that precisely such polity is our goal-in other words, that we truly believe in the tenets of our religion. It is, therefore, quite erroneous to assume that the fears of non-Muslim minorities could be allayed by our discreetly avoiding, as much as possible, any direct references to our ultimate, religious objectives. This only creates in them a suspicion of hypocrisy on our part. The real way to allaying or at least alleviating their fears would be our clear exposition, in as great detail as possible, of the ethical ideals towards which we are striving; but even such an exposition will be of no avail unless we are able to show, in our day-to-day life, that those ideals mean more to us than mere slogans.

Apart from its probable effect on non-Muslims, an evasive postponement of our 'long-term', Islamic objectives in favour of what some people regard (quite wrongly) as momentarily 'expedient' or 'politic', must have a detrimental effect on our community's moral tenor; and can only result in our greater estrangement from the ways of true Islam. Instead of becoming increasingly aware of the ideal goal before them, the Muslims will again become accustomed to think-as they did for many centuries-in terms of 'expediency' and immediate conveniences, and the Islamic objective of Pakistan will most definitely recede into the realm of theoretical idealism-in exactly the same manner as the true objectives of Christianity have receded among the so-called Christian nations of the West.

We do not want that. We want, through Pakistan, to make Islam a reality in our lives. We want Pakistan in order that every one of us should be able to live a truly Islamic life in the widest sense of the word. And it is admittedly impossible for an individual to live in accordance with the scheme propounded by God's Apostle unless the whole society consciously conforms to it and makes the Law of Islam the law of the land. But this kind of Pakistan will never materialize unless we postulate the Law of Islam not merely as an ideal for a vaguely defined future but as the basis, wherever possible, of all our social and personal behaviour at this very hour and minute.

There is [on the other hand] a definite, though perhaps involuntary, tendency on the part of many of our leaders to ignore the spiritual, Islamic background of our struggle and to justify the Muslims' demand for freedom by stressing their unfortunate experiences with the Hindu majority, as well as to base the Muslims' claim to being a separate nation on the differences between their and the Hindus' social usage and cultural expressions.

In short, there is a mounting inclination to consider the fact-for a fact it is-of a separate Muslim nationhood in the conventional, western sense of the word 'nation' instead of considering it in the Islamic sense of ummah or millah? Why should we hesitate to proclaim, loudly and without fear, that our being a nation has nothing to do with the conventional meaning of this word: that we are a nation not merely because our habits, customs and cultural expressions are different from those of the other groups inhabiting the country, but because we mean to shape our life in accordance with a particular ideal of our own?

It cannot be often enough repeated that our adherence to the teachings of Islam is the only justification of our communal existence. We are not a racial entity. We are-in spite of the great progress of Urdu as the language of Muslim India-not even a linguistic entity within the strict meaning of this term. We are not, and never can be, a nation in the sense in which the English or the Arabs or the Chinese are nations. But precisely the fact that we are not, and never can be, a nation in the exclusive, conventional sense of the word is the innermost source of our strength: for it makes us realize that we-we alone in the modern world,-can, if we but want it, bring again to life that glorious vision which arose over the sands of Arabian nearly fourteen centuries ago: the vision of an ummah of free men and women bound together not by the accidental bonds of race and birth, but by their free, conscious allegiance to a common ideal.

If our desire for Pakistan is an outcome of our creative strength and purity; if we attain to that clarity of vision which encompasses the goal of our endeavours long before it is achieved; if we learn to love that goal for its own sake-in the conviction that it is supremely good in an absolute sense (or, as I would prefer to phrase it, in God's sight), and not merely because it appears to be economically advantageous to ourselves and our community, then no power on earth could stop Pakistan from being born and fròm becoming a gateway to an Islamic revival the world over.

And if, on the other hand, our cry for self-determination is due to no more than a fear of being dominated by a non-Muslim majority; if our vision of the fixture is merely negative; if it does not encompass the hope of our being free for something, but contents itself with the beggarly hope of our being free from something; if Islam, instead of being a moral obligation and an end in itself, means no more to us than a habit and a cultural label: then-even then-we might achieve some sort of Pakistan by virtue of our numerical strength in this country; but it would be an achievement far short of the tremendous possibilities which God seems to be offering to us.

It would be only one 'national state' more in a world split up into numberless national states-perhaps no worse than some of the others, but certainly no better than most: while the subconscious dream of the Muslim masses, and the conscious dream of those who first spoke of Pakistan (long before even this name had been thought of) was the birth of a polity in which the Prophet's Message could fully come into its own as a practical proposition.

What the common man desires is not merely a state in which Muslims would have greater economic facilities than they have now, but a state in which God's Word would reign supreme. Not that the 'common man' does not care for economic facilities. He cares, rightly, very much for them. But he feels, no less rightly, that an Islamic theocracy would not only give him all the economic justice and opportunity for material development which he now so sadly lacks, but would enhance his human dignity and spiritual security as well. (Most Muslim scholars have tried to differentiate between the Islamic concept of a state based on the principle of Khilafah or vicegerency and European medieval religious states based on rule by holy and 'infallible' clergy).

To give valid Islamic content, as well as a creative, positive direction to the people's dreams and desires; to prepare them not only politically (in the conventional context of this word) but also spiritually and ideologically for the great goal of Pakistan: this is the supreme task awaiting our leaders. They must not think that to organize the masses and to give voice to our political demands is all that he millah expects them to do. Organization is, no doubt, urgently necessary; political agitation is necessary, but these necessities must be made to serve our ideological goal-and not, as we so often find in these days, allowed to reduce it to secondary rank.

To a Muslim who takes Islam seriously, every political endeavour must, in the last resort, derive its sanction from religion, just as religion can never remain aloof from politics for the simple reason that Islam, being concerned not only with our spiritual development but with the manner of our physical, social and economic existence as well, is a 'political' creed in the deepest, morally most compelling sense of this term. In other words, the Islamic, religious aspect of our fight for Pakistan must be made predominant in all the appeals which Muslim leaders make to the Muslim masses. If this demand is neglected, our struggle cannot possibly fulfil its historic mission.

The need for the ideological, Islamic leadership on the part of our leaders is the paramount need of the day. That some of them-though by far not all-are really aware of their great responsibility in this respect is evident, for example, from the splendid convocation address which Liaquat Ali Khan, the Quaid-e-Azam's principal lieutenant [later first prime minister of Pakistan], delivered at Aligarh a few months ago. In that address he vividly stressed the fact that our movement derives its ultimate inspiration from the Holy Quran, and that, therefore, the Islamic state at which we are aiming should derive its authority from the Shariah alone. Muhammad Ali Jinnah [d. 1948] himself has spoken in a similar vein on many occasions. Such pronouncements, coming as they do from the highest levels of Muslim League leadership, go a long way to clarifying the League's aims.

Never before have Muslim leaders been endowed with such power to guide the destinies of the millah in the right direction-or in the wrong. It is within their power to decide, here and now, whether the Indian Muslims shall becomes Muslims in the true sense of the word and, thus, the core and backbone of a resurgent Islam-or just another 'national group' among many other so-called

Muslim groups and states where Islam is good enough to be displayed as a cultural label, but not good enough to provide the basis on which to build the community's social, economic and political existence. The present leaders of the Muslim League, I repeat it deliberately, have it within their power to make such a decision: for the wave of enthusiasm for Pakistan which has swept over the Muslim masses in this country, and which has united them as they have never been united in the past, has endowed those leaders with a prestige-and a power to lead-the like of which was never enjoyed by the leaders in the past centuries.

Because of this, their moral responsibility is all the greater. In short, it is the foremost duty of our political leaders to impress upon the masses that the objective of Pakistan is the establishment of a truly Islamic polity; and that this objective can never be attained unless every fighter of Pakistan-man or woman, great or small-honestly tries to come closer to Islam at every hour and every minute of his or her life: that, in a word, only a good Muslim can be a good Pakistani.

And this holds good for the leaders themselves as well. They must show in their social behaviour that they regard Islam as a serious proposition and not merely as a slogan. To put it plainly 'that they themselves are trying to live up to the demands of Islam. I do not mean to say that all of them are remiss in this respect. There are among them many people to whom Islam is a living inspiration, and to these our homage is due. But, on the other hand, very many of our leaders have Islam only on their lips-and that only when they address a public meeting or make a statement to the press-while their personal behaviour and outlook is as devoid of Islam as the behaviour and outlook of the average political leader in Europe or America is devoid of Christianity. This must change if our struggle for Pakistan is not to degenerate into a pitiful copy of the 'nationalist' endeavours from which the rest of the Muslim world is suffering.

As I have already said the Muslim masses instinctively realize the Islamic purport of Pakistan, and genuinely desire a state of affairs in which la ilaha ill'Allah would become the starting point of the community's development. But they are inarticulate and confused in their thoughts. They cannot find their way unaided. They must be led. And so, again, we come back to the question of leadership and of its duties. It seems to me that the supreme test of the present-day Muslim leadership will be its ability-or inability-to lead the community not only in the purely political and economic but also in the moral sphere: the ability-or inability-to convince the Muslims that 'God does not change the condition of a people unless they change their inner selves' (Ar-Ra'd 13:11), which means no more and no less than that a community's political and economic status cannot be lastingly improved unless the community as a whole grows in moral stature.

PAKISTAN BEGINNINGS OF SELF-GOVERNMENT

The Government of India Act of 1909—also known as the Morley-Minto Reforms (John Morley was the secretary of state for India, and Gilbert Elliot, fourth earl of Minto, was viceroy)—gave Indians limited roles in the central and provincial legislatures, known as legislative councils.

Indians had previously been appointed to legislative councils, but after the reforms some were elected to them. At the centre, the majority of council members continued to be government-appointed officials, and the viceroy was in no way responsible to the legislature. At the provincial level, the elected members, together with unofficial appointees, outnumbered the appointed officials, but responsibility of the governor to the legislature was not contemplated.

Morley made it clear in introducing the legislation to the British Parliament that parliamentary self-government was not the goal of the British government. The granting of separate electorates and communal representation was welcomed by Muslims but opposed by Congress.

The Muslim League was pleased by the apparent British intention to support and safeguard Muslim interests in the subcontinent. Separate electorates remained a part of the Muslim League platform even after the independence of Pakistan. Congress opposition was understandable. As the majority community in most provinces, Hindus stood to lose from weighted minority representation. Congress also presented itself as a national secular party and could not support identification of voters with a particular community.

The Morley-Minto Reforms were a milestone. Step by step, the elective principle was introduced for membership in Indian legislative councils. The "electorate" was limited, however, to a small group of upper-class Indians. These elected members increasingly became an "opposition" to the "official government." Communal electorates were later extended to other communities and made a political factor of the Indian tendency toward group identification through religion. The practice created certain vital questions for all concerned. The intentions of the British were questioned. How humanitarian was their concern for the minorities? Were separate electorates a manifestation of "divide and rule"?

For Muslims it was important both to gain a place in all-India politics and to retain their Muslim identity, objectives that required varying responses according to circumstances, as the example of Muhammad Ali Jinnah illustrates. Jinnah, who was born in 1876, studied law in England and began his career as an enthusiastic liberal in Congress on returning to India. In 1913 he joined the Muslim League, which had been shocked by the 1911 annulment of the partition of Bengal into cooperating with Congress to make demands on the British. Jinnah continued his membership in Congress until 1919. During this dual membership period, he was described by a leading Congress spokesperson as the "ambassador of Hindu-Muslim unity."

India's important contributions to the efforts of the British Empire in World War I stimulated further demands by Indians and further response from the British. Congress and the Muslim League met in joint session in December 1916. Under the leadership of Jinnah and Pandit Motilal Nehru (father of Jawaharlal Nehru), unity was preached and a proposal for constitutional reform was made that included the concept of separate electorates.

The resulting Congress-Muslim League Pact (often referred to as the Lucknow Pact) was a sincere effort to compromise. Congress accepted the separate electorates demanded by the Muslim League, and the Muslim League joined with Congress in demanding self-government. The pact was expected to lead to permanent and constitutional united action.

In August 1917, the British government formally announced a policy of "increasing association of Indians in every branch of the administration and the gradual development of self-governing institutions with a view to the progressive realization of responsible government in India as an integral part of the British Empire." Constitutional reforms were embodied in the Government of India Act of 1919—also known as the Montagu-Chelmsford Reforms (Edwin Samuel Montagu was Britain's secretary of state for India; the Marquess of Chelmsford was viceroy). These reforms represented the maximum concessions the British were prepared to make at that time. The franchise was extended, and increased authority was given to central and provincial legislative councils, but the viceroy remained responsible only to London.

The changes at the provincial level were significant, as the provincial legislative councils contained a considerable majority of elected members. In a system called "dyarchy," the nation-building departments of government—agriculture, education, public works, and the like—were placed under ministers who were individually responsible to the legislature. The departments that made up the "steel frame" of British rule—finance, revenue, and home affairs—were retained by executive councillors who were often, but not always, British and who were responsible to the governor.

The 1919 reforms did not satisfy political demands in India. The British repressed opposition, and restrictions on the press and on movement were re-enacted. An apparently unwitting example of violation of rules against the gathering of people led to the massacre at Jallianwala Bagh in Amritsar in April 1919. This tragedy galvanized such political leaders as Jawaharlal Nehru (1889-1964) and Mohandas Karamchand Gandhi (1869-1948) and the masses who followed them to press for further action.

The Allies' post-World War I peace settlement with Turkey provided an additional stimulus to the grievances of the Muslims, who feared that one goal of the Allies was to end the Caliphate of the Ottoman sultan. After the end of the Mughal Empire, the Ottoman caliph had become the symbol of Islamic authority and unity to Indian Sunni Muslims. A pan-Islamic movement, known as the Khilafat Movement, spread in India. It was a mass repudiation of Muslim loyalty to British rule and thus legitimated Muslim participation in the Indian nationalist movement. The leaders of the Khilafat Movement used Islamic symbols to unite the diverse but assertive Muslim community on an all-India basis and bargain with both Congress leaders and the British for recognition of minority rights and political concessions.

Muslim leaders from the Deoband and Aligarh movements joined Gandhi in mobilizing the masses for the 1920 and 1921 demonstrations of civil disobedience and noncooperation in response to the massacre at Amritsar. At the same time, Gandhi endorsed the Khilafat Movement, thereby placing many Hindus behind what had been solely a Muslim demand.

Despite impressive achievements, however, the Khilafat Movement failed. Turkey rejected the Caliphate and became a secular state. Furthermore, the religious, mass-based aspects of the movement alienated such Western-oriented constitutional politicians as Jinnah, who resigned from Congress. Other Muslims also were uncomfortable with Gandhi's leadership. The British historian Sir Percival Spear wrote that "a mass appeal in his [Gandhi's] hands could not be other than a Hindu one. He could transcend caste but not community. The [Hindu] devices he used went sour in the mouths of Muslims." In the final analysis, the movement failed to lay a lasting foundation of Indian unity and served only to aggravate Hindu-Muslim differences among masses that were being politicized. Indeed, as India moved closer to the self-government implied in the Montagu-Chelmsford Reforms, rivalry over what might be called the spoils of independence sharpened the differences between the communities..

The political picture in India was not at all clear when the mandated decennial review of the Government of India Act of 1919 became due in 1929. Prospects of further constitutional reforms spurred greater agitation and a frenzy of demands from different groups. The commission in charge of the review was headed by Sir John Simon, who recommended further constitutional change, but it was not until 1935 that a new Government of India Act was passed. Three consecutive round table conferences were held in London in 1930, 1931, and 1932, at which a wide variety of interests from India were represented. The major disagreement concerned the continuation of separate electorates, which Gandhi and Congress strongly opposed. As a result, the decision was forced on the British government. Prime Minister Ramsay MacDonald issued his "communal award," which continued the system of separate electorates at both the central and the provincial level.

The principal result of the act was "provincial autonomy." The dyarchical system was discontinued, and all subjects were placed under ministers who were individually and collectively responsible to the former legislative councils, which were renamed legislative assemblies. (In a few provinces, including Bengal, a bicameral system was established; the upper house continued to be called a legislative council.) Almost all assembly members were elected, with the exception of some special and otherwise unrepresented groups. After the elections, provincial chief ministers and cabinets took office, although the governors had limited "emergency powers." Sindh was separated from Bombay and became a province. The 1919 reforms had earlier been introduced in the North-West Frontier Province. Balochistan, however, retained special status; it had no legislature and was governed by an "agent general to the governor general." At the centre, the act essentially provided for the establishment of dyarchy, but it also provided for a federal system that included the princes. The princes refused to join a system that might force them to accept decisions made by elected politicians. Thus, the full provisions of the 1935 act did not come into force at the centre.

JINNAH'S ISLAMIC CREDENTIAL AND THE TWO-NATION THEORY

The two-nation theory has its roots in Islam's two-world theory that splits humanity into momins and kafirs—believers and infidels. It is the history, the political culture, and the passion of the Muslim to live in Dar-al-Islaam, or the Abode of Islam. Muslims everywhere have always striven to live within it. Islam even makes it the onerous duty of every Muslim, should he be unfortunate enough to find himself therein, to quit Daar-al-Harb (the House of War, or Non-Islam) and to seek refuge in a land ruled by a Muslim state. Pakistan was the dream of the Muslims in India before 1947 and Jinnah has made that dream into a reality.

In the national legislative elections held in 1945 across British India, the Muslim League captured all 30 seats reserved for Muslims in the Central Assembly; and in the elections for state legislatures in 1946, the Muslim League won 439 of the 494 seats allotted for Muslims in all British Indian states. Congress has then ceased to represent the Muslims.

The Cabinet Mission Plan of 16th May, 1946 was intended to divide India into the states grouped into Hindu and Muslim majority groups: (a) Bihar, U.P., Orissa, C.P., Bombay and Madras; (b) Assam and Bengal; (c) Punjab, NWF Province and Sindh.

Congress party agreed to this scheme. The Muslim League accepted it first, but rejected it subsequently, and announced in August 1946, its plan of Direct Action, announced by Jinnah himself. This led to the outbreak of riots in Calcutta in August 1946 and then in Noakhali in Chittagong area of East Bengal. The riots soon spread through Bihar to Rawalpindi in Punjab, and the NWFP. The statement in the House of Commons by Clement Attlee on 22 Feb. 1947, that Britain was handing over power by June 1948, set the smouldering fires into a full blaze. The riots broke out in Rawalpindi district in March 1947, and Nehru flew over the riot affected areas, and was shown the deep well into which Sikh and Hindu women had jumped to save their honour. He then agreed to the principle of partition of Punjab and Bengal, which had been vigorously demanded by the Sikhs all along in Punjab and later by the Hindus in Bengal as well. Jinnah has never condemned the riots and the massacres. The life of Jinnah and his activities demonstrates very clearly a man driven by the idea of an Islamic state for the Muslims of the Indian subcontinent, although it would mean destruction of lives of millions and uprootments of millions more. The revisionists have tried to put a lot of emphasis on the life of Jinnah before 1937, however a close analysis of that life would show a deeply devoted Empire loyalist Muslim living in an Anglo-Saxon world and trying to gain acceptability from the British rulers by emulating the outward styles of them. He was the perfect example of the type of Muslims Syed Ahmed, the founder of the Aligarh University, has advocated, to enhance the interests of the Muslims in British India.

As a successful lawyer he was a very good actor, giving different speech to satisfy different audience, yet at the same time was ruthless and determined to achieve his target – to create a state only according to Islam, where the non-Muslims have to accept the supremacy of the Islamic way of life. This is not secularism in any sense of the term. The constitution of Pakistan, which he had proposed, and, was implemented in 1955, was for the Islamic State of Pakistan, not a secular state.

There is a growing body of opinion in India today, calling for a confederation of India and Pakistan to solve the problem of Kashmir. They, following the clue from the United States, are advocating autonomy of Jammu & Kashmir, visa free entry for the Pakistanis to India, regular trade and commerce between India and Pakistan, forgetting the torturous history of the subcontinent altogether. The appeasement policy towards Pakistan and Bangladesh by the previous government of Vajpayee and the current government of Man Mohan Singh provides ample examples of that route. The unfortunate statement of Advani, to declare Jinnah as a secularist, is the ultimate expression of that wrong policy.

6

Jinnah: Ambassador of Hindu-Muslim Unity

On his return from England in 1896, Jinnah joined the Indian National Congress. In 1906 he attended the Calcutta session as secretary to Dadabhai Naoroji, who was now president of Congress. One of his patrons and supporters, G. K. Gokhale, a distinguished Brahmin, called him 'the best ambassador of Hindu-Muslim unity'. He was correct. When Bal Gangadhar Tilak, the Hindu nationalist, was being tried by the British on sedition charges in 1908 he asked Jinnah to represent him.

On 25 January 1910 Jinnah took his seat as the 'Muslim member from Bombay' on the sixty-man Legislative Council of India in Delhi. Any illusions the Viceroy, Lord Minto, may have harboured about the young Westernized lawyer as a potential ally were soon laid to rest. When Minto reprimanded Jinnah for using the words 'harsh and cruel' in describing the treatment of the Indians in South Africa, Jinnah replied: 'My Lord! I should feel much inclined to use much stronger language. But I am fully aware of the constitution of this Council, and I do not wish to trespass for one single moment. But I do say that the treatment meted out to Indians is the harshest and the feeling in this country is unanimous' (Wolpert 1984: 33).

Jinnah was an active and successful member of the (mainly Hindu) Indian Congress from the start and had resisted joining the Muslim League until 1913, seven years after its foundation. None the less, Jinnah stood up for Muslim rights. In 1913, for example, he piloted the Muslim Wakfs (Trust) Bill through the Viceroy's Legislative Council, and it won widespread praise.

Muslims saw in him a heavyweight on their side. For his part, Jinnah thought the Muslim League was 'rapidly growing into a powerful factor for the birth of a United India' and maintained that the charge of 'separation' sometimes levelled at Muslims was extremely wide of the mark.

On the death of his mentor, Gokhale, in 1915, Jinnah was struck with 'sorrow and grief' (Bolitho 1954: 62), and in May 1915 he proposed that a memorial to Gokhale be constructed. A few weeks later in a letter to The Times of India he argued that the Congress and League should meet to discuss the future of India, appealing to Muslim leaders to keep pace with their Hindu 'friends'.

Jinnah was elected president of the Lucknow Muslim League session in 1916 (from now he would be one of its main leaders, becoming president of the League itself from 1920 to 1930 and again from 1937 to 1947 until after the creation of Pakistan). Jinnah's political philosophy was revealed in the Lucknow conference in the same year when he helped bring the Congress and the League on to one platform to agree on a common scheme of reforms. Muslims were promised 30 per cent representation in provincial councils. A common front was constructed against British imperialism. The Lucknow Pact between the two parties resulted. Presiding over the extraordinary session, he described himself as 'a staunch Congressman' who had 'no love for sectarian cries' (Afzal 1966: 56-62).

This was the high point of his career as ambassador of the two communities and the closest the Congress and the Muslim League came. About this time, he fell in love with a Parsee girl, Rattanbai (Ruttie) Petit, known as 'the flower of Bombay'. Sir Dinshaw Petit, her father and a successful businessman, was furious, since Jinnah was not only of a different faith but more than twice her age, and he refused his consent to the marriage. As Ruttie was underage, she and Jinnah waited until she was 18, in 1918, and then got married. Shortly before the ceremony Ruttie converted to Islam. In 1919 their daughter Dina was born.

By this time even the British recognized Jinnah's abilities. Edwin Montagu, the Secretary of State for India, wrote of him in 1917: 'Jinnah is a very clever man, and it is, of course, an outrage that such a man should have no chance of running the affairs of his own country' (Sayeed 1968: 86).

Jinnah cut a handsome figure at this time, as described in a standard biography by an American professor: 'Raven-haired with a moustache almost as full as Kitchener's and lean as a rapier, he sounded like Ronald Coleman, dressed like Anthony Eden, and was adored by most women at first sight, and admired or envied by most men' (Wolpert 1984: 40). A British general's wife met him at a viceregal dinner in Simla and wrote to her mother in England: After dinner, I had Mr. Jinnah to talk to. He is a great personality. He talks the most beautiful English. He models his manners and clothes on Du Maurier, the actor, and his English on Burke's speeches. He is a future Viceroy, if the present system of gradually Indianizing all the services continues. I have always wanted to meet him, and now I have had my wish. (Raza 1982: 34)

Mrs. Sarojini Naidu, the nationalist poet, was infatuated: to her, Jinnah was the man of the future. He symbolized everything attractive about modern India. Although her love remained unrequited she wrote him passionate poems; she also wrote about him in purple prose worthy of a Mills and Boon romance: Tall and stately, but thin to the point of emaciation, languid and luxurious of habit, Muhammad Ali Jinnah's attenuated form is a deceptive sheath of a spirit of exceptional vitality and endurance. Somewhat formal and fastidious, and a little aloof and imperious of manner, the calm hauteur of his accustomed reserve but masks, for those who know him, a naive and eager humanity, an intuition quick and tender as a woman's, a humour gay and winning as a child's. Pre-eminently rational and practical, discreet and dispassionate in his estimate and acceptance of life, the obvious sanity and serenity of his worldly wisdom effectually disguise a shy and splendid idealism which is of the very essence of the man. (Bolitho 1954: 21-2)

However, Gandhi's emergence in the 1920s—and the radically different style of politics he introduced which drew in the masses—

marginalized Jinnah. The increasing emphasis on Hinduism and the concomitant growth in communal violence worried Jinnah. Throughout the decade he remained president of the Muslim League but the party was virtually non-existent. The Congress had little time for him now, and his unrelenting opposition to British imperialism did not win him favour with the authorities.

In 1929, while Jinnah was vainly attempting to make sense of the uncertain political landscape, Ruttie died. Jinnah felt the loss grievously. He moved to London with his daughter Dina and his sister Fatima, and returned to his career as a successful lawyer. At this point, Jinnah's story appeared to have concluded as far as the Indian side was concerned.

SECURING A FINANCIAL BASE

Jinnah had successfully resolved the dilemma of all those who wished to challenge British colonialism. He had secured himself financially. Sir Sayyed Ahmad Khan had to compromise; Jinnah did not.

This difference was made possible by developments in the early part of the century: Indians could now enter professions which gave them financial and social security irrespective of their political opinions. Earlier, Indians had been seen as either friendly or hostile natives. The former were encouraged, the latter were victimized, often losing their lands and official positions.

Jinnah's lifestyle resembled that of the upper-class English professional. Jinnah prided himself on his appearance. He was said never to wear the same silk tie twice and had about 200 hand-tailored suits in his wardrobe.

His clothes made him one of the best-dressed men in the world, rivalled in India perhaps only by Motilal Nehru, the father of Jawaharlal. Jinnah's daughter called him a 'dandy', 'a very attractive man'. Expensive clothes, perhaps an essential accessory of a successful lawyer in British India, were Jinnah's main indulgence. In spite of his extravagant taste in dress Jinnah remained careful with money throughout his life (he rebuked his ADC for over-tipping the servants at the Governor's house in Lahore in 1947—G. H. Khan 1993: 81). Dina recounts her father commenting on the two communities: 'If Muslims got ten rupees they would buy a pretty scarf and eat a biriani whereas Hindus would save the money.'

In the early 1930s Jinnah lived in a large house in Hampstead, London, had an English chauffeur who drove his Bentley and an English staff to serve him. There were two cooks, Indian and Irish, and Jinnah's favourite food was curry and rice, recalls Dina. He enjoyed playing billiards. Dina remembers her father taking her to the theatre, pantomimes and circuses.

In the last years of his life, as the Quaid-i-Azam, Jinnah increasingly adopted Muslim dress, rhetoric and thinking. Most significant from the Muslim point of view is the fact that the obvious affluence was self-created. Jinnah had not exploited peasants as the feudal lords had done, nor had he made money like corrupt politicians through underhand deals, nor had he been bribed by any government into selling his conscience. What he owned was made legally, out of his skills as a lawyer and a private investor. By the early 1930s he was reportedly earning 40,000 rupees a month at the Bar alone (Wolpert 1984:138)—at that time an enormous income. Jinnah was considered, even by his opponents like Gandhi, one of the top lawyers of the subcontinent and therefore one of the most highly paid. He also had a sharp eye for a good investment, successfully dabbling in property. His houses were palatial: in Hampstead in London, on Malabar Hill in Bombay and at 10 Aurengzeb Road in New Delhi, a house designed by Edwin Lutyens. His wealth gave him an independence which in turn enabled him to speak his mind.

Paradoxically, Jinnah's behaviour reflected as much Anglo-Indian sociology as Islamic theology. His thriftiness to the point of being parsimonious, his punctuality, his integrity, his bluntness, his refusal to countenance sifarish (nepotism) were alien to South Asian society. Yet these were the values he had absorbed in Britain. He later attempted to weld his understanding of Islam to them. His first two speeches in the Constituent Assembly of Pakistan in 1947 reflect some of the ideas of a Western liberal society and his attempts to find more than an echo of them in Islamic history from the time of the holy Prophet. Jinnah was attempting a synthesis.

Creating a Country

In the early 1930s several important visitors came to Jinnah's Hampstead home, requesting him to return to India to lead the Muslim League. Eventually he was persuaded and finally returned in 1935. With little time for preparation, he led the League into the 1937 elections. Its poor showing did not discourage him; instead, he threw himself into reorganizing it. The Muslim League session in 1937 in Lucknow was a turning point and generated wide enthusiasm. A snowball effect became apparent. In 1939, now in his early sixties, Jinnah made his last will, appointing his sister Fatima, his political lieutenant Liaquat Ali Khan and his solicitor as joint executors and trustees of his estate. Although Fatima was the main beneficiary, he did not forget his daughter Dina and his other siblings. He also remembered his favourite educational institutions, especially Aligarh, which helped lay the foundations for Pakistan.

Jinnah's fine clothes and erect bearing helped to conceal the fact that he was in poor physical health. From 1938 onwards he was to be found complaining of 'the tremendous strain' on his 'nerves and physical endurance' (Jinnah's letter to Hassan Ispahani written on 12 April of that year in the Ispahani Collection). From then on he regularly fell ill, yet that was carefully hidden from the public. He remained unwell for much of the first half of 1945. Later in the year he admitted: 'The strain is so great that I can hardly bear it' (to Ispahani, 9 October 1945, Ispahani Collection). His doctors, Dr. Jal Patel and Dr. Dinshah Mehta, ordered him to take it easy, to rest, but the struggle for Pakistan had begun and Jinnah was running out of time.

Although by now called the Quaid-i-Azam, the Great Leader, Jinnah never courted titles. He had refused a knighthood and even a doctorate from his favourite university: In 1942, when the Muslim University, Aligarh, had wished to award him an honorary Degree of Doctor of Laws, he refused saying: 'I have lived as plain Mr. Jinnah and I hope to die as plain Mr. Jinnah. I am very much averse to any title or honours and I will be more happy if there was no prefix to my name.' (Zaidi 1993: volume I, part I, xlv)

Not all Muslims looked up to Jinnah. Many criticized him, some because they found him too Westernized, others because he was too straight and uncompromising. One young man, motivated by religious fervour and belonging to the Khaksars, a religious party, attempted to assassinate him on 26 July 1943. Armed with a knife he broke into Jinnah's home in Bombay and succeeded in wounding him before he was overpowered. Jinnah publicly appealed to his followers and friends to 'remain calm and cool' (Wolpert 1984: 225). The League declared 13 August a day of thanksgiving throughout India.

In 1940 Jinnah presided over the League meeting in which the Lahore Resolution was moved calling for a separate Muslim homeland. In 1945-6 the Muslim League triumphed in the general elections. The League was widely recognized as the third force in India along with the Congress and the British. Even Jinnah's opponents now acknowledged him: Gandhi addressed him as Quaid-i-Azam. The Muslim masses throughout India were now with him, seeing in him an Islamic champion.

By the time Mountbatten came to India as Viceroy in 1947 Jinnah was dying; he would be dead in 1948. Neither the British nor the Congress suspected the gravity of Jinnah's illness. Many years later Mountbatten confessed that had he known he would have delayed matters until Jinnah was dead; there would have been no Pakistan.

There were several dramatic twists and turns on the way to Pakistan, with Jinnah trying to negotiate the best possible terms to satisfy the high expectations and emotions of the Muslims. Pakistan was finally conceded in the summer of 1947, with Jinnah as its Governor-General. It was, in his words, 'motheaten' and 'truncated', but still the largest Muslim nation in the world. In Karachi, its capital, as Governor-General Jinnah delivered two seminal speeches to the Constituent Assembly on 11 and 14 August. Suddenly, at the height of his popularity, Jinnah resigned the presidency of the League.

Despite his legendary reserve and the seriousness of his position, Jinnah retained his quiet sense of humour. As Governor-General, when he was almost worshipped in Pakistan, he was told that a certain young lady had said she was in love with his hands (Bolitho 1954: 213). Shortly afterwards, she was seated near him at a function, and Jinnah mischievously asked her not to keep looking at his hands. The lady was both thrilled and embarrassed at having amused the Quaid-i-Azam.

By now his health was seriously impaired. He was suffering from tuberculosis, and his heavy smoking—fifty cigarettes a day of his favourite brand, Craven A—and punishing work schedule had also taken their toll. Jinnah died on 11 September 1948 at the age of 71. The nation went into deep mourning. Quite spontaneously, hundreds of thousands of people joined the burial procession—a million people, it was estimated. They felt like orphans; their father had died. Dina, on her only visit to Pakistan, recalls 'the tremendous hysteria and grief'.

The grief was genuine. Those present at the burial itself or those who heard the news still look back on that occasion as a defining moment in their lives. They felt an indefinable sense of loss, as if the light had gone out of their lives. (As a typical example take the case of Sartaj Aziz, a distinguished Pakistani statesman. He remembers the impact that hearing of Jinnah's death had on him. He had fainting fits for three days. His mother said that he did not respond in the same manner to his own father's death.) A magnificent mausoleum in Karachi was built to honour Jinnah. This, then, is the bare bones of Jinnah's life.

JINNAH—A GENUINE MUSLIM COMMUNALIST

Two years ago L K Advani created a great controversy by declaring and affirming that Mohammed Ali Jinnah, the founder of Pakistan, was "secular" and that his main objective was the establishment of Pakistan as a "secular State." Perhaps, he came to this positively wrong if not perverted and one-sided conclusion based on only one statement in Jinnah's entire career which he made on 11 August, 1947 (just three days prior to the birth of Pakistan!) to the Pakistan Constituent Assembly in which he declared that Pakistan would function as a "secular" State. Let me quote from his famous speech on that occasion: "You are free, you are free to go to your temple, you are free to go to your mosque or to any other place of worship in the State of Pakistan. You may belong to any religion or caste or creed - that has nothing to do with the business of the State. We are starting in the days when there is no discrimination, no distinction between one community and another, no discrimination between caste or creed. We are starting with the fundamental principle that we are all citizens and equal citizens of one State.... In course of time Hindus would cease to be Hindus and Muslims would cease to be Muslims not in the religious sense because that is the personal faith of each individual, but in the political sense as citizens of the State."

No doubt it seems to be an unambiguous statement to establish Pakistan as a secular State. But what has been the track record of Pakistan during the last 60 years as an independent State? Hindus as a race and as a minority have been eliminated in Pakistan to the extent of 99 per cent. Hindus in minority who constituted more than 10 per cent of the population in Pakistan on 15 August, 1947 have now been reduced to the level of less than 0.05 per cent. This has been brought about by forced conversion of Hindus into Muslims through the known terrorist methods of Islam. Hindu temples have been destroyed without any mercy or compunction with unprecedented Islamic fervour reminiscent of the brutal atrocities of Chengiz Khan, Mohammed of Gazni, Mohamed of Gori, etc.

Until 1920 Jinnah's loyalty was with the Congress party and India, the great undivided India of the time. Thereafter his loyalty shifted, until it was all devoted, so he claims, to the cause of the Muslims in India. To quote the brilliant words of Proful Goradia: "Islam was in danger and he was seen as going to defend it in the shining armour in the form of a Sherwani, the sword of his brilliant mind and riding a rabid steed called the "Muslim League." The Seville Row Suit, the faith in constitutional weaponry and membership of the Congress Party all disappeared. It is difficult to think of another leader whose career is so sharply split into two absolutely opposite directions. It was, as it were, schizophrenia albeit of career and not of mind. The best way to go about understanding the paradox is to trace Jinnah's life with the help of his well known biographies."

Mohammed Ali Jinnah went to England in 1892 at the age of 16. There he studied Law and qualified himself as a Barrister from Lincoln"' Inn. Jinnah was never shy of declaring that he was thrilled by the liberalism of Lord Morley. During his stay in England, he came into personal touch with Dadabhai Naoroji who was the first Indian to be elected to the House of Commons. No wonder, 14 years later Jinnah became Secretary to Dadabhai Naoroji.

Jinnah returned to India in 1896 as a qualified Barrister. English became his chief language and it remained so for the rest of his life, for he never mastered Urdu. Even when he was leading the Muslims into freedom in the late 1930s based on his two nation theory, he had to define the terms of Muslim emancipation in an alien tongue. His clothes also remained English, until his last years of his life, when he adopted the sherwani and shalwar of the Muslim gentlemen. He was fond of pork, which is taboo to Muslims. He never offered the Namas, Muslim prayer. And his manner of address was always English.

Jinnah married Ruttenbai Petit, daughter of Sir Dinshaw Petit, one of the distinguished Parsee aristocrats of Bombay in 1918. She was 18 years old and Jinnah was 42 years old at that time. Jinnah had then become the leader of the Bar and had amassed his fortune. Till 1919, Jinnah was a staunch supporter of Hindu-Muslim unity. In those days, Jinnah gave several speeches in the hope of awakening India to the virtues of Hindu-Muslim unity. With the coming of Mahatma Gandhi in 1919, everything changed.

In 1920, Jinnah resigned from the Home Rule League. Annie Besant, the creator of the Home Rule League, had also resigned earlier. Gandhi was elected in her place and he cleverly changed the title of Home Rule League to "Swaraj Sabha." So long as Annie Besant was the President of the Home Rule League, their demand was "self-government within the British Empire." When Gandhi became the President of Swaraj Sabha, their demand changed to complete Swaraj or freedom from all ties with Briton. Jinnah's reaction was quick and typical. Jinnah did not subscribe to Gandhiji's view that India should cut off all connections with Great Briton. No wonder he resigned from "Swaraj Sabha." This episode demonstrated not only Jinnah's independence, and stubborn devotion to constitutional methods, but also revealed his deep instinctive dislike of Gandhiji's mind and approach.

Mahatma Gandhi was upset and he sent a letter to Jinnah requesting him to return to the Home Rule League to participate in the new opportunities that had opened up before the country. Jinnah refused. He gave a clear and categorical reply to Mahatma Gandhi: "I thank you for your kind suggestion offering me to take my share in the new life that has opened up before the country. If by "new life" you mean your methods and your programme, I am afraid I cannot accept them, for I am fully convinced that it must lead to disaster.... Your methods have already caused split and division in almost every institution that you have approached hitherto. People generally are desperate all over the country and your extreme programme has for the moment struck the imagination mostly of the inexperienced youth and the ignorant and the illiterate. All this means disorganization and chaos. What the consequences of this may be I shudder to contemplate."

The split between Mahatma Gandhi and Jinnah became total and final at the Nagpur session of the Congress held in December 1920. At that session Jinnah protested against Gandhi"s extreme measures. Jinnah told Gandhi: "Your way is a wrong way: mine is the right way - the constitutional way is the right way." When Jinnah could not have his way, he decided to say good bye to the Congress Party.

By 1928, Jinnah was disgusted with Indian Politics and left for London. He was disheartened because neither the Muslims nor the Hindu members of the Congress and the Muslim League had much time for what he contended. He was invited to the first Round Table Conference held in London in January 1931. Again he was invited as a delegate to the second Round Table Conference held towards the end of 1931. However, he was not invited to the third Round Table Conference. The British had rightly assessed that Jinnah had little support of his own people at that time. It was at this point of time, a frustrated and dejected Jinnah, disowned by the Muslims, distrusted by the Hindus and discarded by the British, decided to reassert himself by changing his ways and methods. He threw away the baggage of his past. And with his own hands started digging the grave of Hindu-Muslim unity, to which he had devoted his years till 1918. This was brought about by a combination of unforeseen fortuitous circumstances.

Liaquat Ali Khan went to England in 1933 and persuaded Jinnah to return to India to work for the emancipation of Muslims. Jinnah returned to India in January 1935. He soon got in touch with all the Muslim leaders and quickly reorganized the Muslim League. In short, Jinnah politically converted himself into a 100 per cent rabid Muslim Communalist in order to become the Sultan of at least a part of India. In a matter of 12 years he created the new State of Pakistan in 1947. He had laid the foundation for this by his famous speech at the Lahore session of the Muslim League held on 23 March, 1940 when the Muslim League passed the "Pakistan Resolution."

Jinnah declared on that occasion: "It has always been taken for granted that Musalmans are a minority. The Musalmans are a nation by definition.... The Hindus and Musalmans belong to two different civilizations which are based mainly on conflicting ideas and conceptions. To yoke together two such nations under a single State, one as a numerical minority and the other as a majority, must lead to growing discontent and final destruction of any fabric that may be so built up for the Government of such a State." Thus with great conceptual clarity and conviction Jinnah succeeded in creating a non-secular Islamic State. Alas! Gandhi and Nehru steeped in mutual conceptual confusion and total want of clarity, created a quasi-fraudulent, purposeless, aimless, directionless pseudo-secular non-State!!

HOW AMERICAN VIEWED JINNAH

It is true that an American scholar has written a better biography of the Quaid-i-Azam Muhammad Ali Jinnah but neither the American nor the Pakistani scholars explaining how the Americans viewed the Quaid and his demand of Pakistan have penned hardly any scholarly work down. An American scholar's perspective in this regard may be startling for many.

Before World War II, the American public as well as the officials had little concern with the political developments in India. The

Indian National Congress was assumed to be the chief proponent of the freedom struggle against British imperialism and Gandhi was acknowledged as the epitome of the struggling Asian masses.

Jinnah was first mentioned in the American press when the 'New York Times' reproduced his full speech delivered at the first Round Table Conference in London, in 1930. However, back in 1923, an American author Claude Van Tyne had admitted in his book 'India in Ferment' that the seventy million Muslims of India were a nation and the British government had to accept them as a separate nation. As the Quaid emerged as the undisputed leader of the Indian Muslims, the American press began to follow his political trail. By the end of 1939, the 'New York Times' reported him as an important if not the most important Indian Muslim leader. John Gunther in his book, "Inside Asia" described him as "one of the most important Asian leaders, an eloquent orator whose opposition to the Hindus was bitter and inflamed." Even by December 1939, the unsympathetic 'Time' magazine considered him important enough to run his portrait but noted that "while the great Hindus, Gandhi and Nehru, obviously worked toward an India for Indians, the leader of the Muslims usually thought first about independence for Muslims and afterward about independence for Indians."

However, the 'New York Times' comments that the Muslims constituted the best part of the Indian army and the British were therefore unwilling to antagonise them played a crucial role in formulating American attitudes toward the Quaid and the Indian Muslims in the subsequent years. The same newspaper also noted that Jinnah claimed that autonomous national states would only solve the communal problem and added that 'the Islamic group was ready to give support to Britain in the European war' but cautioned that the "two Indias - Muslim and Hindu were as unlike as Germany and France."

The official American interest in the Quaid can be gauged from the observations of Thomas M. Wilson, the US consul general at Calcutta, in 1941. He believed that due to wartime exigencies the demand for Pakistan could be put aside but felt that it would be a great mistake to dismiss it as of no importance. To his surprise,

March 23 was widely celebrated throughout India as the ' Pakistan Day'.

In the following years different US magazines/newspapers such as 'Newsweek', 'Nation,' 'The New Republic', etc. reported on Jinnah describing him as the chief obstacle to the Indian independence but at the same time powerful enough to thwart the British war effort if his demand for Pakistan was not sympathetically considered. The American government and the public got a better perspective of the Indian imbroglio after an extensive tour of the subcontinent by the 'New York Times' correspondent Herbert L. Mathews. Till then, the US was indoctrinated by the Congress propaganda, which depicted that everyone in India was united on the Congress platform under Gandhi. His first hand dispatches from India, for the first time, clarified that Indians were not united under Congress and "Jinnah, who was contemptuously dismissed in New York as a political tool of the British with little following, was one of the most important factors in the Indian situation." Although the American press was not sympathetic to the Quaid, Mathews was surprised to find out that at least nine out of ten politically conscious Muslims in India were with Jinnah and the League. His reports generated considerable interest in the US State Department.

The American military intelligence officers stationed in India corroborated that Muslim soldiers in the Indian army were deeply loyal to Jinnah and opposed to Gandhi. When British PM Churchill informed the US President Roosevelt that "We must not on any account break with the Muslims who represent 100 million people and the main Army elements on which we must rely for the immediate fighting," the US President had to be accommodative to Churchill's stance. This was buttressed by the US Ambassador W.Averell Harriman's secret message to Roosevelt confirming that about 75 per cent of the Indian troops and volunteers were Muslims and of the balance, less than half, or perhaps only 12 per cent of the total were sympathetic to Congress.

After the fall of Singapore, the American troops were sent to India in 1942. Gandhi opposed this and prepared to "unleash a large-scale 'Quit India' campaign in which American as well as

British forces will be urged to get out of India immediately." On the other hand the American military intelligence noted with great satisfaction that in reply to the 'Quit India' resolution, the Quaid immediately gave orders for the Muslims to "take no part in any disturbance. Not one Muslim in India entered the fray or raised his hand." At the time of the Cripps' Mission, Colonel Louis Johnson was sent to India as the personal representative of the US president. He reported that as the British government was using the Muslim League therefore approval of any plan for self-determination for India was unnecessary. The State Department got alarmed by his pro-Congress attitude and chastised him to not to identify himself closely with any particular group and suggested that from then on the Indian problem should be judged from the military viewpoint. Another person whose reports carried considerable weight in the US establishment at that time was John Paton Davies, Jr. He was the second secretary of the Chinese embassy and was attached to the staff of General Joseph W. Stilwell, who was then heading the US forces in India, China and Burma. He held several meetings with the Quaid. He reported to the US secretary of state that Jinnah stood head and shoulders above any Muslim leader. In a confidential letter to General Stilwell, Davies highlighted that Jinnah did not wish to embarrass the British and therefore supported the war effort.

While commenting on the rumours that the British government subsidised the Muslim League, Davies observed that Jinnah was incorruptible and though agreed that the British did use the League but clarified that they did not own it. Later on, Congress' threatening civil disobedience movement yet again compelled Roosevelt to send a career diplomat William Phillips as his personal representative to India in 1943. He also had several interviews with the Quaid. Though personally he disapproved of Quaid's "dream of sovereign India into separate nations" yet he appreciated Jinnah's statement that he could be counted on "to do nothing to obstruct the war effort since I regard victory against Japan as essential to the good of India." This was very comforting to the Americans because it was generally believed that the Muslims might mutiny if Jinnah told them to. On the whole, Phillips concluded, "while Jinnah had been exploited by the British in their divide and rule policy, the frequent accusations of pro-Congress groups that Jinnah was playing the British game was unacceptable." In addition, quite a few American military and diplomatic personnel conducted dozens of interviews of the Quaid, and the US government on the Indian situation prepared at least four lengthy and extensively researched reports. The League's sweeping electoral success in 1945-46 and the refusal of Nehru and Congress to accept the Cabinet Mission proposals as interpreted by the British and the League convinced the Americans that Quaid's dream of Pakistan was the only solution to the Indian problem.

After the June 3 partition plan, US Secretary of State George C. Marshall cabled to "have the friendliest relations with the new Pakistan state when it is established..." Consequently, when the Quaid assumed the charge of the first governor-general of Pakistan in Karachi in mid August, the US was the only foreign power to send an official delegate in that ceremony. The American press as well as the important US officials openly admitted "Jinnah had proved himself a great statesman not only of Asia but also of the world." Edgar Snow, the author of " The World's Queerest State" acknowledged that even if Jinnah were appraised only as a barrister "he had won the most monumental judgement in the history of bar."

GROWTH OF COMMUNALISM IN INDIA (1937-1947)

The earlier blog has tried to trace the history and growth of communalism upto 1937. However a few eminent bloggers apart from questioning the surmise of the undersigned had also questioned about the facts after 1937. My apologies for the delay in posting this *sequiter* but I had to do some reading myself to be able to answer my learned critics. Once again I have depended heavily on IGNOU and to some extent on 'India's Struggle for Independence' by Vipan Chandra. Your comments, good, bad or indifferent are most welcome. Earlier Caveat Emptor applies to his essay also.)

The year 1937 was a turning point in the history of communalism in India in so far as it concerns the stridency and intensity of politics of hatred. In the elections held for the provincial legislative assembly, the Muslim League won only 109 out of 492 reserved Muslim seats and only 4.8 % of the total Muslim votes showing thereby the lack of popular support for Muslim League even among the Muslim population. It was a well known fact that League's support base was mostly amongst the wealthy and the landlords. As constructive programme for development of popular support always takes the time and also the fact that any constructive socioeconomic programme would have targeted at the wealthy and landed Muslim supporters of the League, the League resorted to the short cut by raising the cry of 'Islam in danger' thereby directly talking to the Muslim masses about the impending 'Hindu Raj'. And what followed was a communal propaganda 'full of fervour, fear, contempt and bitter hatred' (W. C. Smith).

Earlier in October 1934, Gandhiji had withdrawn from the Congress refusing 4-anna membership of the Congress. At Lucknow session of Congress in April 1936 and Faizpur Session in December 1936 presided over by J. L. Nehru, it was decided to contest election to be held in 1937 but the office acceptance was not yet decided. (While Satyamurti and T. Prakasham advocated office acceptance, M. R. Masani was against it.)

As one of my worthy crtitic has said in his rejoinder to the earlier essay that "Devil is not in the detail" I am reproducing the election results of Congress for the provinces : U.P. (United Provinces) 134/228, Bihar 95/152, Madras 159/215, C.P. (Central Province) 70/112, Orissa 36/60, Bombay 87/175, Bengal 60/250, Sind 8/60, Assam 35/108, NWFP (North West Frontier Province) 19/50, Punjab 18/175.

As a corollary to my first paragraph, it would be germane to point out here that the Hindu fundamentalists had fared worse than their Muslim counterpart in these 1937 elections. For example, Hindu Mahasabha had won only 12 seats out of 175 in Punjab. Hence the same choice of extinction faced them as had faced their Muslim counterparts forcing them to embrace a politics of hatred for survival. Their predicament was aggravated in 1938 when Congress disallowed communalists from working within the Congress organization. Consequently, Congress was condemned by them for "supporting our inveterate enemies" and preaching that Hindus were the only Nation living in India. Thus evolved the Hindu fundamentalists' version of 'two nation theory'.

After the outbreak of WW-II, Muslim League was assiduously fostered by the Viceroy Linlithgow and the Pakistan demand was used to counter the Congress demand that the British should promise to free India after the war and as a proof of sincerity, transfer actual control of government to Indians immediately. British wanted a settlement between the League and the Congress before anything concrete could even be contemplated and promised that no political settlement would be made which was unacceptable to the League thereby giving the Jinnah a kind of a 'veto' power which he was to use to catastrophic effect in future.

Cripps Mission of March-April 1942, though constituted with the avowed intention of 'the earliest possible realisation of self-government in India', actually promised Dominion status and that too after the war, nomination of people of princely states in the proposed Constituent Assembly by their princes, control of British over defence in the new executive council and implicit backdoor recognition of Pakistan via the 'local option clause' by which the princely states were allowed to directly negotiate with the British if they chose to reject the constitution to be framed. At a time when the Pakistan demand was seriously even thought about by the Indians, its sympathetic consideration by the British was a great service to the cause of Pakistan.

At the end of WW-II, at the initiative of Viceroy Wavell, the congress leaders were freed from jail in mid June 1945 and invited to Shimla to work out an interim political arrangement under which the Indians would be responsible for running the country. But Jinnah decided to test his above mentioned power of 'Veto' by insisting that only the League had the right o nominate Muslim members to the executive Council. This was embarrassing to the government as well as this denied representation to the Muslims of the Unionist Party which had staunchly supported the British during the war. But as the present and future interests were considered more important than the past loyalties, Wavell announced the breakdown of talk rather than bypass the League thereby upholding the 'veto' promised to the League by Linlithgow.

Elections held in the winter of 1945-46 to the Central and Provincial Legislative assemblies were fought by the League with a straight forward communal slogan-" A vote for the League and Pakistan was a vote for Islam." And it was a choice between the Gita and the Koran. Needless to say, the League made a clean sweep of the Muslim seats in the polls.

The Cabinet Mission was sent to India in march 1946 to establish a national government and constitutional arrangement for transfer of power. The then British PM Attlee, in sharp contrast to Wavell's position, declared on 15 March 1946 that "a minority would not be allowed to place a veto on the progress of majority." He mission believed that Pakistan wuldnot be a viable entity and hence made a plan to safeguard the interests of Muslim minority within the overall framework of unity of the country. Three sections were planned which would have their own constitution. Group A: Madras, Bombay, United Provinces. Bihar, Central Provinces and Orissa; Group B: Punjab, NWFP and Sind and group C: Bengal and Assam. Common centre would look after defence, Foreign Affairs and communication. A province could leave the group to which it was assigned after the first general elections and after 10 years it could demand modification of both the group and union constitution. But the ambivalence over grouping *i.e.* it was compulsory or optional led to a deadlock and eventual failure of Cabinet Mission as both the League and the Congress took this a vindication of their stand. The League taking advantage of Nehru's speech about the sovereignty of the constituent assembly to amend the rules of procedure of Cabinet Mission withdrew its acceptance.

Interim government was formed on 2 September 1946 with Nehru as its de facto head and reversing the earlier stand of the British to placate and take the League with it. This infuriated the League to actualize its threat of Direct Action the call for which was give on 16 August 1946 in Calcutta with a new slogan 'Larke lenge Pakistan' (We will fight and get Pakistan.) Communal frenzy was provoked by Muslim groups in Bengal with the League's Bengal ministry headed by Suhrawardy looking on and leading to 'the Great Calcutta Killings'. Effect was felt in Noakhali in East Bengal, Bihar in October 1946 and in UP, Bombay, Punjab and

NWFP in the subsequent months. This forced the British to go back to their reconciliatory approach towards the League. Wavel and even the Secretar of State for India Pethick Lawrence believed that in the absence of League civil war would become inevitable in India. Consequently, the League joined the interim government on 26 October 1946 and started continuing their fight from within the government.

Wavell was replaced by Mountbatten and Attlee reaffirmed his government's resolve to withdraw from India latest by '30 June 1947'. The League went on a final offensive, brought down the coalition Punjab government led by Khizr Hyat Khan of unionist party. 3 June plan was devised to accommodate both the parties-by creating a sovereign Pakistan to accede to Jinnah's demand but to make it as small as possible so as to accommodate the 'unity' demand of the congress. Dominion status was to be given to India and Pakistan on 15 August 1947 and other demands of congress *viz.* princely states to be with India, were acceded to as it was making a greater sacrifice. The country gained independence at a great cost and to paraphrase Jinnah "a truncated and moth eaten country" was born. A country where Muslims have more freedom than the country which was ostensibly created for them.

7

The Role of Jinnah in the Formation of Pakistan

Father of the Nation Quaid-i-Azam Muhammad Ali Jinnah's achievement as the founder of Pakistan, dominates everything else he did in his long and crowded public life spanning some 42 years. Yet, by any standard, his was an eventful life, his personality multidimensional and his achievements in other fields were many, if not equally great. Indeed, several were the roles he had played with distinction: at one time or another, he was one of the greatest legal luminaries India had produced during the first half of the century, an 'ambassador of Hindu-Muslim unity, a great constitutionalist, a distinguished parliamentarian, a top-notch politician, an indefatigable freedom-fighter, a dynamic Muslim leader, a political strategist and, above all one of the great nation-builders of modern times. What, however, makes him so remarkable is the fact that while similar other leaders assumed the leadership of traditionally well-defined nations and espoused their cause, or led them to freedom, he created a nation out of an inchoate and downtrodden minority and established a cultural and national home for it. And all that within a decade.

For over three decades before the successful culmination in 1947, of the Muslim struggle for freedom in the South-Asian subcontinent, Jinnah had provided political leadership to the Indian Muslims: initially as one of the leaders, but later, since 1947, as the only prominent leader-the Quaid-i-Azam. For over thirty years, he had guided their affairs; he had given expression, coherence and direction to their legitimate aspirations and cherished dreams; he had formulated these into concrete demands; and, above all, he had striven all the while to get them conceded by both the ruling British and the numerous Hindus the dominant segment of India's population. And for over thirty years he had fought, relentlessly and inexorably, for the inherent rights of the Muslims for an honourable existence in the subcontinent. Indeed, his life story constitutes, as it were, the story of the rebirth of the Muslims of the subcontinent and their spectacular rise to nationhood, phoenix-like.

Quaid-e-Azam, Muhammad Ali Jinnah was born on 25th December 1876 at Vazeer Mansion Karachi, was the first of seven children of Jinnahbhai, a prosperous merchant. After being taught at home, Jinnah was sent to the Sindh Madrasasah High School in 1887. Later he attended the Mission High School, where, at the age of 16, he passed the matriculation examination of the University of Bombay. On the advice of an English friend, his father decided to send him to England to acquire business experience. Jinnah, however, had made up his mind to become a barrister. In keeping with the custom of the time, his parents arranged for an early marriage for him before he left for England.

In London he joined Lincoln's Inn, one of the legal societies that prepared students for the bar. In 1895, at the age of 19, he was called to the bar. While in London Jinnah suffered two severe bereavements—the deaths of his wife and his mother. Nevertheless, he completed his formal studies and also made a study of the British political system, frequently visiting the House of Commons. He was greatly influenced by the liberalism of William E. Gladstone, who had become Prime Minister for the fourth time in 1892, the year of Jinnah's arrival in London. Jinnah also took a keen interest in the affairs of India and in Indian students. When the Parsi leader Dadabhai Naoroji, a leading Indian nationalist, ran for the English Parliament, Jinnah and other Indian students worked day and night for him. Their efforts were crowned with success, and Naoroji became the first Indian to sit in the House of Commons.

When Jinnah returned to Karachi in 1896, he found that his father's business had suffered losses and that he now had to depend on himself. He decided to start his legal practice in Bombay, but it took him years of work to establish himself as a lawyer.

It was nearly 10 years later that he turned toward active politics. A man without hobbies, his interest became divided between law and politics. Nor was he a religious zealot: he was a Muslim in a broad sense and had little to do with sects. His interest in women was also limited to Ruttenbai—the daughter of Sir Dinshaw Petit, a Bombay Parsi millionaire—whom he married over tremendous opposition from her parents and others. The marriage proved an unhappy one. It was his sister Fatima who gave him solace and company.

Three years later, in January 1910, Jinnah was elected to the newly-constituted Imperial Legislative Council. All through his parliamentary career, which spanned some four decades, he was probably the most powerful voice in the cause of Indian freedom and Indian rights. Jinnah, who was also the first Indian to pilot a private member's Bill through the Council, soon became a leader of a group inside the legislature. Mr. Montagu (1879-1924), Secretary of State for India, at the close of the First World War, considered Jinnah "perfect mannered, impressive-looking, armed to the teeth with dialecties..."Jinnah, he felt, "is a very clever man, and it is, of course, an outrage that such a man should have no chance of running the affairs of his own country."

For about three decades since his entry into politics in 1906, Jinnah passionately believed in and assiduously worked for Hindu-Muslim unity. Gokhale, the foremost Hindu leader before Gandhi, had once said of him, "He has the true stuff in him and that freedom from all sectarian prejudice which will make him the best ambassador of Hindu-Muslim Unity: And, to be sure, he did become the architect of Hindu Muslim Unity: he was responsible for the Congress-League Pact of 1916, known popularly as Lucknow Pact-the only pact ever signed between the two political organisations, the Congress and the All-India Muslim League, representing, as they did, the two major communities in the subcontinent. The Congress-League scheme embodied in this pact was to become the basis for the Montagu-Chemlsford Reforms, also known as the Act of 1919. In retrospect, the Lucknow Pact represented a milestone in the evolution of Indian politics. For one thing, it conceded Muslims the right to separate electorate, reservation of seats in the legislatures and weightage in representation both at the Centre and the minority provinces. Thus, their retention was ensured in the next phase of reforms. For another, it represented a tacit recognition of the All-India Muslim League as the representative organisation of the Muslims, thus strengthening the trend towards Muslim individuality in Indian politics. And to Jinnah goes the credit for all this.

Thus, by 1917, Jinnah came to be recognised among both Hindus and Muslims as one of India's most outstanding political leaders. Not only was he prominent in the Congress and the Imperial Legislative Council, he was also the President of the All-India Muslim and that of the Bombay Branch of the Home Rule League. More important, because of his key-role in the Congress-League entente at Lucknow, he was hailed as the ambassador, as well as the embodiment, of Hindu-Muslim unity.

In subsequent years, however, he felt dismayed at the injection of violence into politics. Since Jinnah stood for "ordered progress", moderation, gradualism and constitutionalism, he felt that political terrorism was not the pathway to national liberation but the dark alley to disaster and destruction. Hence, the constitutionalist Jinnah could not possibly, countenance Mohandas Karamchand Gandhi's novel methods of Satyagrah (civil disobedience) and the triple boycott of government-aided schools and colleges, courts and councils and British textiles. Earlier, in October 1920, when Gandhi, having been elected President of the Home Rule League, sought to change its constitution as well as its nomenclature, Jinnah had resigned from the Home Rule League, saying: "Your extreme programme has for the moment struck the imagination mostly of the inexperienced youth and the ignorant and the illiterate. All this means disorganisation and chaos". Jinnah did not believe that ends justified the means.

In the ever-growing frustration among the masses caused by colonial rule, there was ample cause for extremism. But, Gandhi's doctrine of noncooperation, Jinnah felt, even as Rabindranath Tagore (1861-1941) did also feel, was at best one of negation and despair: it might lead to the building up of resentment, but nothing constructive. Hence, he opposed tooth and nail the tactics adopted by Gandhi to exploit the Khilafat and wrongful tactics in the Punjab in the early twenties. On the eve of its adoption of the Gandhian programme, Jinnah warned the Nagpur Congress Session (1920): "you are making a declaration (of Swaraj within a year) and committing the Indian National Congress to a programme, which you will not be able to carry out". He felt that there was no short-cut to independence and that Gandhi's extra-constitutional methods could only lead to political terrorism, lawlessness and chaos, without bringing India nearer to the threshold of freedom.

The future course of events was not only to confirm Jinnah's worst fears, but also to prove him right. Although Jinnah left the Congress soon thereafter, he continued his efforts towards bringing about a Hindu-Muslim entente, which he rightly considered "the most vital condition of Swaraj". However, because of the deep distrust between the two communities as evidenced by the countrywide communal riots, and because the Hindus failed to meet the genuine demands of the Muslims, his efforts came to naught. One such effort was the formulation of the Delhi Muslim Proposals in March, 1927. In order to bridge Hindu-Muslim differences on the constitutional plan, these proposals even waived the Muslim right to separate electorate, the most basic Muslim demand since 1906, which though recognised by the congress in the Lucknow Pact, had again become a source of friction between the two communities. Surprisingly though, the Nehru Report (1928), which represented the Congress-sponsored proposals for the future constitution of India, negated the minimum Muslim demands embodied in the Delhi Muslim Proposals.

In vain did Jinnah argue at the National convention (1928): "What we want is that Hindus and Mussalmans should march together until our object is achieved...These two communities have got to be reconciled and united and made to feel that their interests are common". The Convention's blank refusal to accept Muslim demands represented the most devastating setback to Jinnah's life-long efforts to bring about Hindu-Muslim unity, it meant "the last straw" for the Muslims, and "the parting of the ways" for him, as he confessed to a Parsee friend at that time. Jinnah's disillusionment at the course of politics in the subcontinent prompted him to migrate and settle down in London in the early thirties. He was, however, to return to India in 1934, at the pleadings of his co-religionists, and assume their leadership. But, the Muslims presented a sad spectacle at that time. They were a mass of disgruntled and demoralised men and women, politically disorganised and destitute of a clear-cut political programme.

ACTIVITIES OF JINNAH

Jinnah was the most Westernized political leader in all the annals of Indian Islam; no other Muslim political leader could match him in terms of modernity and a modern outlook. He was completely at home with the Anglo-Indian society in cosmopolitan Bombay and metropolitan London. During his chequered career, Jinnah encountered an exceedingly large number of non-Muslim leading personalities and a host of British officials, more than any other Muslim leader and had interacted with them for some four decades. However, during that time Jinnah married a Zoroastrian girl only after getting her converted to Islam. So much so for the 'Secularist' Jinnah.

Since 1897, Jinnah was active in Anjuman-I-Islam, Muslim Bombay's foremost religio-political body. In 1906, Jinnah opposed the demand for separate electorates, but before long his opposition thawed when he realized that the demand had "the mandate of the community" of the Muslims in India. In 1910, he was elected to the Imperial Council on a reserved Muslim seat. From then on, he came in close contact with Nadwah, Aligarh and the All India Muslim League (AIML), and he was chosen by the AIML to sponsor a bill on Waqf alal Aulad, a problem of deep concern to Muslims since the time of Syed Ahmad Khan.

He joined the AIML formally in October 1913 (although he gave up his membership of the Congress in 1920 opposing Gandhi's policy to confront the British) and became its President in 1916. One result of his efforts was the Congress-Muslim League Lucknow Pact of 1916, which settled the controversial separate electorate for the Muslims, paving the way for Pakistan in future.

For Jinnah, while national freedom for both Hindus and Muslims continued to be the supreme goal, the means adopted to achieve it underwent a dramatic change. The ultimate objective was to ensure political power for Muslims. The period after 1937 Jinnah has developed close friendship with Mohammed Iqbal, the spiritual founder of the concept of Pakistan. Jinnah called Muslims 'a nation', stressing their distinct religion, culture, language, and civilization, and calling on them to "live or die as a nation". He even called the League flag 'the flag of Islam', arguing, "you cannot separate the Muslim League from Islam.

In an address to Gaya Muslim League Conference in January 1938, Jinnah begun mapping out his new worldview. He said, "When we say 'This flag is the flag of Islam' they think we are introducing religion into politics - a fact of which we are proud. Islam gives us a complete code. It is not only religion but it contains laws, philosophy, and politics. In fact, it contains everything that matters to a man from morning to night."

In his address at Patna session of the Muslim League (26-29 December 1938) he declared: - "The behaviour of the Congress Ministers in the six or seven provinces in which they had gained power under the 1935 Act was that they had compelled Muslim children to accept 'Bunde Matram' as their national song though it was idolatrous and a hymn of hate against Muslims."

In his historic declaration for Pakistan in the Muslim League conference in Lahore in 1940, he spelled out his reasons for reaching out towards the 'Pakistan' goal arguing that, "Islam and Hinduism... are not religions in the strict sense of the word, but are... different and distinct social orders", that "the Hindus and Muslims belong to two different religious philosophies, social customs, literature", "to two different civilizations", that they "derive their inspiration from different sources of history"... (with) different epics, different heroes, and different episodes."

In his marathon talks with Gandhi in September 1944, Jinnah demanded the constituency for the plebiscite to decide upon the Pakistan demand would comprise only the Muslims, and not the entire population of the areas concerned. After independence, as head of the state he had founded, Jinnah talked in the same strain.

He talked of securing "liberty, fraternity and equality as enjoined upon us by Islam" (25 August 1947); of "Islamic democracy, Islamic social justice and the equality of manhood" (21 February 1948); of raising Pakistan on "sure foundations of social justice and Islamic socialism which emphasized equality and brotherhood of man" (26 March 1948); of laying "the foundations of our democracy on the basis of true Islamic ideals and principles" (14 August 1948); and "the onward march of renaissance of Islamic culture and ideals" (18 August 1947).

He called upon the mammoth Lahore audience in 30 October 1947, to build up "Pakistan as a bulwark of Islam", to "live up to your traditions and add to it another chapter of glory", adding, "If we take our inspiration and guidance from the Holy Quran, the final victory, I once again say, will be ours" (30 October 1947).

As for the specific institutions of the new state, he exhorted the armed forces to uphold "the high traditions of Islam and our National Banner" (8 November 1947); and commended the State Bank research organization to evolve "banking practices compatible with Islamic ideals of social and economic life" and to "work our destiny in our own way and present to the world an economic system based on true Islamic concept of equality of manhood and social justice" (1 July 1948).

For Jinnah, "the creation of a State of our own was a means to an end and not the end in itself. The idea was that we should have a State in which we could live and breathe as free men and which we could develop according to our own lights and culture and where principles of Islamic social justice could find free play" (11 October 1947).

He told Edwards College students that "this mighty land has now been brought under a rule, which is Islamic, Muslim rule, as a sovereign independent State" (18 April 1948). He even described Pakistan as "the premier Islamic State" (February 1948).

Jinnah's broadcast to the people of the United States (February 1948) was in a similar vein: "I do not know what the ultimate shape of this constitution is going to be, but I am sure that it will be of a democratic type, embodying the essential principles of Islam. Today, they are as applicable in actual life as they were 1300 years ago. Islam and its idealism have taught us democracy. ....We have many non- Muslims—Hindus, Christians, and Parsis—but they are all Pakistanis. They will enjoy the same rights and privileges as any other citizens and will play their rightful part in the affairs of Pakistan."

This is the repetition of what Jinnah said on 11 August 1947, which was quoted by many as the proof that Jinnah was 'Secularist par Excellence', but it is misleading to say the least. Jinnah has said clearly that he wanted equal treatments of people of all religions within an Islamic state, not in a secular state.

While he laid a good deal of stress on Islamic ideals and principles, he ruled out theocracy, saying, "Pakistan is not a theocracy or anything like it. Islam demands from us the tolerance of other creeds." Technically speaking, theocracy means a government "by ordained priests, who wield authority as being specially appointed by those who claim to derive their rights from their sacerdotal position". Of all Jinnah's pronouncements, his 11 August 1947 address has received the greatest attention since the birth of Pakistan, and spawned a good deal of controversy. That address contains: "I think we should keep that in front of us as our ideal and you will find that in course of time Hindus would cease to be Hindus and Muslims would cease to be Muslims, not in the religious sense because that is the personal faith of each individual, but in the political sense as citizens of the state."

Jinnah's pronouncement was purely a political speech designed to please the gathered Britishers of some of the highest ranks, including Lord Mountbatten and to appease the Hindu minorities in Pakistan in order to protect the Muslims from the growing threat of communal violence in India. A close study all of Jinnah's pronouncements during 1934-48, and most of his pronouncement during the pre-1934 period, shows that the word, 'secular' (signifying an ideology) does not find a mention in any of them. Even when confronted with the question, he evaded it—as the following extracts from his 17 July 1947 press conference indicates:

Question: "Will Pakistan be a secular or theocratic state?" Mr. M.A. Jinnah: "You are asking me a question that is absurd. I do not know what a theocratic state means." A correspondent suggested that a theocratic State meant a State where only people of a particular religion, for example, Muslims, could be full citizens and Non-Muslims would not be full citizens. Mr. M.A. Jinnah: "Then it seems to me that what I have already said is like throwing water on duck`s back (laughter). When you talk of democracy, I am afraid you have not studied Islam. We learned democracy thirteen centuries ago."

JINNAH'S PAKISTAN

DAWN of November 6 carried a news item under the headline 'PML body proposes challenging military rule.' It read : 'Pakistan Muslim League's legal committee headed by former law minister Khalid Anwer on Friday recommended to the Coordination Council of Pakistan Muslim League (N) to challenge the military takeover of the country in the Supreme Court.'

What will these partymen plead? "We hereby solemnly swear that in the exercise of our gross ineptitude, effective corruption, insatiable greed, dangerous intolerance, combined with all other imaginable failings, we have brought about the downfall of what we held to be democracy. We amended the Constitution of the Republic of Pakistan at will, suspending all rules of procedure while doing so, with the aim of making our Leader all-powerful and impregnable. We successfully managed to totally corrupt each and every institution of state, other than the army.

We did not reckon with our leader's stupidity in taking on, for a second time, the Pakistan Army or that his reckless ambition would make him commit the criminal offence of effectively 'highjacking' an aeroplane of his own national airline and endangering the lives of some 200 passengers. We created a situation in which the Chief of Army Staff and his men were forced to throw us out, suspend the mangled and mauled Constitution, and take over the governance of the country for an unspecified period of time."

No doubt the judiciary will judge wisely and well. Now, what makes a democrat. A baggy shalwar, a kamiz, and an unbuttonable waistcoat covering what is known as a 'healthy' (meaning overfed) body? Does a uniform prevent a fit and trim man from being a democrat? We should count ourselves fortunate that we have a man who received a liberal education at St. Patrick's High School in Karachi, taught by Father Stephen Raymond, Ossie Nazareth and the likes of such men to differentiate right from wrong, religion from religiosity, good from bad, and to appreciate and experience what life has to offer.

After matriculating he went to study at Foreman Christian College at Lahore. This man, we feel, will not follow the dictatorial and democratic pattern of enlisting religion on his side, or if the religious leaders are not compliant, going to the extent of foisting upon us a new kind of perverted religion subservient to his ends. We must trust that he will do his best to rebuild Pakistan as envisaged by its founder, Mohammed Ali Jinnah. (US Ambassador William Milam on November 5 in Islamabad whilst speaking at a conference on American Studies stated that America is not anti-Islamic, and that the present change in the country could be used as an opportunity to return to the vision which Mr Jinnah had for Pakistan.)

General Pervez Musharraf was four-year-old, getting ready to go to school, when Jinnah on August 11, 1947 enunciated his 'creed' to his constituent assembly meeting for the first time at Karachi. This speech was a fine bit of rhetoric, but far too moral, truly democratic, free of bigotry and loaded with justice to be able to be digested by the philistines of that era and by those who have followed down the fifty-two degenerative years. Far too many loyal Pakistanis who have occupied leadership roles from the day Jinnah died right down to the ending of this century would have been far more at ease had he never made this particular speech. It has inspired fear in successive governments, has been a point of bitter dissent in its interpretation, and has even been officially distorted in print. It has been this nation's misfortune that we have never, after Jinnah's lifetime, showed the slightest desire to live up to the principles he set for us.

Before the flag of Pakistan had even been hoisted, that August day he told the future legislators : "You are free, free to go to your temples, you are free to go to your mosques or to any other places of worship in this State of Pakistan. You may belong to any religion or caste or creed-that has nothing to do with the business of the State."

Now, this particular passage has always been the main bugbear of the insecure, the feeble of faith, and the cowards who live by self-deception. The very next day it was found to be too irksome, it inspired fear. In his speech, Jinnah also proclaimed that "the first duty of a government is to maintain law and order, so that life, property and religious beliefs of its subjects are fully protected by the State." Amongst the evils which he vowed would not be tolerated were bribery, corruption, blackmarketing, and "this great evil-the evil of nepotism and jobbery."

The definition of 'jobbery' : 'the practice of corruptly turning a public office, trust, etc., to private gain or advantage; the perpetration of jobs.' Such is the daily bread of powermongers. What Jinnah failed to foresee was that within less than two years such practices would be just a few of the prerequisites for the survival and maintenance of power of those who would rule after him.

Fortunately for him, Jinnah did not live long enough to see his dream betrayed by men unworthy even to utter his name. He died before total disillusionment could set in (though he had his suspicions that it was on its way) and broke his heart. From what we know of him, he was that rare being, an incorruptible man in all the many varied meanings of the word corruption, purchasable by no other, swayed by no other, perverted by no other; a man of honour, integrity and high ideals. That the majority of his countrymen have been found wanting in these qualities is this country's tragedy.

What the General must now remember is that Jinnah also failed to perceive in his countrymen their penchant for pernicious sycophancy, the malignant weapon of the ambitious, that was to drag down many a man, make fools of many more, and with which leaders of this nation have found themselves unfit to combat. They succumb, time after time.

Power seekers are adept in the art of sycophancy, if adept in nothing else. Declamations of 'my imperishable and devoted loyalty,' 'you are not merely an individual, but an institution,' 'your services are indispensable for the greater good of the country,' 'you embody the national interest,' all roll glibly off many servile tongues, and are transferred with the greatest of ease from each transient master to the next. The supreme example of adulation : 'When the history of this country is written by objective historians, your name will be placed even before that of Mr Jinnah,' written to Iskander Mirza by loyal Zulfikar Ali Bhutto, is closely rivalled by Mushahid Hussain's declaration that the Muslim Leaguers were but 'slaves of Mian Nawaz Sharif's thoughts.'

THE ELECTION CAMPAIGN FOR PAKISTAN

Since the creation of Pakistan experiments have been made to as-certain the will of the people regarding the reconstruction of national institutions. From time to time, various governments envisaged plans, schemes and proposals, to strengthen and streamline the structure of private and public establishments, according to the emerging needs. However, the process of reformation, during the last so many years, evidently failed to satisfy the national requirements as well as the public opinion.

Once again the nation is passing through the election experiment to be held from 18th of August. The election campaign, with each passing day is gaining momentum throughout the country. In a democratic society, elections are considered as an integral part of the political system, destined to change the government, peacefully, by the majority votes.

In the parliamentary system, prevailing in Britian since centuries, the will of the people, ascertained through the ballot, became the beacon of light for the people at home and abroad. Inspired by the peaceful means of transfer of power, many British colonies adopted the parliamentary system for the good governance of their country. Pakistan, being an important part of the British Empire, opted for the parliamentary system, based on British conventions. However, since independence, the country witnessed very many changes in the form and format of the government, mutilating the very pattern of the parliamentary structure. Even the constitution of the country was abrogated, changed, modified and amended to suit the desire of the ruling class.

Now, under the guidance of President Musharraf, new reforms have been introduced to associate the common man with the representative institutions. For the first time in the history of Pakistan the women were granted 30 percent representation in the assemblies. The Local Bodies elections being held on the non-party basis providing opportunity to the honest and capable candidates to contribute their share in the development of healthy society, free from the prevailing corruption. The elections will be a test for the politicians who claim to enjoy popularity among the electorates. In order to hold free and impartial elections, the Election Commission has prescribed a code of conduct to be followed by the candidates. It is a basic requirement of the election procedure, which will strengthen the democratic traditions. During the British rule elections were envisaged to be held in the peaceful atmosphere, free from the intimidation of officials as well as the resourceful and influential candidates. Even the Elections of 1945-46 were considered very transparent which paved the way for the ultimate success of Muslim League's candidates. The electorates were provided opportunity to exercise the right of vote according to their conscience.

At this critical juncture, the pressure tactics were vehemently condemned by Quaid-i-Azam who in his press conference at Karachi on 6th September 1945 stated that: "It would be highly improper for me to interfere or to influence the activities, proceedings and decisions of the Parliamentary Board, Provincial or Central, or for that matter, of any tribunal set up by the League. No inducement can ever be given to any person; howsoever high he may be, in joining the Muslim League. It will be corruption to do so and no honest man can be a party to it."

While discussing the election issues, it must be realized that the destiny of the Subcontinent was decided during the elections of 1945-46. The elections established, beyond any doubt, the claim of the All India Muslim League as the sole representative organization of 10 million Muslims of India. Hitherto, League's assertions to represent the entire Muslim community were disputed and emphatically denied by the Indian National Congress, stressing on its national character, having in its fold the eminent Muslims of various castes and communities, supporting its policy and programme. The Muslims belonging to Congress, publicized by the Congress press as 'Nationalist Muslims', invigorated the position of the Congress in the political parlays between the Congress and the League. The government of India too subscribed the Congress views about the Muslim minority.

The Congress forcefully advocated that all the sections of Indian population, desire and demand, a democratic united India, free from the communal exploitation.

The British government supported the Congress stance and the general public in England, influenced by the Congress propaganda, treated the Muslim League as a communal organization, struggling to safeguard the interests of upper class Muslims, particularly the landed aristocracy. To achieve the freedom of India, the Congress launched the violent campaign of 'Quiet India' against the Government of India in August 1942. The government suppressed the agitation. In spite of the crackdown on its members, leaders and activists, who were arrested and kept in confinement till July 1945, the party position remained intact, powerful enough to encounter the government against any decision, contrary to its aims and objects.

As regards the British government, although it emerged victorious against Germany and Japan in the Second World War (1939-45), it substantially lost the moral and material capacity to subdue and subordinate the spirit of Indian nationalism. According to political perceptions in England, the Indian circumstances were becoming unfavourable for the government and it would be impossible to crush any violent agitation against the British rule. Consequently, the British government asked Lord Wavell, the Viceroy of India to invite Indian leaders for consultations. On June 14, 1945, Lord Wavell, in his broadcast announced that: " I have been authorised by His Majesty's Government to place before the Indian political leaders proposals designed to ease the present political situation and to advance India towards her goal of full self government." He also announced holding elections saying that: " The appropriate time for fresh elections for the Central and Provincial legislatures will be discussed at the Conference."

Before concluding his broadcast he expressed the noble sentiments: " Finally, I would ask you all to help in creating the atmosphere of goodwill and mutual confidence that is essential if we are to make progress. The destiny of this great country and of the many millions who live in it depends on the wisdom and good understanding of the leaders, both of action and of thought, British and Indian, at this critical moment of India's history."

The Simla Conference deliberated on the Indian problems till July 14 without reaching any settlement between the principal political parties. Maulana Abdul Kalam Azad, President of the Congress remarked about the breakdown of the conference as: "... the position taken by Mr. Jinnah was that the Muslim League on behalf of the Muslim should nominate Muslim members in the new Executive Council. The Congress found that such a position would be inconsistent with its basic national character. "

However, Lord Wavell took the responsibility and announced that:" I wish to make it clear that the responsibility for the failure is mine."He also stated that the general elections would be held in the coming winter.

The elections became the most important, crucial and urgent problem to be faced by the national parties. It was more important for the Muslim League, which was still consolidating its position among the Muslim masses. Sensing the importance of elections, Muhammad Ali Jinnah, before leaving Simla, issued a statement on 16th July, emphasising that: " Every province and every district must be thoroughly and systematically organized and the result of the elections would be the acid test and the verdict given at the polling booths will be the main criterion by which the solidarity and unity of Musalmans will be judged both in India and abroad all over the world."

He invited Muslims attention towards financial assistance stating that: "I have not made any appeal for funds since 1942, as there was no need for it but I want to impress upon our people that we do require money now to face these elections all over the vast Subcontinent of India in eleven provinces as well as for the centre. I hope that my appeal will meet with cordial and generous response."

Thus the President of the League started the election campaign, just after the failure of the Simla Conference. He issued statements, addressed public meetings, circulated appeals, and received numerous deputations, emphasing the importance of the success of League's candidates. On 31st October, he pronounced that " The elections will give a clear verdict on the issue whether the Muslims of India stands for Pakistan or for Akhand Hindustan. It is therefore a question of life and death with Muslims of India. If we are defeated in the elections, then we would be nowhere, but I have full faith in you and, I see clearly that Musalmans of India today understand the issues before them. We have no press, nor financial support the Congress has, but, we Muslims, are politically more conscious than Hindus are, the handicaps notwithstanding."

The election campaign started by the Muslim League stirred all sections of Muslim population. The appeal for funds made by the Quaid demanding that: "Give me the silver bullets and I will finish the job." inspired the Muslims who contributed generously for the election fund.

Even the school students devoted their pocket money for the cherish goal of Pakistan. The Muslim women having no monetary resources threw away their ornaments before the fund raising parties in excitement. The students of the Muslim University Aligarh played a pivotal role in the election campaign. More than six hundred students spread away in the far-flung areas canvassing and collecting votes for the ML candidates. They approached Muslims of every walk of life to support the national cause of Pakistan and succeeded in counteracting the powerful material means, employed by the Congress to defeat League's Candidates. The student army found by the League in the election battle, fought pitched battles with the anti-League voters from one corner of India to another. The credit for the success of the League undoubtedly goes to the student community.

Another important factor, which consolidated the position of the League, was the participation of ulema and sufis. The religious divines entered in the election campaign from different sides and changed the nature of elections from the political battle into the religious Jihad. The spiritual element introduced by the religious personages sanctified the struggle and the ordinary Muslim, hitherto reluctant to side and support the League, treating it a West-oriented organization, joined the campaign that decided the future of India. The invaluable support extended by the divines shortened the distance for the realisation of Pakistan.

Eminent ulemas and spiritual leaders such as, Maulana Shabbir Ahmad Usmani, Maulana Abdul Hamid Badayuni, Dewan Syed Ale Rasul Ali Khan of Ajmer, Pir Ladlay Hussain of Gulharga, Khwaja Ghulam Sadeed-ud-din of Tonsa, Sajjada Nasheen of Pakpattan, Syed Ghulam Mohiuddin Chisti of Golra, Maulana Qamar-ud-din of Saeeyal, Pir Syed Jamiat Ali Shah of Alipore, Maulana Syed Fazal Shah of Jalalpur and many more participated in the election campaign. The spiritual leaders directed their followers to only vote for the Muslim League candidates. The Fatawas issued by the ulemas and messages propagated by the spiritual heads created a deep impression that Pakistan enjoyed the blessing of the God Almighty. It goes without saying that without the support of the religious leaders it was nearly impossible for the League to secure cent percent votes in the election of Central Legislative Assembly, which decisively produced favourable results in the Provincial Assembly elections subsequently held in 1946. The contribution of ulemas for the creation of Pakistan must be realised as a most significant factor to be remain a living force in the contemporary history of Pakistan.—The author is former Senior Research Fellow, Quaid-i-Azam Academy.

A Dream Destination

In the subcontinent, there emerged many movements in the 19th and 20th centuries with extensive impacts and aspirations. These movements with their specific endeavour achieved colossal popularity and successes. Pakistan Movement is one of those movements, resulting in a separate state for the Muslims of the Indian subcontinent. The first brick in the foundation of Pakistan was laid in 712 A.D. when Muhammad Bin Qasim anchored at Debal Port, freed the Muslim women and children from the prisons of Raja Dahir and constructed the first mosque at the town. Quaid-i-Azam Muhammad Ali Jinnah acclaimed the event in these words:

"The Pakistan Movement started when the first Muslim put his foot on the soil of Sindh, the gateway of Islam in India".

Muslims came to the Indian subcontinent as rulers. They were in minority and had a religion different from that of the majority whom they dominated. The locals accepted Islam in large numbers but even then the majority of non-Muslims remained high. The rotten governmental system and characterless behaviour of the last Mughal rulers paved the way for the downfall of the Mughal dynasty. Muslim rule in India was not ousted by the Hindu majority but by outsiders-the East India Company and the British. These outsiders received support from all religious communities, but the most disturbing stage came when the British showed their intention to establish majority rule under their supervision, which was called democracy. This created deep fear among the Muslims who saw their future as slaves of the Hindu majority.

The Muslims of the subcontinent, because of the stigma attached to them for their role in the 1857 war of independence, were groping in the dark.

After that, the British provided opportunities and facilities to the Hindus as their allies in every aspect of life, while the Muslims were ignored. The Hindus in turn fully availed this opportunity to harm the Muslims and destroy their culture. The Muslims, however, were aware of the fact that the Hindu majority would overwhelm them. The Hindus were far ahead in the fields of trade, commerce and technology. British-backed Hindus launched many movements to restrain Muslim culture and even their existence and convert them to Hinduism.

For this purpose, the Hindus started a movement to establish Hindi language in the subcontinent instead of Urdu. However, the Urdu language came to birth in the subcontinent in the Muslim era and it was common in Hindus and Muslims. Therefore, there were two main reasons as to why the Hindus detested this language. First, it recalled the Muslim regime in the region and secondly, all the literature of Muslim culture and religion had been translated in this language. In 1867, the Hindus of Benaras started a movement to declare the Urdu language as foreign and demanded to establish Hindi language in the subcontinent.

In 1875, Arya Samaj movement was begun to oust the Muslims from subcontinent. Under this movement, the Muslims were declared "Aliens". Following the creation of the Indian National Congress in 1885, the Muslim leaders saw through the game of this "National" movement and cautioned their people of the hovering hazards. The establishment of Muslim League in 1906 was a challenge to the Indian National Congress. Maulana Hasrat Mohani presented a plan to the Government for a country envisaging two separate states for the Hindus and Muslims. Chaudhary Rehmat Ali further developed this concept. He displayed great wisdom and foresight by putting forth not only a name but in large measure the scheme that ended in the inception of Pakistan. Maulana Muhammad Ali, Maulana Shaukat Ali and Maulana Zafar Ali Khan spread the message of Pakistan through their logical lectures and articles in newspapers.

At the end of 19th century, the Muslims had to face much difficulty to survive. At the same time, they were the target of both the British and the Hindus. At this critical hour, Sir Syed Ahmed Khan guided the Muslim nation and practically took steps to save its status. He equated education with power and declared that the Muslims could improve their political, social and economic condition only through the medium of modern and scientific education. He cultivated the concept of a separate Muslim nation on the basis of religion, culture and history. He inspired the Muslims of the subcontinent to demand a separate homeland where they could arrange their lives and affairs of the State according to the dictates of Holy Quran and Sunnah. The early 20th century, the period of 1908-1914 was most disturbing for the Muslims of the subcontinent. It was not only the local Indian affairs, which were frustrating them politically, but the activities of the imperialists in the rest of the Muslim world were also a source of much anguish.

The anti-Muslim attitude of the Indian National Congress and other activities goaded the Muslims to become politically stronger. On 30th December 1906, Mohammedan Educational Conference was organised, in which a new political platform was announced for Muslims named "All-India Muslim League".

The Government of India Act of 1909-also known as the Morley-Minto Reforms—gave Indians limited role in the central and provincial legislatures, known as legislative councils. For Muslims, it was important both to gain a place in the Indian politics and to retain their Muslim identity, objectives that required varying responses according to the circumstances, as the example of Muhammad Ali Jinnah illustrates. Jinnah began his carrier as an enthusiastic liberal in the Congress. But in 1913, he joined the Muslim League, which had been shocked by the 1911 annulment of the partition of Bengal into cooperating with Congress to make demands on the British. Jinnah continued his membership with Congress until 1919. During this dual membership period, he was described by leading Congress spokesperson as the "Ambassador of Hind-Muslim Unity". Jinnah, with his tiring efforts, brought the two parties on one agenda in 1916, which is called Misaq-e-Lakhnao. The Muslims of subcontinent observed October 27, 1919 as "Khilafat Day". Khilafat Movement was launched at the end of 1st World War to pressurise the British to accomplish their promise to retain the Caliphate in Turkey. This movement encouraged the Muslims and produced political enthusiasm among them. Muslim clerics started taking part in politics.

In this movement, however, the most outstanding contribution was of Dr. Sir Muhammad Iqbal, the great philosopher and poet and symbol of Muslim nationalism. On his return from Europe in 1908, he started his great task of reforming the Muslims through his poetry. His entire poetry is based on the Quranic philosophy of Islam, by which Muslims, especially the educated, were awakened. Allama also recognised the Two-Nation Theory. He was actually the dreamer of a new Muslim state of Pakistan.

The demand for Pakistan became popular during the Second World War and Muslim community was organised under the banner of the All-India Muslim League. Branches of the party were opened even in the remote corners of the subcontinent. Literature in the form of pamphlets, books, magazines and newspapers was produced and distributed to explain the rationale for demanding Pakistan. With an overwhelming majority of the Indian Muslims now convinced about the imperative need for

Pakistan, the entire Muslim population of the Indian subcontinent rallied around the Quaid-e-Azam who under the platform of the Muslim League led them to their dream destination-Pakistan.

Remembering Role of Ulema in Pakistan Movement

In 1940 the Muslim League formally endorsed the partitioning of British India and the creation of Pakistan as a separate Muslim state. During pre-independence talks held in 1946, therefore, the British government found that the stand of the Muslim League on separation and that of the Congress on the territorial unity of India were strongly irreconcilable. The British then decided on partition and on August 15, 1947, transferred power dividedly to India and Pakistan. The latter, however, came into existence in two parts: West Pakistan, as Pakistan stands today, and East Pakistan, now known as Bangladesh. The two were divided by 1,600 km (1,000 miles) of Indian territory.

The separate homeland that is now named 'Pakistan' was obviously a direct outcome of insurmountable struggle and a raft of sacrifices by audacious Muslims of subcontinent from all walks of life. Apart from the role of politicians of the subcontinent in the struggle of freedom for Muslims of India, the contribution of writers, theologians, journalists, students, women and mainly Ulema and mashaikh is worth remembering. They all channelled their energies and sources in the making of the Muslim nation and the idea of what is called two-nation theory. In pith, the credit for the success of the struggle cannot be attributed to a mere single section of the society. Irrespective of professions and strata of society, each and every Muslim was motivated and moblised to take active part. Broadly speaking, almost all the Ulema and mashaikh as well as other prominent leaders belonging to all schools of thought from the entire subcontinent readily propped up the cause of what was named 'Pakistan Movement'.

Of the Ulema and mashaikh, Allama Shabbir Ahmed Usmani was the outstanding personality who rendered really valuable services for mobilizing and gearing up the movement of Pakistan. He and other noted Ulema and Mashaikh had a great number of followers spread over the subcontinent, who put their hearts in speeding up movement of separate homeland for the Muslims of the united India.

Hence, the services of the Ulema and Mashaikh in the movement of Pakistan proved strong backing and boosted efforts carried out by the Muslims of the subcontinent for a separate Muslim state, where they would spend their lives in accordance with Islamic laws and principles without any fear. Their services included educating their disciples and awakening the general masses to the need of Pakistan for the Muslims of the subcontinent, making physical and personal contacts with the people even in distant areas, convening of public meetings and ingraining the idea of inevitable necessity of an independent country in their minds.

Moreover, while complying with the instructions and directions of the Quaid-i-Azam in strict manner under the able guidance and instructions, the Ulema and Mashaikh spread the message in all corners of the subcontinent, infused the Muslims and worked ceaselessly to achieve the goal.

Maulana Shabbir Ahmed lent his full support in the election campaigns of the Muslim League and even pleaded in favour of Quaid-i-Azam against all opposition, directed from other ill-advised and ill-informed rather blind Ulema and Mashaikh. He always publicly announced his complete faith in the honesty and integrity of Quaid-i-Azam and even exhorted the Muslims to vote to the Muslim League. For, it was struggling hard for carving out a new Muslim State on the global map where the Islamic laws and traditions shall possibly be formulated and practiced. He advised the Muslims not to lend an ear to Hind-influenced Muslims or the nationalist Muslims. On one occasion, he said that any one who casts his vote for the opponents of the Muslim League must think of the eventual aftermaths of his action in terms of the interests of his nation and the answers that would be called upon to yield on the Day of Judgment.

Therefore, the role of our Ulema and Mashaikh in the Pakistan Movement is really highly laudable and worth of writing in letters of gold. They prevailed upon their followers for awakening the common people, they toured the country in spite of the difficulties in the means of communication, they addressed meetings and enabled the nation to reach that goal which they have resolved for.

In this connection, the names of Pir Jamaat Ali Shah, Mian Ghulam Ullah Sharaqpuri, Pir Ghulam Mohyuddin Golravi, Allama Allauddin Siddiqui, Allama Shabbir Ahmed Usmani and many other noted religious leaders will ever be remembered with regard to the superb services they rendered for the cause of Pakistan's making. It is worth mentioning here that when the matter of Aligarh University's progress and later that of the financial needs of the Muslim League for its development rose, Hazrat Pir Jamaat Ali Shah subscribed lakhs of rupees on his behalf and on that of his followers. In the same way, when the 1945 elections were in full swing, Khawaja Hasan Nizami of Taunsa and other deities asked their followers to work for the success of the Muslim League.

Apart, the grand historic congregation of Benares, which was attended by more or less six thousand Ulema and Mashaikhs as well as hundreds of thousands of students from every sphere of life delivered real support to the Pakistan Resolution in 1940, and so made the task of the achievement of Pakistan considerably easier.

Similarly, the landmark convention of the All-India Muslim League in 1946 was attended by a great number of Ulema and the Mashaikh including Pir Jamaat Ali Shah, Maulana Jamal Mian of Farangi Mahal (Lucknow) as well as the inspiring personality of Maulana Abdul Hamid of Badaun in Uttar Pradesh. As recorded in Pak-India history, aforementioned religious leaders and scholars enjoyed deep and intensive influence of the common people and had a large number of followers and adherents. Given the reasons, these Ulema and Mashaikh proved a strong source of greater strength and sacrifice for the Muslim League, who devoted themselves to the cause of Pakistan Movement for freedom.

After reviewing Pakistan's history, one comes to a conclusion that religious scholars have been a great source for building the nation in one way or the other. Convinced by the fact that they continue to enjoy the status of strong opinion leaders in our society with ever-rising number of their followers, their role can be utilized for the country's socioeconomic development other than just spreading and teaching Islam. It has been observed that isolating them from putting their efforts and minds for the country's socioeconomic and political development is a major cause behind the outlook they present.

However, one hardly disagrees to the idea that Ulema can be made play their proactive role in helping the government in its fight against sectarianism and in promoting national harmony and tolerance in the society, help project a real and peaceful image of Islam in the world, help other Muslim countries to counter anti-Islamic propaganda, help eradicate drug abuse from society and help the government to control birth rate by augmenting population awareness in their speeches. Being a due role of the religious scholars and orators towards society's uplift in all spheres of life, they should preach their followers and disciples through their lectures and sermons to work at all possible levels for society's socio-cultural and politico-economic development by contributing their efforts to combat society's different burgeoning problems. For example, corruption, rape, dowry, hoarding, illiteracy, AIDS, rising population, pollution, child labour, bigotry, chauvinism, terrorism, religious extremism and fanaticism, etc.

There are some so-called religious scholars in the country who have played havoc to the country's image. They preached nothing but extremism, fanaticism, sectarianism and hatred against other religious outfits to the extent. Several religious organisations, many of them albeit banned to continue to operate freely under different names, circulated inflammatory material and brainwashed the minds of youths towards fanning religious hatred, extremism, fanaticism and sectarianism; thereby, peaceful youths were turned militants. The time proved such obnoxious roles as destructive roles rather than constructive. As a result, Pakistani society continues to suffer awfully.

It is high time religious scholars realised their due role and rearranged themselves and contributed to salvage the ailing society. Its equally obligatory on them to preach Islam in its true spirit that stands for tolerance, brotherhood, tranquillity and peace without harming or preaching hatred against another religion or religious outfit.

8

Demand for Pakistan

"We are a nation", they claimed in the ever eloquent words of the Quaid-i-Azam-*"We are a nation with our own distinctive culture and civilization, language and literature, art and architecture, names and nomenclature, sense of values and proportion, legal laws and moral code, customs and calendar, history and tradition, aptitudes and ambitions; in short, we have our own distinctive outlook on life and of life. By all canons of international law, we are a nation"*. The formulation of the Muslim demand for Pakistan in 1940 had a tremendous impact on the nature and course of Indian politics. On the one hand, it shattered for ever the Hindu dreams of a pseudo-Indian, in fact, Hindu empire on British exit from India: on the other, it heralded an era of Islamic renaissance and creativity in which the Indian Muslims were to be active participants. The Hindu reaction was quick, bitter, malicious.

Equally hostile were the British to the Muslim demand, their hostility having stemmed from their belief that the unity of India was their main achievement and their foremost contribution. The irony was that both the Hindus and the British had not anticipated the astonishingly tremendous response that the Pakistan demand had elicited from the Muslim masses. Above all, they failed to realize how a hundred million people had suddenly become supremely conscious of their distinct nationhood and their high destiny. In channelling the course of Muslim politics towards Pakistan, no less than in directing it towards its consummation in the establishment of Pakistan in **1947**, non played a more decisive role than did Quaid-i-Azam Muhammad Ali Jinnah. It was his powerful advocacy of the case of Pakistan and his remarkable strategy in the delicate negotiations, that followed the formulation of the Pakistan demand, particularly in the postwar period, that made Pakistan inevitable.

CRIPPS SCHEME

While the British reaction to the Pakistan demand came in the form of the Cripps offer of **April, 1942**, which conceded the principle of self-determination to provinces on a territorial basis, the Rajaji Formula (called after the eminent Congress leader C.Rajagopalacharia, which became the basis of prolonged Jinnah-Gandhi talks in **September, 1944**), represented the Congress alternative to Pakistan. The Cripps offer was rejected because it did not concede the Muslim demand the whole way, while the Rajaji Formula was found unacceptable since it offered a "motheaten, mutilated" Pakistan and the too appended with a plethora of preconditions which made its emergence in any shape remote, if not altogether impossible. Cabinet Mission The most delicate as well as the most tortuous negotiations, however, took place during 1946-47, after the elections which showed that the country was sharply and somewhat evenly divided between two parties-the Congress and the League-and that the central issue in Indian politics was Pakistan.

These negotiations began with the arrival, in **March 1946**, of a three-member British Cabinet Mission. The crucial task with which the Cabinet Mission was entrusted was that of devising in consultation with the various political parties, a constitution-making machinery, and of setting up a popular interim government. But, because the Congress-League gulf could not be bridged, despite the Mission's (and the Viceroy's) prolonged efforts, the Mission had to make its own proposals in May, 1946. Known as the Cabinet Mission Plan, these proposals stipulated a limited centre, supreme only in foreign affairs, defense and communications and three autonomous groups of provinces. Two of these groups were to have Muslim majorities in the northwest and the northeast of the subcontinent, while the third one, comprising the Indian mainland, was to have a Hindu majority. A consummate statesman that he was, Jinnah saw his chance. He interpreted the clauses relating to a limited centre and the grouping as "the foundation of Pakistan", and induced the Muslim League Council to accept the Plan in June 1946; and this he did much against the calculations of the Congress and to its utter dismay.

Tragically though, the League's acceptance was put down to its supposed weakness and the Congress put up a posture of defiance, designed to swamp the League into submitting to its dictates and its interpretations of the plan. Faced thus, what alternative had Jinnah and the League but to rescind their earlier acceptance, reiterate and reaffirm their original stance, and decide to launch direct action (if need be) to wrest Pakistan. The way Jinnah manoeuvred to turn the tide of events at a time when all seemed lost indicated, above all, his masterly grasp of the situation and his adeptness at making strategic and tactical moves. Partition Plan By the close of 1946, the communal riots had flared up to murderous heights, engulfing almost the entire subcontinent. The two peoples, it seemed, were engaged in a fight to the finish. The time for a peaceful transfer of power was fast running out. Realizing the gravity of the situation. His Majesty's Government sent down to India a new Viceroy-Lord Mountbatten. His protracted negotiations with the various political leaders resulted in 3 June (1947) Plan by which the British decided to partition the subcontinent, and hand over power to two successor States on 15 August, 1947. The plan was duly accepted by the three Indian parties to the dispute-the Congress the League and the Akali Dal (representing the Sikhs).

DEMAND FOR A SEPARATE STATE

From then onwards, the Muslim League policy was clear and unmistakable. It did not want one India with a clear Hindu majority, which through a parliamentary system of government and so-called democratic process would nullify Muslim rights and interests. The Pakistan Resolution was the Muslim answer to Congress ambitions. The Quaid did not have to define Pakistan. All knew what he meant. Beverley Nichols, visiting India in 1943, asked the Quaid how he would describe the vital principle of Pakistan. "In five words," replied the Quaid, "the Muslims are a nation."

With the adoption of the Pakistan ideal, Muslim nationalism came into its own. It had taken Muslims three quarters of a century to finally decide what they wanted. "They had tried everything," says Dr. KK Aziz, a renowned scholar, "a revolt in 1857, friendship with Britain, opposition to the Congress, extremist agitation, cooperation with the Congress, belligerent neutrality, negotiations, appeals, threats." The march of history had made a nation of a community. No longer, writes Dr. Aziz, did they eat out their heart in sullen impotence, trusting in the beneficence of the British or the goodwill of the Hindus. To the Congress claim that India was a National State, the Muslims answered with the brand new idea of separate Muslim nationalism.

Why did the Muslim demand Pakistan? Because, they feared the prospect of Hindu domination. Z A Suleri gave three main reasons behind the demand for Pakistan: Muslims having ruled India before the advent of the British were entitled to rule at least the Muslim majority areas; Hindu and Muslim philosophies of life and ways of life were so far apart from each other that it was "impossible for them to live together;" Muslims were convinced that their economic and social problems could be solved only by an approach to Islam, and this was impractible until they had a state of their own. Carimbhoy Ibrahim was of the view that the attitude of the Congress had always been communal and that it had never taken the Muslims into confidence when it wielded power. It always wanted to establish Hindu raj by introducing the Vidya Mandir Scheme, the Wardha Scheme, the "Bande Mataram" song and other Hindu practices and beliefs. Not once in any way had it shown a desire to accommodate the Muslims. Thus, 83 years after the formal end of the Mughal empire, the Muslims of South Asia firmly decided on the political future they wished to shape for themselves. The struggle for Pakistan had begun.

How, one may ask, did the Founding Fathers accomplish such a monumental task? Through unflinching resolve, patriotic zeal and singleness of purpose. They battled against formidable odds before they could reach the frontiers of the Promised Land. But, sad to relate, within a few years of the Quaid's demise, a band of usurpers raised their ugly heads. They crippled the Muslim League, blacklisted old and venerable politicians, threw caution to the winds, embarked on a reckless career and played havoc with what the founder had achieved. They even lost one half of the country. The other half that survived is also under threat. Pakistan is in a jam. Its political, economic and social fabric is in tatters. "The centre cannot hold. The best lack all convictions, while the worst are full of passionate intensity." Could we bring back the spirit of the forties? Yes, we can, if a stroke of good fortune brings forth a small group of thoughtful, committed citizens endowed with the same resolve, passion and dedication that had fired the hearts of the Men of 1940. Time is running out. How much longer shall destiny test our patience?

CONTRIBUTION OF AHMADI MUSLIMS IN MAKING AND CONSOLIDATION OF PAKISTAN

It is generally known that Mr. Muhammad Ali Jinnah (fondly called as Quaid-e-Azam) single handedly founded Pakistan. While the Indian leaders notably Mahatma Gandhi, Pandit Nehru and a host of Congress leaders spent many years in Jail and launched several civil disobedience Movements, but this thin and slim outstanding lawyer called Jinnah carved out an Independent Islamic state called "Pakistan" in seven years from nowhere. From Lahore Resolution of March 23, 1940 to crucial talks in June 1946, battles were won by this remarkable statesman, Mr. M. A. Jinnah. This astounded the India's Viceroy Lord Mountbatten. He was amazed at the remarkable skills of this sharp and tactful statesman at negotiations. His determination stronger than the rock of Gibraltar and his unquestionable integrity were the sterling qualities that landed Muslims of India a homeland of their own.

Few known this fact that Mr. M. A. Jinnah had quit the Indian political scene and out of the frustration left Indian politics. He retreated to London (UK) after attending the second Round Table Conference in 1932, where he established his legal practice. It was a great loss to Muslims in India. It provided immense relief to Indian Congress, as their main adversary left the field. He was persuaded back to India by no other person than Hadrat Mirza Bashir-ud-Din Mahmud Ahmad, the Head of Ahmadiyya Movement. This divine figure surveyed the Indian political horizon and found no honest and outstanding Muslim figure to lead the Muslims of India, the Muslims who lost their empire in India after five centuries of Mughal rule.

Hadrat Sahib asked the then Ahmadiyya Missionary in London (UK) Mr. Abdur Raheem Dard to get in touch with Mr. M. A. Jinnah who initially turned down all overtures. It took Mr. Dard three hours face to face talk successfully persuaded him to return to India. Mr. Jinnah was most reluctant, but he eventually changed his mind. The Sunday Times London (April 9, 1933) carried a report of a reception that was held by the Imam of London Mosque, Mr. Dard, where Mr. Jinnah frankly acknowledged the fact that: "The eloquent persuasion of Imam left me no way of escape."

Sardar Shaukat Hayat in his book "The Nation that lost its soul" mentions the following event: "One day, I got a message from Quaid-e-Azam saying "Shaukat, I believe you are going to Batala, which I understand is about five miles from Qadian, please go to Qadian and meet Hadrat Sahib and request him on my behalf for his blessings and support for Pakistan's cause. After the meeting (in Batala) I reached Qadian about midnight, I sent a word that I had brought a message from Quaid-e-Azam. Hadrat Sahib came down immediately and enquired what were Quaid's wishes. I conveyed his message for prayer and for his support for Pakistan. He said: "Please convey to the Quaid-e-Azam that we have been praying for his mission from the very beginning. Where the help of his followers is concerned, no Ahmadi will not stand against any Muslim Leaguer."

The second feat, during that crucial period after elections, was achieved when Sir Zafrullah Khan who prevailed upon Khizar Hayat Khan Tiwana to resign at a time when Mr. Tiwana enjoyed complete confidence of the Punjab Assembly, paving the way for the Muslim League to appear on the horizon. Hadrat Mirza Bashir-ud-Din Mahmud Ahmad was watching with dismay the unholy alliance between the Viceroy and the Congress Party, as an Interim Indian Government was formed in 1946 without Muslim participation. Mr. Jinnah threatened to launch a protest movement.

On September 23, 1946, this divine figure arrived in Delhi along with a team of advisors and remained in Delhi at the residence of Sir Zafrullah Khan for three weeks. He held high level discussions with top Indian leaders, Mr. M. A. Jinnah, Mahatma Gandhi, Pandit Nehru, Nawab of Bhopal, Khawja Nazimuddin, Sardar Niashtar and Nawab Chattari. Hadrat Sahib also wrote a letter to Lord Wavell indicating to him that the Muslim League enjoyed the total support of the Indian Muslims. A day before his departure for Qadian, Lord Wavell invited the Muslim League to join the Interim Cabinet of India. The daily Nawa-i-waqt in its issue of October 14, 1946 quoted Hindu Daily Milap "This act tantmounts to torpedeoing of the Indian Independence Movement."

In the crucial stages of delicate negotiations that Mr. Jinnah conducted with the British Government, the ulema led by Ahrars (the Muslim clergy) abetted, instigated and funded by the Indian Congress, opposed Mr. Jinnah at every step. The Indian Congress party had dozens of powerful leaders, they had a powerful machinery and unlimited cash was available to defeat the single handed effort of a lone figure Mr. Jinnah. Despite heavy odds, despite heavy opposition by the Muslims priesthood led by Ahrars, Mr. Jinnah won and won convincingly because he enjoyed the prayers of this divine figure who called him to India. The real tragedy of Pakistan is that this very pack of ulema who opposed the Making of Pakistan overnight became the lovers of Pakistan.

Sir Muhammad Zafrullah Khan - a devout Ahmadi who did his bai'at at the hand of the Hadrat Mirza Ghulam Ahmad, the founder of Ahmadiyya Movement on September 16, 1907. Sir Zafrullah Khan had been a judge of the Indian Federal Court as well as the President of Indian Muslim League (1931) and had a judicial mind, he was asked to look at the draft of the Lahore Resolution (March 23, 1940) and he did do the fine tuning of the LAHORE RESOLUTION, the language and the constitutional complexity of the resolution. When the partition of India was to take place in 1947, the Lord Mountbatten set up a Boundary Commission to determine the new boundaries of two independent states of India and Pakistan. This Commission was headed by Sir Radcliffe. The Congress party of India had already "bought" Lord Mountbatten by naming him the first Governor General of India. Quaid-e-Azam was fully aware of the great stakes that the Boundary

Commission had for Pakistan. The main question was how to divide Punjab into two - one going to India and the other to Pakistan. Mr. Jinnah selected the best legal brain - an Ahmadi - Sir Zafrullah Khan and on one occasion described him as his son. The aggressive and forceful arguments that Sir Zafrullah Khan marshalled in presentation of the case evoked widespread praises.

A week before Pakistan came into being, in a letter dated August 8, 1947 to Sir Zafrullah Khan by the then President of the Punjab Muslim League Mr. Iftikhar Hussain Khan, Nawab of Mamdot wrote: "Now that the Boundary Commission has concluded its hearings. I wish to express deep sense of gratitude which I and all other Muslims of Punjab feel towards you.

Your unremitting toil in collection of material, your brilliant presentation of our case and your profound interpretation of law and history have won universal admiration. In this most critical hour of our history you have rendered an inestimable service to the Millat and created a lasting place in the hearts of all Muslims. We can never forget how willingly you agreed to interrupt your important discussions in London, and to return and fulfil this private mission. The knowledge that your zeal was inspired solely by your love for Islam fill our hearts with pride and gratitude."

A distinguished Muslim, Maulana Muhammad Ali Jauhar, paid tribute to the work of the Ahmadiyya Movement in fighting for an independent Muslim state in India with these words, "It will be ungrateful if we do not mention (the Second Khalifa) and his well- disciplined Community who have devoted all their efforts, irrespective of doctrinal differences, towards the welfare of the Muslims.

These gentlemen are, on the one hand, taking an active interest in the politics of Muslims and, on the other, energetically engaged in promoting the unity, organisation, trade and preaching among Muslims. The time is not far away when the attitude of this organised sect of Islam will provide guidance for the Muslim nation in general and for those persons in particular who are idly sitting under the domes of Bismillah and making boastful and empty claims of service to Islam". The Second Khalifa and the Ahmadiyya Movement were also to play an important role in securing fundamental social and political rights for Muslims in Kashmir who were ruled autocratically by a Hindu maharajah.

Soon after August 14, 1947, Pakistan appeared on the international map because of the powerful and forceful representation of Sir Zafrullah Khan in the United Nations. He was the first Foreign Minister of Pakistan. He represented Pakistan on Kashmir dispute in the Security Council in 1948. Sir Zafrullah Khan later became a great fighter of the Arab cause in the United Nations. He fought a powerful fight for the independence of Libya, Somalia, Eritrea, Sudan, Tunis, Morocco, and Indonesia during 1948-54. He was a Vice President of the International Court of the Justice at the Hague during 1958-61. He was a President of the UN General Assembly in 1962. He then became the President of the International Court of the Justice at the Hague in 1970-73.

The contribution of Ahmadis in all walks of life of Pakistan is TOTAL AND COMPLETE, one is simply amazed, how this small community of over four millions accomplished so much and gave their best. A grandson of the founder of the Movement Hadrat Mirza Ghulam Ahmad, Mian Muzaffar Ahmad, generally known as M. M. Ahmad nurtured the dream and vision of his uncle. He became the Finance Minister 1970-71 of Pakistan.

Two Ahmadi brothers, General Akhtar Hussain Malik and General Abdul Ali Malik, gave their best to the defence of Pakistan. There are others, like Brigadier Iftikhar Janjua and scores of others Ahmadi Colonels and majors. This bravery and selfless desire to defend the motherland was not confined to Army alone. In a book, "Air battle of Pakistan" commissioned by then Air Marshal Nur Khan, there are references to Ahmadi Pilots. According to Air commodore (later Air Marshal) Abdur Rahim a dangerous Air mission was planned and volunteers were asked and it was clear that it is possible none of the pilots would be able to come back, among dozens of officers only five pilots volunteered and all of them were Ahmadis and all of them returned safely after the mission was accomplished.

This may sound astounding but events indicate that in every operation whether planning or combat in which there was a semblance of success, there was or were Ahmadis involved.

Ahmadis performed their duties in a manner which make them feel humble and grateful to Allah for having afforded them this opportunity to serve Islam and Pakistan.

An Ahmadi brings Noble Prize to Pakistan and put Pakistan on the map of International Science. Pakistan has a poor educational record. According to a recent survey its literacy rate is 34.8%, as against this, Ahmadis have 99% literacy rate and it is because of their love of knowledge.. They follow a saying of Holy Prophet, it says: In pursuit of education if you have to go China, go and pursue it. And Ahmadis followed this command of their beloved literally. It is no wonder that the only Nobel Prize winner in the whole Muslim world is an Ahmadi - Dr. Abdus Salam.

Ahmadis under the guidance of Hadrat Mirza Bashir-ud-Din Mahmud Ahmad not only helped in the conception, creation, establishment and consolidation of Pakistan, but also the prayers of the Prince of Islam, Hadrat Mirza Tahir Ahmad, the illustrious son, is now sustaining Pakistan. History offers few parallels where a people who face daily persecution in all walks of daily life, treated as second as class citizens and are not even enrolled as voters in Pakistan keep continue praying for the integrity and solidarity of Pakistan under the spiritual guidance of their master, Hadrat Mirza Tahir Ahmad (aba).

A NATION CALLING FOR A HOME

That there are factors, administrative, linguistic or cultural, which are the predisposing causes behind these demands for separation, is a fact which is admitted and understood by all. Nobody minds these demands and many are prepared to concede them. But, the Hindus say that the Muslims are going beyond the idea of separation and questions, such as what has led them to take this course, why are they asking for partition, for the annulment of the common tie by a legal divorce between Pakistan and Hindustan, are being raised.

The answer is to be found in the declaration made by the Muslim League in its Resolution that the Muslims of India are a separate nation. It is this declaration by the Muslim League, which is both resented and ridiculed by the Hindus. The Hindu resentment is quite natural. Whether India is a nation or not, has been the subject-matter of controversy between the Anglo-Indians and the Hindu politicians ever since the Indian National Congress was founded. The Anglo-Indians were never tired of proclaiming that India was not a nation, that 'Indians' was only another name for the people of India. In the words of one Anglo-Indian "to know India was to forget that there is such a thing as India." The Hindu politicians and patriots have been, on the other hand, equally persistent in their assertion that India is a nation. That the Anglo-Indians were right in their repudiation cannot be gainsaid. Even Dr. Tagore, the national poet of Bengal, agrees with them. But, the Hindus have never yielded on the point even to Dr. Tagore.

This was because of two reasons. Firstly, the Hindu felt ashamed to admit that India was not a nation. In a world where nationality and nationalism were deemed to be special virtues in a people, it was quite natural for the Hindus to feel, to use the language of Mr. H. G. Wells, that it would be as improper for India to be without a nationality as it would be for a man to be without his clothes in a crowded assembly. Secondly, he had realized that nationality had a most intimate connection with the claim for self-government. He knew that by the end of the 19th century, it had become an accepted principle that the people, who constituted a nation, were entitled on that account to self-government and that any patriot, who asked for self-government for his people, had to prove that they were a nation. The Hindu for these reasons never stopped to examine whether India was or was not a nation in fact. He never cared to reason whether nationality was merely a question of calling a people a nation or was a question of the people being a nation. He knew one thing, namely, that if he was to succeed in his demand for self-government for India, he must maintain, even if he could not prove it, that India was a nation.

In this assertion, he was never contradicted by any Indian. The thesis was so agreeable that even serious Indian students of history came forward to write propagandist literature in support of it, no doubt out of patriotic motives. The Hindu social reformers, who knew that this was a dangerous delusion, could not openly contradict this thesis. For, anyone who questioned it was at once called a tool of the British bureaucracy and enemy of the country. The Hindu politician was able to propagate his view for a long time. His opponent, the Anglo-Indian, had ceased to reply to him. His propaganda had almost succeeded. When it was about to succeed comes this declaration of the Muslim League— this rift in the lute. Just because it does not come from the Anglo-Indian, it is a deadlier blow. It destroys the work which the Hindu politician has done for years. If the Muslims in India are a separate nation, then, of course, India is not a nation. This assertion cuts the whole ground from under the feet of the Hindu politicians. It is natural that they should feel annoyed at it and call it a stab in the back.

But, stab or no stab, the point is, can the Musalmans be said to constitute a nation? Everything else is beside the point. This raises the question : What is a nation? Tomes have been written on the subject. Those who are curious may go through them and study the different basic conceptions as well as the different aspects of it. It is, however, enough to know the core of the subject and that can be set down in a few words. Nationality is a social feeling. It is a feeling of a corporate sentiment of oneness which makes those who are charged with it feel that they are kith and kin. This national feeling is a double edged feeling. It is at once a feeling of fellowship for one's own kith and kin and an anti-fellowship feeling for those who are not one's own kith and kin. It is a feeling of "consciousness of kind" which on the one hand binds together those who have it, so strongly that it over-rides all differences arising out of economic conflicts or social gradations and, on the other, severs them from those who are not of their kind. It is a longing not to belong to any other group. This is the essence of what is called a nationality and national feeling.

Now apply this test to the Muslim claim. Is it or is it not a fact that the Muslims of India are an exclusive group? Is it or is it not a fact that they have a consciousness of kind? Is it or is not a fact that every Muslim is possessed by a longing to belong to his own group and not to any non-Muslim group? If the answer to these questions is in the affirmative, then the controversy must end and the Muslim claim that they are a nation must be accepted without cavil.

What the Hindus must show is that notwithstanding some differences, there are enough affinities between Hindus and Musalmans to constitute them into one nation, or, to use plain language, which make Muslims and Hindus long to belong together. Hindus, who disagree with the Muslim view that the Muslims are a separate nation by themselves, rely upon certain features of Indian social life which seem to form the bonds of integration between Muslim society and Hindu society.

In the first place, it is said that there is no difference of race between the Hindus and the Muslims. That the Punjabi Musalman and the Punjabi Hindu, the U. P. Musalman and the U. P. Hindu, the Bihar Musalman and the Bihar Hindu, the Bengal Musalman and the Bengal Hindu, the Madras Musalman and the Madras Hindu, and the Bombay Musalman and the Bombay Hindu are racially of one stock. Indeed there is more racial affinity between the Madras Musalman and the Madras Brahmin than there is between the Madras Brahmin and the Punjab Brahmin. In the second place, reliance is placed upon linguistic unity between Hindus and Muslims. It is said that the Musalmans have no common language of their own which can mark them off as a linguistic group separate from the Hindus. On the contrary, there is a complete linguistic unity between the two. In the Punjab, both Hindus and Muslims speak Punjabi. In Sind, both speak Sindhi. In Bengal, both speak Bengali. In Gujarat, both speak Gujarati. In Maharashtra, both speak Marathi. So in every province. It is only in towns that the Musalmans speak Urdu and the Hindus the language of the province. But outside, in the mofussil, there is complete linguistic unity between Hindus and Musalmans. Thirdly, it is pointed out that India is the land which the Hindus and Musalmans have now inhabited together for centuries. It is not exclusively the land of the Hindus, nor is it exclusively the land of the Mahomedans.

Reliance is placed not only upon racial unity but also upon certain common features in the social and cultural life of the two communities. It is pointed out that the social life of many Muslim groups is honeycombed with Hindu customs. For instance, the Avans of the Punjab, though they are nearly all Muslims, retain

Hindu names and keep their genealogies in the Brahmanic fashion. Hindu surnames are found among Muslims. For instance, the surname Chaudhari is a Hindu surname but is common among the Musalmans of U.P. and Northern India. In the matter of marriage, certain groups of Muslims are Muslims in name only. They either follow the Hindu form of the ceremony alone, or perform the ceremony first by the Hindu rites and then call the Kazi and have it performed in the Muslim form.

In some sections of Muslims, the law applied is the Hindu Law in the matter of marriage, guardianship and inheritance. Before the Shariat Act was passed, this was true even in the Punjab and the N. W. F. P. In the social sphere the caste system is alleged to be as much a part of Muslim society as it is of Hindu society. In the religious sphere, it is pointed out that many Muslim *pirs* had Hindu disciples; and similarly some Hindu *yogis* have had Muslim *chelas*. Reliance is placed on instances of friendship between saints of the rival creeds. At Girot, in the Punjab, the tombs of two ascetics, Jamali Sultan and Diyal Bhawan, who lived in close amity during the early part of the nineteenth century, stand close to one another, and are reverenced by Hindus and Musalmans alike. Bawa Fathu, a Muslim saint, who lived about 1700 A.D. and whose tomb is at Ranital in the Kangra District, received the title of prophet by the blessing of a Hindu saint, Sodhi Guru Gulab Singh. On the other hand, Baba Shahana, a Hindu saint whose cult is observed in the Jang District, is said to have been the *chela* of a Muslim *pir* who changed the original name (Mihra), of his Hindu follower, into Mir Shah.

All this, no doubt, is true. That a large majority of the Muslims belong to the same race as the Hindus is beyond question. That all Mahomedans do not speak a common tongue, that many speak the same language as the Hindus cannot be denied. That there are certain social customs which are common to both cannot be gainsaid. That certain religious rites and practices are common to both is also a matter of fact. But the question is: can all this support the conclusion that the Hindus and the Mahomedans on account of them constitute one nation or these things have fostered in them a feeling that they long to belong to each other?

There are many flaws in the Hindu argument. In the first place, what are pointed out as common features are not the result of a conscious attempt to adopt and adapt to each other's ways and manners to bring about social fusion. On the other hand, this uniformity is the result of certain purely mechanical causes. They are partly due to incomplete conversions. In a land like India, where the majority of the Muslim population has been recruited from caste and out-caste Hindus, the Muslimization of the convert was neither complete nor effectual, either from fear of revolt or because of the method of persuasion or insufficiency of preaching due to insufficiency of priests. There is, therefore, little wonder if great sections of the Muslim community here and there reveal their Hindu origin in their religious and social life. Partly it is to be explained as the effect of common environment to which both Hindus and Muslims have been subjected for centuries. A common environment is bound to produce common reactions, and reacting constantly in the same way to the same environment is bound to produce a common type. Partly are these common features to be explained as the remnants of a period of religious amalgamation between the Hindus and the Muslims inaugurated by the Emperor Akbar, the result of a dead past which has no present and no future.

As to the argument based on unity of race, unity of language and inhabiting a common country, the matter stands on a different footing. If these considerations were decisive in making or unmaking a nation, the Hindus would be right in saying that by reason of race, community of language and habitat the Hindus and Musalmans form one nation. As a matter of historical experience, neither race, nor language, nor country has sufficed to mould a people into a nation. The argument is so well put by Renan that it is impossible to improve upon his language. Long ago in his famous essay on Nationality, Renan observed: "that race must not be confounded with nation. The truth is that. there is no pure race; and that making politics depend upon ethnographical analysis, is allowing it to be borne upon a chimera....Racial facts, important as they are in the beginning, have a constant tendency to lose their importance. Human history is essentially different from zoology. Race is not everything, as it is in the sense of rodents and felines."

Speaking about language, Renan points out that: "Language invites re-union; it does not force it. The United States and England, Spanish America and Spain speak the same languages and do not form single nations. On the contrary, Switzerland which owes her stability to the fact that she was founded by the assent of her several parts counts three or four languages. In man there is something superior to language, —will. The will of Switzerland to be united, in spite of the variety of her languages, is a much more important fact than a similarity of language, often obtained by persecution."

As to common country, Renan argued that: "It is no more the land than the race that makes a nation. The land provides a substratum, the field of battle and work; man provides the soul; man is everything in the formation of that sacred thing which is called a people. Nothing of material nature suffices for it"

Having shown, that race, language, and country do not suffice to create a nation, Renan raises in a pointed manner the question, what more, then, is necessary to constitute a nation? His answer may be given in his own words: "A nation is a living soul, a spiritual principle. Two things, which in truth are but one, constitute this soul, this spiritual principle. One is in the past, the other in the present. One is the common possession of a rich heritage of memories; the other is the actual consent, the desire to live together, the will to preserve worthily the undivided inheritance which has been handed down. Man does not improvise. The nation, like the individual, is the outcome of a long past of efforts, and sacrifices, and devotion. Ancestor-worship is therefore, all the more legitimate; for our ancestors have made us what we are. A heroic past, great men, glory,—1 mean glory of the genuine kind,—these form the social capital, upon which a national idea may be founded. To have common glories in the past, a common will in the present; to have done great things together, to will to do the like again,—such are the essential conditions for the making of a people. We love in proportion to the sacrifices we have consented to make, to the sufferings we have endured. We love the house that we have built, and will hand down to our descendant. The Spartan hymn, 'We are what you were; we shall be what you are,' is in its simplicity the national anthem of every land.

"In the past an inheritance of glory and regrets to be shared, in the future a like ideal to be realised; to have suffered, and rejoiced, and hoped together; all these things are worth more than custom houses in common, and frontiers in accordance with strategical ideas; all these can be understood in spite of diversities of race and language. I said just now, 'to have suffered together' for indeed, suffering in common is a greater bond of union than joy. As regards national memories, mournings are worth more than triumphs; for they impose duties, they demand common effort."

Are there any common historical antecedents which the Hindus and Muslims can be said to share together as matters of pride or as matters of sorrow? That is the crux of the question. That is the question which the Hindus must answer, if they wish to maintain that Hindus and Musalmans together form a nation. So far as this aspect of their relationship is concerned, they have been just two armed battalions warring against each other. There was no common cycle of participation for a common achievement. Their past is a past of mutual destruction—a past of mutual animosities, both in the political as well as in the religious fields. As Bhai Parmanand points out in his pamphlet called "The Hindu National Movement":—"In history the Hindus revere the memory of Prithvi Raj, Partap, Shivaji and, Beragi Bir, who fought for the honour and freedom of this land (against the Muslims), while the Mahomedans look upon the invaders of India, like Muhammad Bin Qasim and rulers like Aurengzeb as their national heroes" In the religious field, the Hindus draw their inspiration from the Ramayana, the Mahabharata, and the Gita. The Musalmans, on the other hand, derive their inspiration from the Quran and the *Hadis*. Thus, the things that divide are far more vital than the things which unite. In depending upon certain common features of Hindu and Mahomedan social life, in relying upon common language, common race and common country, the Hindu is mistaking what is accidental and superficial for what is essential and fundamental.

The political and religious antagonisms divide the Hindus and the Musalmans far more deeply than the so-called common things are able to bind them together. The prospects might perhaps be different if the past of the two communities can be forgotten by both, Renan points out the importance of forgetfulness as a factor in building up a nation: "Forgetfulness, and I shall even say historical error, form an essential factor in the creation of a nation; and thus it is that the progress of historical studies may often be dangerous to the nationality. Historical research, in fact, brings back to light the deeds of violence that have taken place at the commencement of all political formations, even of those the consequences of which have been most beneficial. Unity is ever achieved by brutality. The union of Northern and Southern France was the result of an extermination, and of a reign of terror that lasted for nearly a hundred years. The king of France who was, if I may say so, the ideal type of a secular crystalliser, the king of France who made the most perfect national unity in existence, lost his prestige when seen at too close a distance. The nation that he had formed cursed him; and today the knowledge of what he was worth, and what he did, belongs only to the cultured.

"It is by contrast that these great laws of the history of Western Europe become apparent. In the undertaking which the king of France, in part by his justice, achieved so admirably, many countries came to disaster. Under the crown of St. Stephen, Magyars and Slavs have remained as distinct as they were eight hundred years ago. Far from combining the different elements in its dominions, the house of Hapsburg has held them apart and often opposed to one another.

In Bohemia, the Czech element and the German element are superimposed like oil and water in a glass. The Turkish policy of separation of nationalities according to religion has had much graver results. It has brought about the ruin of the East. Take a town like Smyrna or Salonica; you will find there five or six communities each with its own memories, and possessing among them scarcely anything in common. But the essence of the nation is, that all its individual members should have things in common; and also, that all of them should hold many things in oblivion.

No French citizen knows whether he is a Burgundian, an Alan, or a Visigoth; every French citizen ought to have forgotten St. Bartholomew, and the massacres of the South in the thirteenth century. There are not ten families in France able to furnish proof of a French origin; and yet, even if such a proof were given it would be essentially defective, in consequence of a thousand unknown crosses, capable of deranging all genealogical systems."

The pity of it is that the two communities can never forget or obliterate their past. Their past is imbedded in their religion, and for each to give up its past is to give up its religion. To hope for this is to hope in vain.

In the absence of common historical antecedents, the Hindu view that Hindus and Musalmans form one nation falls to the ground. To maintain it is to keep up a hallucination. There is no such longing between the Hindus and Musalmans to belong together as there is among the Musalmans of India.

It is no use saying that this claim of the Musalmans being a nation is an after-thought of their leaders. As an accusation, it is true. The Muslims were hitherto quite content to call themselves a community. It is only recently that they have begun to style themselves a nation. But an accusation, attacking the motives of a person, does not amount to a refutation of his thesis. To say that because the Muslims once called themselves a community, they are, therefore, now debarred from calling themselves a nation is to misunderstand the mysterious working of the psychology of national feeling. Such an argument presupposes that wherever there exist a people, who possess the elements that go to the making up of a nation, there must be manifested that sentiment of nationality which is their natural consequence and that if they fail to manifest it for sometime, then that failure is to be used as evidence showing the unreality of the claim of being a nation, if made afterwards. There is no historical support for such a contention.

As Prof. Toynbee points out : "It is impossible to argue *a priori* from the presence of one or even several of these factors to the existence of a nationality; they may have been there for ages and kindled no response and if is impossible to argue from one case to another; precisely the same group of factors may produce nationality here, and there have no effect."

This is probably due to the fact, as pointed out by Prof. Barker, that it is possible for nations to exist and even for centuries, in unreflective silence, although there exists that spiritual essence of a national life of which many of its members are not aware. Some such thing has no doubt happened in the case of the Musalmans. They were not aware of the fact that there existed for them the spiritual essence of a national life. This explains why their claim to separate nationality was made by them so late. But, it does not mean that the spiritual essence of a national life had no existence at all.

It is no use contending that there are cases where a sense of nationality exists but there is no desire for a separate national existence. Cases of the French in Canada and of the English in South Africa, may be cited as cases in point. It must be admitted that there do exist cases, where people are aware of their nationality, but this awareness does not produce in them that passion which is called nationalism. In other words, there may be nations conscious of themselves without being charged with nationalism. On the basis of this reasoning, it may be argued that the Musalmans may hold that they are a nation but they need not on that account demand a separate national existence; why can they not be content with the position which the French occupy in Canada and the English occupy in South Africa? Such a position is quite a sound position. It must, however, be remembered that such a position can only be taken by way of pleading with the Muslims not to insist on partition. It is no argument against their claim for partition, if they insist upon it.

Lest pleading should be mistaken for refutation, it is necessary to draw attention to two things. First, there is a difference between nationality and nationalism. They are two different psychological states of the human mind. Nationality means "consciousness of kind, awareness of the existence of that tie of kinship." Nationalism means "the desire for a separate national existence for those who are bound by this tie of kinship." Secondly, it is true that there cannot be nationalism without the feeling of nationality being in existence. But, it is important to bear in mind that the converse is not always true.

The feeling of nationality may be present and yet the feeling of nationalism may be quite absent. That is to say, nationality does not in all cases produce nationalism. For nationality to flame into nationalism two conditions must exist. First, there must arise the "will to live as a nation." Nationalism is the dynamic expression of that desire. Secondly, there must be a territory which nationalism could occupy and make it a state, as well as a cultural home of the nation. Without such a territory, nationalism, to use Lord Acton's phrase, would be a "soul as it were wandering in search of a body in which to begin life over again and dies out finding none." The Muslims have developed a "will to live as a nation." For them nature has found a territory which they can occupy and make it a state as well as a cultural home for the newborn Muslim nation. Given these favourable conditions, there should be no wonder, if the Muslims say that they are not content to occupy the position which the French choose to occupy in Canada or the English choose to occupy in South Africa, and that they shall have a national home which they can call their own.

9

Pakistan Resolution in Retrospect

Pakistan owes her emergence to four outstanding leaders – Sir Syed Ahmad Khan (1817-98), Maulana Muhammad Ali (1878-1931), Muhammad Ali Jinnah (1876-1948), and Allama Muhammad Iqbal (1877-1938). These leaders provided intellectual and political leadership to Indian Muslims during the ninety years (1858-1947) of the British imperial dominance.

Surprisingly though, all of them were thorough-bred nationalists at one time or another. But, betimes, they got disillusioned and shied away willy-nilly from their Hindu compatriots, either because of Hindu ethnocentrism in the late 19th century or Congress's rather exclusive, unitary nationalism in the 1920s and 1930s. That makes Pakistan, in part, a product of these Hindu, myopic approaches, asymmetrical with the prime dictates of the ground realities in a multi-nation and multi-cultured subcontinent. In part it was, of course, a product of the Muslims' quest for an equitable share in power, a quest designed primarily to organise their society on the basis of their pristine value structure.

Interestingly, three of these four leaders – Sir Syed, Iqbal and Jinnah – had initially started out as full blooded nationalists, but were obliged to end up, finally, at threshold of Muslim "separatism". And that, of course, after a good deal of traumatised reappraisals. So did Maulana Muhammad Ali, who joined mainstream nationalist politics midway through his career. But he was the foremost "nationalist" leader along with Gandhi during the Khilafat and Non-Cooperation Movement (1920-22), and he also presided over the subsequent Cocanada Congress session (1923), a unique honour for a Muslim, an honour that was inexplicably denied to Jinnah, though he occupied the top echelon of Congress leadership for several years and was considered the embodied symbol of Hindu-Muslim unity. Yet, within seven years, Muhammad Ali would vehemently denounce Gandhi's much-trumpeted Civil Disobedience Movement, launched in April 1930. In his presidential address to the All India Muslim Conference at Bombay on April 23, 1930, he declared, "We refuse to join Mr Gandhi, because his movement is not a movement for the complete independence of India but for making the seventy millions of Indian Musalmans dependents of the Hindu Mahasabha". And he was cheered by over 20,000 Muslims that had gathered on the occasion (Times of India, April 24, 1930).

Jinnah's postures and predilections during his long political life (1904-48) were a microcosm of Muslim India's during the period. For some seventeen years (1904-20), he had stood on the Congress's platform, pleading the Congress cause and envisioning a truly nationalist destiny for India. For another sixteen years (1921-37), though out of Congress for good, he was still working for a nationalist destiny; he was still striving for a Hindu-Muslim settlement and he was still collaborating with the Congress and its leadership. In pursuit of his mission, he devised several constitutional formulae, but all to no avail.

At the Congress-sponsored All Parties National Convention at Calcutta in December 1928, called to consider and ratify the Nehru Report (1928) as the blueprint of India's future constitution, Jinnah had put forward the six minimum Muslim demands for acceptance. But all of them were outvoted one by one. In vain did Jinnah argue: "... what we want is that the Hindus and Muslims should march together until our object is obtained... I want you... to rise to that statesmanship which Sir Tej Bahadur describes. Minorities cannot give anything to the majority... If they are small points, why not concede? It is up to the majority and majority alone can give." In aggregate terms, the most acrimonious and acerbic controversy in Indian politics in the late 1920s (since the

Nehru Report) and all through the 1930s had hinged around the basic issue of Hindu "Unitarianism" vs Muslim Federalism. The difference in the approaches was sharply reflected in the formation of ministries in the Hindu and Muslim majority provinces in mid 1937. While the Muslim provinces went for coalition governments, the Hindu provinces under the Congress's aegis opted for exclusive, one party government.

Till early 1937, however, Jinnah was still his "nationalist" self; preaching his credo eloquently; trying to unite Hindus, Muslims and Sikhs. But, alas, Jinnah came to be caught on the wrong wicket. For one thing, at about this time, Pandit Nehru, the Congress Rashtrapathi (1936-38), began expounding his controversial "two-forces" formula, which counted Muslims out of India's politic body as a religio-political entity. He fired his first salvo in that direction on September 18, 1936, saying that "... the real contest is between two forces - the Congress representing the will for freedom of the nation and the British Government in India and its supporters who oppose this urge and try to suppress it. Intermediate groups, whatever virtue they may possess, fade out or line up with one of the principal forces. The issue for India is that of independence. He who is for it must be with the Congress and if he talks in terms of communalism he is not keen on independence."

To this formula Nehru returned, on January 10, 1937. Shorn of its sophistry and anti-imperialist tone, this represented a challenge to Muslim individuality in Indian politics, an individuality which they had nurtured and claimed since the times of Sir Syed Ahmad Khan. It also represented not only a challenge to the continued existence of the Muslim League (AIML), but also a moment of truth for Jinnah who had led that body continuously since 1919, except for his three years of self-exile (1931-34) in England.

Yet Jinnah's response was surprisingly conciliatory, if only because he still hoped for a rapprochement with the Congress. In his speech at Calcutta's Muhammad Ali Park, on January 4, 1937, he said "I refuse to line up with the Congress. I refuse to accept this proposition. There is a third party in this country and that is

Muslim India.... We are not going to be camp followers of any party". (Italics for emphasis) Despite this timely rebuttal, he held out the olive branch, saying, "We are willing as equal partners to come to a settlement with our sister communities in the interest of India." And Jinnah reaffirmed this stance repeatedly for the next six months.

The deep divergence that characterised the Hindu-Muslim, Congress-League, thinking in 1937 stemmed from the basic dichotomy between Hindu "Unitarianism", a la the Nehru Report, and Muslim federalism, a la Jinnah's Fourteen Points (1929). In essence, it centred on the issue that whether India was uni-national or bi-national, whether it was uni-cultured or bi-cultured. In denying the "intermediate groups" the right to existence and in denying "all third parties' in the historical sense, Nehru was not only denying the AIML the right to exist or its due importance; more important: he was denying the Muslims the right to organize themselves politically on a platform of their own or on a platform other than that of the Congress. In other words, he was denying them their distinct individuality in India's body politic as a religio-political entity.

Jinnah, as opposed to this, felt that India was multinational and multi-cultured; that Muslims had the right to maintain their separate entity; that Muslim India represented the "third party" in India's body politic; that they should refuse to be "camp followers of any party" and that, above all, Muslims should organise themselves politically to make the third party claim a fait accompli. As a corollary to this claim, he demanded equality of status for Muslims. Of course, he repeatedly offered to coalesce with the Congress in the struggle for freedom, but only if the Muslims were "assured of their political freedom".

Thus, he told a meeting at the residence of Syed Ali Zaheer, presided over by the pro-Congress Syed Wazir Hasan, on May 9, 1937, "While we shall not knock at the Government House, we shall not also bow before Anand Bhawan", the Congress headquarters at Allahabad. Six weeks earlier, in late March 1937, he had told the AIML Council in categorical terms why he considered the Muslims' merger with the Hindus, and the AIML's with the Congress, almost impossible. It was impossible for Muslims to merge with Hindus because "their language, culture and civilization are quite different", he argued. National self-government, he said, was his creed; but Muslims "must unite as a nation and then live or die as a nation" (italics for emphasis).

The Muslims were considered a minority at this stage of India's political evolution. But "minorities", argued Jinnah in the Indian Legislative Assembly on February 7, 1935, while speaking on the Report of the Joint Parliamentary Committee on Indian Constitutional Reforms, "means a combination of things. It may be that a minority has a different religion from the other citizens of a country. Their language may be different, their race may be different, their culture may be different, and the combination of all these various elements – religion, culture, race, language, arts, music, and so forth – makes the minority a separate entity in the State, and the separate entity as an entity wants safeguards. Surely, therefore, we must face this question as a political problem; we must solve it and not evade it..."

Thus, what was at issue in the Congress-League, Nehru-Jinnah, controversy was, above all, the status of Muslims in Indian politics. Their status, in turn, depended upon whether India was uni-national or bi-national. The Congress's political conduct in 1937, remarked Penderel Moon in his Divide and Quit, meant that "there would be no room on the throne of India, save for Congress and Congress stooges".

The developing Congress's policy, thus, gave Muslims a foretaste of what the Hindu un-remitted centralism and homogenic ambitions meant. Under the sort of nationalist dispensation envisaged by the Congress, Muslims would surely be relegated to a back seat. Their values would be at a discount, their cultural identity in jeopardy. Above all, they would have no hope of shaping their spiritual, social, and cultural life according to their own ethos. All this meant culturicide, pure and simple. The Congress's conduct and rule were thus, in gross violation of 'minority' rights, civil society, and of adequate, if not good, governance – issues which, under the prevalent Westphalian Model (1648), with its overriding credo of the sovereignty of 'nations' and the 'sanctity' of borders, had not acquired the measure of importance and criticality which they have had since the demise of the Soviet Union (1991), the prime anti-Human Rights paradigm in the twentieth century. All this obviously posed a new and serious challenge to Muslims as a religio-cultural entity.

In immediate terms, it was this situation, at once despairing and agonising, that turned Muslim thinking towards Pakistan. If the Islamic way of life could not be preserved in an all-India set up, it should be saved wherever it was possible. Pakistan, or more accurately the demand for it, was thus a last-ditch attempt: an attempt to centralise, to quote Iqbal, "the life of Islam as a cultural force" in a specified territory, so that "the most living portion of the Muslims of India" could develop to the fullest in that territory, their "spiritual, cultural, economic and social life according to their own genius", to quote Jinnah, – a development which was practically impossible under the sort of dispensation envisaged by the Hindu-dominated Congress. Such, in short, were the urges and motivations that, in immediate terms, led to the formulation of the demand for Pakistan.

At another level, with the grim prospect of having been denied a place on the throne of India, what alternative did the Muslims have except for forging a throne for themselves in their majority provinces? And Pakistan simply meant only that much - and nothing more. Hence, in 1940, Muslims had no choice but to go to the Pakistan platform – unless they were prepared to be decimated as a religio-political entity in India's body politic.

PAKISTAN RESOLUTION

It is a historical fact that after the events of 1857 and the subsequent consolidation of the British Raj in India, the political thinkers and intellectuals of the Subcontinent started to think about the political, religious cultural and social future of India. As a result, many ideas, plans, proposals and schemes were put forward for the partition of India and the formation of a separate Muslim state. Apart from indigenous proposals, British parliamentarians, writers and others were also thinking in terms of the bifurcation of India.

The first such scheme for the partition or division of India was voiced by a British Parliamentarian John Bright in June 1858. Addressing the House of Commons he suggested "five or six large presidencies with complete autonomy, ultimately becoming independent States." After two decades, in December 1877, he again reiterated that "he is seeing several independent and sovereign states in India when British withdrawal had been affected."

After 1857, since the Muslims of India were grossly marginalised in the social, religious and political fields, they were not inclined to accept the demand for partition of India into two independent and autonomous states. Although the actual struggle for the establishment of a proposed Muslim state started in March 1940 from the platform of the All India Muslim League (AIML), it nonetheless has a long historical background. Sir Syed Ahmed Khan was the first Muslim thinker who stressed that Hindus and Muslims are two different nations, hence any attempt to fuse them into one nation would fail. Accordingly in 1867, before the Divisional Commissioner of Banaras, he very clearly said "I am convinced both these nations will not join whole heartedly in any thing. At present, there is no hostility between the two communities, but on account of the so-called educated it will increase immediately in future. He who lives will see." After the establishment of the Indian National Congress in 1885, his conviction became firmer when he said "Indian National Congress is a Hindu organisation and it can not provide safeguard to the interests of Muslims."

Although Sir Syed Ahmad Khan did not present in principle, any plan or proposal for the partition of India, yet he provided a basis to the Indian Muslims for thinking about their future.

From to 1940, more than one hundred proposals and schemes for the partition of India were presented by different quarters. In these proposals, the principal of partition was presented mostly on administrative and communal grounds; however, these proposals not only popularised but also paved the way for the vivid description and elucidation of the Two Nation Theory. It is amazing that the first scheme for the partition of India was presented by John Bright in 1858, a Britisher. On the 4th of June

1858, while participating in a discussion in the British Parliament concerning the Government of India, he was of the opinion, "A great country like India cannot be administered by Britain for a long time, one day we will have to let them rule. Hence it is necessary to abolish the Governorship and instead of keeping a colony, and for administrative purposes, India should be divided into five presidencies." It is however strange that in 1947, the last scheme after some 90 years, was also presented by Viceroy Lord Mountbatten- a British.

In 1887, Theodore Beck, educated at Cambridge and the Principal of M. A. O. College at Aligarh, after reviewing the political and social condition of India observed that "Muslims are a separate nation, rule of majority is impossible; Muslims will never agree to be ruled by the Hindu majority." The second scheme for the partition of India was proposed by a renowned Muslim Scholar Jamaluddin Afghani who in 1879, proposed a broader Muslim state. He was of the opinion that there should be a Muslim State incorporating the northwest Muslim majority provinces of India, Afghanistan and Muslim Central Asia.

During the tenure of Viceroy Lord Ripon, in 1883 a British writer Wilfred Scawen Blunt, visited India and held negotiations with different leaders. He wrote in his book Ideas about India that "practically India is to be divided as such that all Northern provinces under the Muslim Government while the South provinces under a Hindu government".

A great Muslim journalist and novelist Maulana Abdul Haleem Sharar, after analysing the deteriorating conditions of the Indian Muslims and the chances of future Hindu-Muslim riots, felt that if the current problems were to be solved, the partition of India was a must. In 1899, another British intellectual and the principal of MAO College Aligarh, Theodore Morison proposed that the only solution to the Indian political uncertainty was to centralise the Indian Muslims in one province or tract of the country, for instance, the north of India from Peshawar to Agra.

From 1899 to 1913, no clear proposal for the partition of India came out, although some political and communal incidents and events took place which strengthened the faith of the Muslims in the Two Nation Theory. Amidst all this, the Governor of United Provinces Sir Anthony MacDonald's order to replace Urdu as the official language was a main event which permitted the use of the Devnagri language in place of Persian and Urdu in government offices. This order was very perturbing for the Muslims of India. At this stage a companion of Sir Syed, Nawab Mohsinul Mulk founded the Urdu Defence Council and protested against the Governor's order. In 1901, another organisation was formed by Nawab Wiqarul Mulk named "Muhammadan Political Organisation"; the main objective of the organisation was to voice the Muslim grievances and demands before the Indian Government. In the same year Viceroy Lord Curzon after bifurcating Punjab established northern frontier area as a province.

But the most shocking event was revealed on October 16, 1905, when Lord Curzon decided to divide the province of Bengal into two. This was a blessing for the Muslims of India but was against the interests of the Hindus.

In 1906, the All India Muslim League (AIML) came into being. In 1908, the Muslims of India achieved more successes through the efforts of AIML; with the help of new reforms, the right for separate electorate for the Muslims was accepted. The Minto-Morley Reforms in 1909 ensured that the Muslims would be free to choose their own candidates. According to the same reforms, the Administrative Council of Viceroy was expanded and changed into Imperial Legislative Council. Almost simultaneously, on December 12, 1911, at his coronation ceremony, King George V announced the cancellation of the division of Bengal. This was a painful moment for the Muslims, while the Hindus who were continuously raising voices against this decision, celebrated joyously. These events forced the Muslims of India to struggle for their rights as a separate community.

On 10th May, 1913, a newspaper called Comrade published a comic column written by a journalist named Wilayat Ali Bambooq where he said, "to solve the Hindu-Muslim problem, Hindus and Muslims must be separated from each other. North India must be handed over to Muslims, while the rest may be handed over to Hindus".

From 1913 to June 1917 five proposals came out about India's constitutional and administrative future but in September 1917 the two Khairi Brothers, Abdul Jabbar and Abdul Sattar, played a prominent role in advancing the idea of a Muslim state in India. During the period 1913 to 1917, a vital change occurred in the political scenario of the Subcontinent through the efforts of M A Jinnah, who was actively participating in politics from the platform of the Indian National Congress and the Legislative Council. He joined the AIML in 1913 and made efforts to create communal harmony between Hindus and Muslims. He was gaining popularity on both sides but some ideologies were not in favour of Jinnah's efforts.

In 1918, Sir Aga Khan in his book "India in Transition" proposed a plan of a huge federation of South Asia with India as its nucleus and centre. From 1919 to 1923, some other politicians and social scientists proposed schemes. Prof. Muhammad Sarwar in his book Afadat wa Malfuzat-i-Hazrat Maulana Ubaidullah Sindhi, wrote that in 1924 an anti-British personality Ubaidullah Sindhi in his manifesto issued from Istanbul in 1924, observed that each region of India was to be called "Swarajiya Republic" and the collection (India) was to be known as the Indian Federal Swarajiya Republican State". The Federal Capital was to be at Delhi.

Apart from Sindhi's observation, Maulana Hasrat Mohani, a renowned poet and politician was the first Indian who moved a resolution demanding, "Complete independence" for India from the Congress platform during its 1920 annual session and again in his presidential address delivered before the ML's annual session at Ahmadabad in Dec 1921. Three years later, Maulana Hasrat presented a slightly amended proposal in his meeting with the Hindu leaders in 1924. Mohani proposed his scheme on two grounds: that no country could be really free under dominion status and that the Muslims would receive a better deal under the independent Federal structure. In the same year Lala Lajpat Rai a Congress leader, founder of the Hindu Mahasabha and a journalist, wrote several articles on the Hindu-Muslim problem and on Pan-Islamism. In May 1925, Khilafat leader Maulana

Muhammad Ali Jauhar, while commenting on Sardar Gul Khan's proposal in his journal Comrade, said "Muslims have no desire to rule over Hindu areas". Maulana Muhammad Ali never gave any concrete suggestion about the partition of India but from his writings and speeches it is indicated that he had a very clear idea about the partition of India.

Apart from Patric Fagan's assumption that Muslims will fight for their domination in north India, few other opinion came forward in 1925 which are on record. In the same year some teachers and students of the Aligarh Muslim University prepared a scheme of partition in which they suggested that India should be rearranged on the basis of a new theory of nationality. The scheme was published in the form of a pamphlet and distributed on the occasion of jubilee celebration of the Aligarh Muslim University.

Journalist Murtaza Ahmad Khan Maikash, Syed Sardar Ali Khan and Nawab Zulfiqar Ali Khan, Sir Ross Masud also presented their proposals but all were superseded by the proposal made by Allama Iqbal in his presidential address. Allama Iqbal proposed that "I would like to see the Punjab, North-West Frontier Province, Sindh, and Balochistan amalgamated into a Single state. Self-government within the British Empire or without the British Empire, the formation of a consolidated North-West Indian Muslim appears to me to be he final destiny of the Muslims, at least of North-West India." In the same address, Iqbal also said "the principal of European democracy can not be applied to India without recognising the fact of communal groups. The Muslim demand for the creation of a Muslim India within India is, therefore, perfectly justified" The proposal of Iqbal was not only welcomed by the Muslim circles but also gained popularity and importance even in non-Muslim circles.

In 1933, a very thought provoking declaration was made by Choudhary Rahmat Ali, a student of Cambridge University. After passing the examination of Law, during the Round Table Conferences in January 1933, Rahmat Ali issued a declaration entitled "Now or Never: Are we to live or perish forever?" In his declaration, Rahmat Ali demanded a Muslim homeland. The homeland of the Muslims of the Subcontinent was named in the first sentence of the declaration as 'Pakistan', according to which "...we mean the five Northern units of India, *viz.*, Punjab, North-West Frontier Province (Afghan Province), Kashmir, Sind and Balochistan." Choudhary Rahmat Ali's proposal embodied in his declaration, gained significance and importance due to two reasons: first, he issued this declaration at a time when the Round Table Conferences were in session in London; second, that Rahmat Ali was the only person who suggested a name "Pakistan" for his proposed Muslim homeland. After Rahmat Ali's declaration, a flood of opinions and suggestions burst forth in India and internationally. The word "Pakistan" became immensely popular.

In August 1933, the Joint Parliamentary Select Committee of British Empire discussed the said declaration with the visiting deputation of the Indian Muslims. From 1933 to 1936, no clear proposal came forward.

In April 1934, Jinnah was elected the president of the AIML again. He reorganised the League with the purpose to participate in the elections which were due to be held under the India Act of 1935.At this crucial stage Allama Muhammad Iqbal extended his full support to Jinnah. During 1936 and 1937 he was in touch with Jinnah and was continuously writing to him on the issues which the Muslim India was facing. In his letter on 28, May 1937, Iqbal commenting and elucidating the seriousness of the Muslim India's situation wrote that to solve these problems it is necessary to redistribute the country and to provide one or more Muslim states with absolute majorities. 1937 to early 1940 were the years when many a proposal, suggestion, scheme and observation came forward about the partition of India on Hindu Muslim basis from all the corners of the country.

1940 was the landmark of the demand for partition because in that year AIML in its annual session held in March 1940 at Lahore in the supreme leadership of the Quaid-i-Azam Muhammad Ali Jinnah presented its separate Muslim homeland plan. The plan was embodied in a resolution, which was initially called Lahore Resolution, which later became famous as Pakistan Resolution. The entire struggle of All India Muslim League after March 1940 was concentrated around this Resolution till the creation of Pakistan in August 1947. Syed Sharifuddin Pirzada, Professor Sharif al Mujahid and K K Aziz in their research work summarised these proposals and schemes with authentic sources and came to the conclusion that the historic Pakistan Resolution was not the end but the beginning which led to the creation of Pakistan.

TEXT OF THE RESOLUTION

While approving and endorsing the action taken by the Council and the Working Committee of the All-India Muslim League, as indicated in their resolutions dated the 27th of August, 17th & 18th September and 22nd of October, 1939, and 3rd of February, 1940 on the constitutional issue, this Session of the All-India Muslim League emphatically reiterates that the scheme of federation embodied in the Government of India Act 1935, is totally unsuited to, and unworkable in the peculiar conditions of this country and is altogether unacceptable to Muslim India.

It further records its emphatic view that while the declaration dated the 18th of October, 1939 made by the Viceroy on behalf of His Majesty's Government is reassuring in so far as it declares that the policy and plan on which the Government of India Act, 1935, is based will be reconsidered in consultation with various parties, interests and communities in India, Muslims in India will not be satisfied unless the whole constitutional plan is reconsidered de novo and that no revised plan would be acceptable to Muslims unless it is framed with their approval and consent.

Resolved that it is the considered view of this Session of the All-India Muslim League that no constitutional plan would be workable in this country or acceptable to the Muslims unless it is designed on the following basic principles, *viz.*, that geographically contiguous units' are demarcated into regions which should be constituted, with such territorial readjustments as may be necessary that the areas in which the Muslims are numerically in a majority as in the North Western and Eastern Zones of (British) India should be grouped to constitute "independent States" in which the constituent units should be autonomous and sovereign.

That adequate, effective and mandatory safeguards should be specifically provided in the constitution for minorities in these units in the regions for the protection of their religious, cultural, economic, political, administrative and other rights and interests in consultations with them and in other parts of (British) India where the Musalmans (Muslims) are in a majority adequate, effective and mandatory safeguards shall be specifically provided in constitution for them and other minorities for the protection of their religious, cultural, economic, political, administrative and other rights and interests in consultation with them.

This session further authorises the Working Committee to frame a scheme of constitution in accordance with these basic principles, providing for the assumption finally by the respective regions of all powers such as defense, external affairs, communications, customs and such other matters as may be necessary.

This session further authorises the Working Committee to frame a scheme of constitution in accordance with these basic principles, providing for the assumption finally by the respective regions of all powers such as defense, external affairs, communications, customs and such other matters as may be necessary. The sad part is calling for the resolutions proper implementation will give you the title of traitor..

A lasting irony is that many of the people involved in the resolution ended up being marginalised from pakistani politics.

The word "Pakistan" was actually never mentioned in the 1940 Lahore Resolution. It emphasied on the creation of a separate homeland for the Muslims of India.

A bit of background here is necessary. M. A. Jinnah joined Congress in 1906 and remained a member till 1919. He joined the Muslim League in 1913. He was known as the "Ambassador of Hindu-Muslim unity" up until the Nehru Report of 1928. Jinnah termed it as "Hindu Report" and condemned it and finally parted ways with the Congress of India. Jinnah, in turn, put forward his famous Fourteen Points that would satisfy Muslim interests - in particular, the retention of separate electorates or the creation of "safeguards" to prevent a Hindu-controlled legislature. Jinnah's proposals were rejected, and from then on cooperation between Hindus and Muslims in the independence movement was rare.

It was during the 1930s that the idea of Two-Nation Theory took stronghold thanks mostly due to the efforts of one Muslim poet philosopher. In his presidential address to the Muslim League session at Allahabad in 1930, the Sir Allama Muhammad Iqbal visualized the establishment of a Muslim state comprising of North-Western region of India.

In subsequent speeches and writings, Iqbal reiterated the claims of Muslims to be considered a nation "based on unity of language, race, history, religion, and identity of economic interests". Allama Iqbal in his famous letters to Mr. Jinnah elaborated his scheme for a separate Muslim State in its political and cultural context and convinced him of the soundness of his concept.

However, Iqbal gave no name to his projected state. That was done by a group of students at Cambridge in Britain who issued a pamphlet in 1933 entitled "Now or Never" by Choudhry Rehmat Ali. They opposed the idea of federation, denied that India was a single country, and demanded partition into regions, the Northwest receiving national status as a "Pakistan". They explained the terms follows: "Pakistan...is...composed of letters taken from the names of our homelands: that is Punjab, Afghani, [N.W.F.P.], Kashmir, Sindh, Tukharistan, Afghanistan, and Balochistan. It means the land of the Paks, the spiritually pure and clean." The demand for Pakistan was formally endorsed by Muslim League by 1940 under the charismatic leadership of M.A Jinnah.

The Lahore Resolution

Qarardad-e-Lahore, commonly known as the Pakistan Resolution (*Qarardad-e-Pakistan*), was a formal political statement adopted by the Muslim League at the occasion of its three-day general session on 22-24 March 1940 that called for greater Muslim autonomy in British India. This has been largely interpreted as a demand for a separate Muslim state, Pakistan. The resolution was presented by A. K. Fazlul Huq.

Although the idea of founding the state was introduced by Allama Iqbal in 1930 and the name Pakistan had been proposed by Choudhary Rehmat Ali in his Pakistan Declaration in 1933, Muhammad Ali Jinnah and other leaders had kept firm belief in

Hindu-Muslim unity. However, the volatile political climate and religious hostilities gave the idea stronger backing

1. *Background:* With the beginning of the Second World War in September 1939, the Viceroy of India Lord Linlithgow declared India's entrance into the war without consulting the provincial governments. In this situation, Jinnah called a general session of the All India Muslim League in Lahore to discuss the circumstances and also analyze the reasons for the defeat of Muslim League in the Indian general election of 1937 in some Muslim majority provinces.
2. *Proceedings:* Choudhry Khaliquzzaman seconding the Resolution with Jinnah presiding the session

   The session was held between 22 March and 24 March, 1940, at Minto Park (now Iqbal Park), Lahore. The welcome address was made by Nawab Sir Shah Nawaz Mamdot. In his speech, Jinnah recounted the contemporary situation, stressing that the problem of India was no more of an inter-communal nature, but manifestly an international. He criticised the Congress and the nationalist Muslims, and espoused the Two-Nation Theory and the reasons for the demand for separate Muslim homelands. According to Stanley Wolpert, this was the moment when Jinnah the former ambassador of Hindu-Muslim unity totally transformed himself into Pakistan's great leader.

Sikandar Hayat Khan, the Chief Minister of the Punjab, drafted the original Lahore Resolution, which was placed before the Subject Committee of the All India Muslim League for discussion and amendments.

The Resolution text unanimously rejected the concept of United India on the grounds of growing inter-communal violence and recommended the creation of an independent Muslim state.

After the presentation of annual report by Liaquat Ali Khan, the Resolution was moved in the general session by A.K. Fazlul Huq, the Chief Minister of undivided Bengal and was seconded by Choudhry Khaliquzzaman who explained his views on the causes which led to the demand of a separate state. Subsequently, Maulana Zafar Ali Khan from Punjab, Sardar Aurengzeb from the

NWFP, Sir Abdullah Haroon from Sindh, and Qazi Esa from Balochistan, and other leaders announced their support. In the same session, Jinnah also presented a resolution to condemn the Khaksar massacre of 19 March, owing to a clash between the Khaksars and the police, that had resulted in the loss of lives.

3. *The Statement:* The principle text of the Lahore Resolution was passed on 24 March. In 1941 it became part of the Muslim League's constitution. In 1946, it formed the basis for the decision of Muslim League to struggle for one state for the Muslims. The statement declared: No constitutional plan would be workable or acceptable to the Muslims unless geographical contiguous units are demarcated into regions which should be so constituted with such territorial readjustments as may be necessary. That the areas in which the Muslims are numerically in majority as in the North-Western and Eastern zones of India should be grouped to constitute independent states in which the constituent units shall be autonomous and sovereign.

Additionally, it stated: That adequate, effective and mandatory safeguards shall be specifically provided in the constitution for minorities in the units and in the regions for the protection of their religious, cultural, economic, political, administrative and other rights of the minorities, with their consultation.

Arrangements thus should be made for the security of Muslims where they were in a minority.

4. *Commemoration:* Muslim League Working Committee at the Lahore session
   - To commemorate the event, *Minar-e-Pakistan,* a 60 meters tall distinctive monument in the shape of a minaret has been built at the site in Iqbal Park Lahore, where the resolution was passed.
   - 23 March is a national holiday in Pakistan, celebrated as Republic Day to commemorate Lahore Resolution as well as the day in 1956 when the country became the first Islamic Republic in the world.

MUSLIM'S STRUGGLE FOR INDEPENDENT STATEHOOD

The Lahore session of the Muslim League (ML) on March 23, 1940, was historic and momentous. It was the biggest concourse of Indian Muslims in their political history since the fall of the once-mighty Mughal Empire in 1857 and the advent of British colonial rule in the subcontinent. More than 100,000 Muslim activists from every nook and corner of the Subcontinent congregated on that day in the historic city of Lahore and proclaimed to the world their determination to make the Pakistan Resolution for Independence and Muslim Statehood the goal of their struggle under the leadership of the Quaid-i-Azam Muhammad Ali Jinnah.

Even then there were some Doubting Thomases but by and large, the Muslim masses throughout India welcomed the Pakistan Resolution which was hammered out by the nation's leaders in the mammoth gathering in the Minto Park (renamed the Iqbal Park) on the starry night of March 23, 1940. The Muslim nation now hugged the path of independence and statehood shown by Allama Iqbal in the 1930 session of the All India Muslim League in Allahabad. Ten years had passed since that historic event and the political will of the Muslim nation had now acquired the strength of steel. The engine of their political struggle, namely the All India Muslim League, was now strong enough to lead them on the pathway to Pakistan.

A year earlier, the Quaid-i-Azam Muhammad Ali Jinnah had given loud and clear hints to the nation and foreign powers that the die would be cast in the next Lahore session of the All India Muslim League (AIML), after which the battle for creating Pakistan will ensue and "Pakistan" will be the battle cry of the Muslim nation. The watch-words of "Faith Unity and Discipline" were the munitions which the Quaid-i-Azam gave to the nation for waging the battle for Pakistan. The most dependable powerhouse in the struggle for Pakistan was the Muslim nation's unity.

The international impact of the Muslim League's Lahore session was colossal. Teams of newsmen had come to Lahore from all parts of the world to report the proceedings of the session and the decisions taken. The BBC was giving copious coverage to the ML's

Lahore session; the American Radio networks were not lagging behind. The Quaid-i-Azam Muhammad Ali Jinnah who was a brilliant communicator for the foreign media, himself took care of the arrangements for briefing newsmen. He had mobilised some of the most talented and articulate young men and women of pro-Muslim League families from Punjab to liaise with the foreign media representatives for the coverage of the ML's Lahore session.

In the forefront of the young lobbyists designated by the Quaid-i-Azam to liaise with the foreign media representatives was the dynamic Mumtaz Shahnawaz whose illustrious mother, Begum Jahanara Shahnawaz was a leading light in the Muslim League High Command and the glittering Reception Committee for the Lahore ML session. The Muslim Leaders had learnt some good lessons from the way the Congress organised its annual sessions. Tazi, as this highly-read Muslim female intellectual was known in League circles in Lahore, was a powerful spokeswoman for the ML and its Pakistan demand.

Many years later when I was serving as the Minister for Information at the Pakistan Embassy in London, I met some veteran British Journalists who had covered for their media organisations in the UK, the ML's Lahore session in March 1940. They spoke highly of the excellence of the media arrangements for this convention.

In Cairo, in 1960, I met an eminent Arab journalist who had covered the ML's Lahore session and interviewed the Quaid-i-Azam. "Lahore is a glorious city, with the most imposing evidence of the greatness of Mughal architecture", he said to me. Visitors to Lahore found the people of Lahore immensely hospitable and a sense of pride in their Islamic Faith imbued them with zeal and élan for Pakistan. In later years, I heard from some Muslims who attended the ML's Lahore session that the Muslim tonga-drivers (drivers of horse drawn carriages- then a popular mode of travel on Lahore's streets) refused to accept fares from the Muslims visiting Lahore for the ML's session. Owners of wayside food shops gave free food to the visitors for the ML's session. The spear-wielding Khaksars who were angered by the brutal police firing on March 19, were mesmerised into becoming followers of the Quaid-i-Azam and were performing security duties to protect the giant Muslim League pandal (canopy) in the Minto Park, the venue of the ML's session in Lahore. The Quaid-i-Azam had issued press statements condemning the Punjab police firing on the unarmed Khaksars and urged the coalition ministry of Sir Sikander Hayat Khan who was the then Chief Minister of Punjab, to pay compensation to the bereaved families and to punish the officers who ordered the police firing. The Quaid-i-Azam had urgently summoned Nawab Bahadur Yar Jung from Hyderabad Deccan to use his good offices for placating the chief of the Khaksars to help maintain peace in Lahore during the ML's session. The Quaid's visit to the Mayo Hospital to console the bereaved families of the Khaksars had a magical effect on Lahore's political atmosphere and groups of Khaksars trekked to the Minto Park and took oaths to safeguard the pandal and protect the Muslim Leaguers in Minto Park. It was an incredible change of political weather in Lahore. Thus a plank of the conspiracy by hostile forces to derail the ML session was smashed by the Quaid-i-Azam's foresight, tact and diplomacy.

The forces inimical to Muslims had learnt beforehand that the ML session would be called upon to pass a resolution for the partition of India to create two independent states, one for the Hindus and the other for the Muslims. Neither the Congress, nor the Unionists in the Punjab, favoured the partition of India. The British wanted their Indian Empire to stay a whole. British newsmen noted and duly reported the Quaid's two hour speech in which he expounded on the Muslim case for independent statehood under the banner of Pakistan. They noted in their reportage that although the Quaid spoke in the English language which was not mother tongue of the majority of the audience, they listened to him in rapt attention and their vociferous cheering and deafening shouts of "Quaid-i-Azam Zindabad" and "Muslim League Zindabad" demonstrated that their hearts beat in unison with that of their Quaid. A Muslim Pathan from the highlands of the Northwest Frontier commented, "I may not understand the English language but I am with Jinnah because he is true and honest and seeks our good".

The Lahore session of the Muslim League saw a glittering assemblage of the provincial and local ML leaders from all parts of the Subcontinent. It was a magnificent demonstration of Muslim unity and pleased and elated Jinnah beyond words. Maulvi Fazlul Haque popularly known as the Lion of Bengal who was one of the sponsors and proposers of the Pakistan Resolution in the ML's Lahore session, expounded on the merits and objectives of the Pakistan Resolution. He catalogued the many injustices done to the Muslims by the Congress rulers of the seven provinces wherein the Congress ruled for some two and a half years after the 1935 General Election in the subcontinent under the British-drafted Government of India Act. While supporting the Resolution vociferously, the Muslim League leader from the United Provinces, Choudhry Khaliquzzaman, thundered denunciation of the Congress Raj and the efforts of the Congress leaders to divide the Muslims in order to deprive them of their just rights. He said, "The Muslims of the United Provinces (U.P) would not get the benefits of Pakistan because their minority status would not place them in the Muslim-majority Pakistan scheme but the U.P. Muslims would be happy to see their brethren in the Muslim majority areas as a part of independent Pakistan". He expressed full confidence in the leadership of the Quaid-i-Azam Muhammad Ali Jinnah.

Speaking on behalf of the Muslims of the Central Provinces (CP) Syed Abdur Rauf Shah declared that the Muslims of CP fully supported the Muslim League's demand for an independent Pakistan. He added "please do not be worried by the injustices that would befall the Muslims of Central provinces under an independent Hindu India. God is our protector; we have strong hearts and faith in God's protection. We want Pakistan to be a safe home for our Muslim brethren. Keep aloft the banner of Islam. We are under Allah's protection. We want Islam to thrive in Pakistan and Allah's blessings on Muslims in the Muslim majority areas that would form independent Pakistan".

From the Bombay province, I Chundrigar said that the injustices heaped on Muslims under the Congress rule in seven Provinces, had compelled the Muslims to seek Pakistan, a free state of their own, instead of being doomed to minority status in a Hindu-dominated India. For them Pakistan was the best choice.

From the Bihar Muslim League, Nawab Muhammad Ismail supported the Pakistan Resolution and eulogised the brotherly attitude of the people of the Punjab towards the Muslims from the provinces where they were in a minority. Nawab Ismail said that the Muslims of Bihar would make every sacrifice to see their Muslim brethren in the Muslim-majority provinces united and free in a single independent Muslim State to be called Pakistan. He declared amid cheering, "Mr Jinnah is the voice and true spokesman of the Subcontinent's Muslims who are united in demanding independent Muslim Statehood under the banner of the Muslim League".

From Balochistan, Qazi Muhammad Isa voiced thunderous support for the Pakistan Resolution. He said that the ill-treatment of Muslims in the seven provinces ruled by the Congress for two and a half years had forced the Muslims to demand Pakistan and the partition of India. The Muslims of Balochistan, like the Muslims of the NWFP would strive their utmost to safeguard the interests of the Muslims in the rest of India. "They are our brothers in Faith: and their defence is our moral and religious duty."

Similar sentiments of Islamic fraternity were projected in the speeches of Haji Abdullah Haroon and Ghulam Hussain Hidayatullah from the Sindh province.

The province of Sindh had prospered and the Muslims felt safe in a separate Sindh province. The Sindh Provincial Assembly had earlier passed a resolution calling for the creation of an independent state, composed of the Muslim-majority areas of the Subcontinent.

Projecting the views of the Muslims of Madras province in Support of the Pakistan Resolution, Abdul Hamid Khan said that for the past three decades the Muslim League had been fighting for the independence of the Subcontinent and the end of colonial rule and it had extended cooperation to the Congress in the freedom struggle but the Muslims were ill-treated under Congress rule in seven provinces of India and this had opened their eyes. They were now justified in demanding an independent state of their own in the subcontinent. He therefore fully supported the Pakistan Resolution in the Muslim League session.

Chundrigar declared that the Bombay Muslims supported the Pakistan Resolution in the ML session because they apprehended Hindu oppression on Muslims in a Hindu-majority India as was their bitter experience under Congress Raj in seven provinces in India for two and a half years. Pakistan was therefore the best solution of the vexing communal problem.

One of the most powerful speeches in favour of the Pakistan Resolution was delivered by the renowned freedom fighter and journalist, Maulana Zafar Ali Khan, Editor of the Daily Zemindar. He said, "I today feel as if I am living in a Muslim environment of freedom and Islamic belief. For years I have championed the cause of freedom for this Subcontinent and worked for Hindu-Muslim cooperation in the struggle for freedom for the entire Subcontinent's teeming millions. But I have felt disillusioned by the Conduct of the Congress rulers. For them independence means the right to oppress and ill-treat the non-Hindu minorities. The Congress rulers have not undertaken any economic enterprise to benefit the Muslim masses in India. I am skeptical of any Constitution or political setup that would doom Muslims to the unenviable status of a powerless, downtrodden minority; subservient to the Congress rulers. I therefore support the Pakistan Resolution in the Muslim League's Lahore Session" From the Muslim ruled State of Hyderabad Deccan, Nawab Bahadur Yar Jang gave the fullest measure of support to the Pakistan Resolution and praised the dynamic leadership of the Quaid-i-Azam who had skippered the Muslim nation to the ramparts of independence and the goal of Pakistan was now within the easy grasp of the Muslims.

Hours after midnight, the Pakistan Resolution in its final form, as approved by the Subjects Committee, was read to the huge audience followed by its Urdu translation. An outburst of cheers from every section of the audience greeted the Resolution and thus it was passed by unanimous acclamation. The foundation of Pakistan was thus laid and battle lines for winning Pakistan were drawn. As dawn was about to be ushered in by the Heavens on earth, the Quaid-i-Azam, resplendent in his white Achkan and Choridar Pyjama rose to thank the participants in the Muslim League session and God Almighty for His benign mercy and guidance. He looked at the profile of the Mughal-built Badshahi Mosque in the distance and near it was the tomb of Allama Iqbal. In emotion-charged words Jinnah said "We are now taking the path Allama Iqbal had shown us in the Muslim League's Allahabad session in 1930. We will achieve for the Muslim nation the Muslim majority State he envisioned and independence and separate statehood are now our goals. The Muslim League will lead us to our goal-Pakistan".

On August 14, 1947, the Muslim majority independent State of Pakistan was established. Poet Iqbal's dream won a reality.

A powerful impact of the Muslim League's March 1940 Lahore session and the adoption of the Pakistan Resolution therein was a sense of self-confidence that gripped the Muslim nation from the hoary heights of the towering Karakoram peaks to Cape Comorin in South India. The success of the Lahore session of the Muslim League and the splendid unity and organisation it demonstrated, gave the Muslim League excellent international publicity and the concept of Pakistan, which was enshrined in the Lahore Resolution, gained worldwide currency.

The word Pakistan did not appear in the text of the Resolution but the name of Pakistan, coined by a group of Muslim students of the Cambridge University in the United Kingdom led by Choudhry Rehmat Ali as the nomenclature for the new Muslim State they proposed for the Subcontinent, caught the fancy and imagination of the Muslim masses in the Subcontinent. Thus "Pakistan" was embedded in the hearts and minds of the Muslims in the Subcontinent as the name of the sovereign and independent state promised to them by their Great Leader, the Quaid-i-Azam Muhammad Ali Jinnah on March 23, 1940, in Lahore. Pakistan symbolised for them the golden haven of their hopes and expectations that would make them the free citizens of a great Muslim country. The agony and pain the Muslim masses had experienced for two and a half years under the rule of the Hindu-dominated Congress had welded them into a single nation and they hugged the dream of Pakistan with their hearts and souls. Even the Quaid-i-Azam Muhammad Ali Jinnah who at one time strove for Hindu-Muslim unity in seeking freedom and independence for the Subcontinent, was now a champion of Muslim separatism, demanding the Partition of India and the creation of two independent States, one for the Muslims and the other for the Hindus.

The March 23, 1940, Pakistan Resolution of the Muslim League in Lahore was the first salvo fired in the battle for Pakistan and in barely seven years of an epic political struggle, the Muslims made their dream state of Pakistan a massive reality. There is eminent truth in the verdict of the Quaid-i-Azam's American biographer, Stanley Wolpert, (Jinnah of Pakistan) "that few individuals significantly alter the course of history, fewer still modify the map of the world. Hardly anyone can be credited with creating a nation state. Muhammad Ali Jinnah did all three. Jinnah virtually conjured that country into statehood... by the force of his indomitable will. His place of primacy in Pakistan's history looms like a lofty minaret over the achievements of all his contemporaries in the Muslim League...."

The beacon of Muslim statehood lit by the Quaid-i-Azam in the Muslim League's Lahore session in 1940 ignited the fires of Muslim political renaissance in thousands of Muslim communities all over India and gave new faith and fire to the Muslims of the Subcontinent in the movement for their political emancipation under the banner of the All India Muslim League. I cannot forget the words of Lord Mountbatten which he uttered at the launching in London of his biography by Ziegler, "if there had not been Mr. Jinnah there would have been no Pakistan". The Lahore session of the Muslim League in March 1940 set the seal of universal Muslim allegiance to the Quaid-i-Azam as the best spokesman of the Muslim nation in the Subcontinent.

The Quaid-i-Azam's sister, Mohtarma Fatima Jinnah told me in 1978 that the Quaid-i-Azam bore the strain of the ML's Lahore session with heroic courage and it seemed that the spectacle of Muslim unity in Lahore and the goal of Pakistan announced in Lahore had boosted his willpower anew. "I want to live longer to be able to see the birth of Pakistan," he said to his loving sister a few hours after the ML's Lahore session had ended as scheduled and the delegates were preparing to return to their respective hometowns and tell their Muslim countrymen more about what had been accomplished in Lahore in the national march on the high road to independence and Pakistan.

My mother, Begum Syed Abdul Hafiz, who attended the ML's Lahore session as a woman member of the delegation from the United Provinces (UP) told me that many of the delegates, before leaving Lahore went to the shrine of Data Ganj Baksh and prayed for the well-being of the people of Lahore and sought God's support for the early success of the Pakistan Movement that would usher into being the Muslim State of Pakistan. The ML's Lahore convention had given the Muslims an unbreakable spirit of fraternal comradeship.

10

Iqbal, Jinnah, and Pakistan: The Vision and the Reality

Iqbal saw the vision, Jinnah gave it a concrete shape, so goes the popular story about the creation of Pakistan, perhaps the only modern nation other than Israel that owes its existence to a nationalism inspired by religion. But the similarity ends there. Israel was created as the homeland for all Jews. Though the term occurs in Iqbal's writing too, he did not have in mind a homeland for Muslims at large, not even for all the Muslims of South Asia. What Iqbal had envisioned in 1930 was a territorial fulfilment of the "final destiny of the Muslims at least of North-West India," who were later in the same paragraph described as being "the most living portion of the Muslims of India whose military and police service has made the British rule possible in this country," and who "will eventually solve the problem of India as well as of Asia." A bit further on Iqbal said, "I demand the formation of a consolidated Muslim state in the best interests of India and Islam.

For India, it means security and peace resulting from an internal balance of power; for Islam, an opportunity to rid itself of the stamp that Arabian Imperialism was forced to give it, to mobilise its law, its education, its culture, and to bring them into closer contact with its own original spirit and with the spirit of modern times." Several points can be noted here. Iqbal tacitly excluded the Muslims of Bengal, although they also formed a majority within their region and had in fact briefly enjoyed a separate state of their own. Typically for Iqbal, whose favourite image in poetry was the "royal falcon," the salvation of Islam and India lay with the "virile and martial" races of Punjab, North-West Frontier, Balochistan, and Sind, the areas where the Muslims were relatively backward in education and economic and social status.

One cannot accuse Iqbal of blatant regionalism—he was scathing about what he called "Punjab Ruralism"—rather one should be aware of the romantic streak that underlay his remarks: his faith in the strength of the untainted primitive that would transform both India and Islam, ridding the former of Western political imperialism and the latter of Perso-Arabic cultural imperialism. Depending solely on his faith, Iqbal, Janus-like, had one face toward the past—a recovery of the pristine nature of Islam- - and another toward the future—a society fully assonant with modern times. Such a posture is easy in the realm of ideals, where all contradictions melt away in the heat of one's vision. In the realm of reality, Iqbal had to demand a Muslim majority state, with the proviso that the more undiluted the majority the better. It was only coincidental that Iqbal's envisioned consolidated state happened to be the region to which he belonged.

Be that as it may, Iqbal's vision reached its territorial fulfilment in the post-1971 Pakistan with its boundaries almost what he had in mind and with its minuscule non-Muslim population. How does one, then, view the pre-1971 history of Pakistan? As an aberration? Should one regard the current Fundamentalist Phase as a fresh beginning, or should one say that after what Professor Ziring calls the Punjabi, the Pathan and the Sindhi phases things have come full circle and we are back at a new Muhajir phase? Must history repeat itself in Pakistan? That is why one must be extremely careful extrapolating relationships between visions and realities.

Iqbal remained a visionary till his end, although his vision did not remain limited to the Muslims of the North-West India. In 1937, in a private and confidential letter to Jinnah, he wrote, "Personally I think that the Muslims of North-West India and Bengal ought at present to ignore Muslim minority provinces. This is the best course to adopt in the interests of both Muslim majority and minority provinces." Even as Iqbal expanded his vision to include Bengal, Jinnah's Muslim League was gearing itself to launch a major campaign "to protect Islam and the Muslims" in those same minority provinces. It was the hue and cry raised against the atrocities allegedly perpetrated by the Congress ministries in the United Provinces and Bihar that eventually gave the League the nationwide stature and strength to challenge the regional parties in the so-called Muslim majority province where it had not fared well at all. One may well conclude that for quite a while Jinnah and others in the Muslim League paid little attention to Iqbal's vision. We have no evidence on record to indicate otherwise. The only immediate response in 1930 was from Ch. Rahmat Ali and his associates at Cambridge who were themselves not taken seriously. We don't have Jinnah's letters to Iqbal, but reading between the lines of Iqbal's correspondence one gathers the impression that Jinnah was rather dubious of the whole thing. In 1937 Iqbal wrote at length on the matter of separate states and warned Jinnah about the rising demand in the Punjab. He repeatedly asked Jinnah to hold the annual session of the League in Lahore. Jinnah, however, stayed away, not only in 1937 but also in 1938. Only after Iqbal's death did the League hold its historic session of 1940 in Lahore, where the Pakistan Resolution was passed. Thus Iqbal's idea went a-begging for a long while, as did Ch. Rahmat Ali's Pakistan Scheme. Their time came only when the nature of the political arena changed and it became expeditious for the Muslim League in its strategy to overcome the regional groups and emerge as the authoritative voice of the Muslims of India. As sketched by Professor Metcalf, it was not that the ideology overwhelmed the minds of the leaders by its sheer irrefutability, it was that the leaders adopted the ideology when the limited provincial arenas became more open and more likely to be effected by national events. This development in the final analysis was perhaps more dependent on the decisions made by the British colonial power than on what was said by either the Congress or the Muslim League.

Looking back—no doubt with the advantage of hindsight—one can see that at the time Iqbal made his initial proposal there were only two core issues: (1) provincial autonomy within a loose federal scheme; and (2) a realignment of state boundaries, including the partition of some states, to better reflect the linguistic and ethnic loyalties of the people of those states. The matter of provincial autonomy seemed particularly important to the Muslims, who feared a strong centre controlled by a non-Muslim majority. The Nehru Report (1928) was perhaps the last Congress document that meaningfully sought to come to some understanding with the Muslims of India while treating them as a communal whole. More importantly, it was the last Congress statement in favour of a relatively loose federal system for future India. Rejected by the League, by 1930 the Nehru Report had been forsworn even by the Congress. The "Progressives," led by Motilal's son Jawaharlal, preferred a polity which should consist of weak states and a strong centre, a scheme they thought necessary given the objective conditions in India. A strong centre was also very attractive for the Hindu communal elements, who during the Twenties had come to be quite powerful within the Congress. This ironic coalition doomed forever any chance of creating a loose federal system in India. It also made it impossible for the Muslim League, *i.e.* Jinnah, to give up anything in the way of separate electorate, weightage in seats, or autonomous states. It was against this background that Iqbal made his bold, ideological statement in Allahabad, while Jinnah was in London at the Round Table Conference making a last-ditch effort on behalf of his cherished goals of constitutional reforms and protection of the rights of the Muslims within a unitary India. It was the growing intransigence of the Hindu communal elements and the shortsighted self-righteousness of the other leaders within the Congress, and not just some intrinsic truth in Iqbal's message, that gradually turned Jinnah into a votary—at least publicly—of the higher communalism of Iqbal.

Nevertheless, Jinnah remained flexible. As late as 1946, he would have gone along with an All India federal system if the Congress had agreed to the Cabinet Mission plan in its entirety. As for the ideological bias behind Iqbal's vision—the Two-Nation theory—Jinnah negated it in no uncertain terms on 11 August 1947, in his very first speech to the Constituent Assembly of Pakistan. There is not a single remark in that speech that pertains to the concept that the Hindus and the Muslims are two separate nations with two separate destinies. In fact, the word Islam does not even occur in it. Jinnah exhorts the members of the Constituent Assembly to keep in mind the problems of law and order, bribery and corruption, black-marketing, and nepotism and jobbery, but not one word is said about any expected unfolding of the pristine nature of Islam. According to Jinnah, religion had "nothing to do with the business of the State." While Iqbal believed that Islam itself was no less a polity, Jinnah declared to his listeners:

"If you change your past and work together in a spirit that everyone of you, no matter to what community he belongs, no matter what relations he had with you in the past, no matter what is his colour, caste or creed, is first, second and last a citizen of this State with equal rights, privileges and obligations, there will be no end to the progress you will make. We should begin to work in that spirit and in course of time all these angularities of the majority and minority communities, the Hindu community and the Muslim community—because even as regards Muslims you have Pathans, Punjabis, Shias, Sunnis and so on, and among the Hindus you have Brahmins, Vashnavas, Khatris, also Bengalees, Madrasis, and so on—will vanish. We should keep that in front of us as our ideal and you will find that in course of time Hindus would cease to be Hindus and Muslims would cease to be Muslims, not in the religious sense, because that is the personal faith of each individual, but in the political sense as citizens of the State."

Notwithstanding Professor Syed's arguments, one still wonders what Iqbal might have thought of Jinnah's remarks if he had been alive. After all, in that same address of 1930, Iqbal had asked his listeners: "Is religion a private affair? Would you like to see Islam, as a moral and political ideal, meeting the same fate in the world of Islam as Christianity has already met in Europe? Is it possible to retain Islam as an ethical ideal and to reject it as a polity in favour of national politics in which religious attitude is not permitted to play any part?"

Obviously Iqbal's own answer to these questions was a resounding no. It thus becomes difficult to go along with the notion that Iqbal had a vision which Jinnah put into reality as Pakistan. More likely that Jinnah found in Iqbal's vision a potent rallying cry for the Muslims at a particular moment in the political history of colonial India, a common enough kind of political opportunism. On the other hand, it may even be more plausibly argued, as suggested by S. M. Ikram, that a major shift had already taken place in the previously politically backward Muslim majority provinces and their new leadership was making itself felt in national councils, leading to a "marked shift in the community's political objectives." In other words, the rallying cry had become so loud by 1940 that Jinnah had to adopt it for his own, much in the way he had earlier championed separate electorates after he was convinced that they were what the community desired even though he was personally against them, not out of any opportunism but out of his conviction in a certain style of political behaviour. It was not the irrefutability of some ideology but the inevitability generated by diverse forces—many of them beyond Jinnah's control—which forced his conversion.

It is also clear that Iqbal and Jinnah did not always see eye to eye. The 1916 pact between the League and the Congress, a crowning achievement for Jinnah, was roundly criticised by Iqbal, who was opposed to any scheme that adversely affected, even in the slightest way, the majority position of the Muslims in the Punjab. In 1928, Iqbal resigned as Secretary of the All India Muslim League because he felt that the League was hedging on the issue of full provincial autonomy. In the thirties, Iqbal was dubious of any attempt to create ties between the League and the Unionist Party in the Punjab. He gave full support to a splinter group, the Punjab Provincial Muslim League, after it was set up in 1936, and repeatedly protested to Jinnah about the so-called Jinnah-Sikandar Pact of 1937. Nehru, in his *Discovery of India*, quotes a comment that Iqbal made to him a few months before his death: "What is there in common between Jinnah and you? He is a politician, you are a patriot." Jinnah was aware of Iqbal's prominent position—his hold over the Indian Muslim imagination—and his high regard for Iqbal was no doubt also genuine. But it is also true that he often followed an independent line and, as said earlier, if one carefully reads Iqbal's letters to Jinnah, it seems that Jinnah usually avoided taking the ideological stances urged upon him by Iqbal.

Why then did Iqbal choose Jinnah for his confidences? He apparently did so because, ideological differences aside, he believed in Jinnah's integrity, because Jinnah was the only Muslim leader with an unchallenged national status, and because Jinnah had no provincial or regional ties of any kind. Iqbal was struggling to crystallise an ideology—what he called a "communalism of a higher kind"—that would reflect, on the one hand, the universals of Islam as seen by Iqbal and, on the other, take advantage of the particular demographic configuration in India. Iqbal could confide in Jinnah because Jinnah was an outsider.

The leaders from the Muslim majority provinces, judging by their behaviour at the time, could not be expected to give up their class interests for the sake of Iqbal's communal gains. On the other hand, the leaders from the Muslim minority areas could justifiably be very suspicious of any political scheme that left them out in the cold. Iqbal needed Jinnah and his Muslim League. Likewise, Jinnah needed a rallying cry that would make the League invulnerable against the Congress as well as against the regional parties in the Muslim majority states. Earlier, Gandhi had captured the Indian political scene with his mixture of religion and politics. The popularity of the frenzied Khilafat movement had also shown how easy it was to bring the Muslims of India to a common platform in the name of religion. Jinnah and the League decided to go the same way. Their politics of protecting separate electorates and reservation of seats turned into a programme to protect Islam. Given the heightened communal antagonism at the time and the fact that the impending implementation of the federal part of the Government of India Act of 1935 made the regional parties eager to obtain some national affiliation, the new programme of the Muslim League and its permanent President met with total success on both the fronts.

The leaders of the Muslim minority provinces, reacting against the short-sighted policies of the Congress, carried the cry of "Protect Islam" to the Muslim masses and enrolled them by hundreds of thousands into the ranks of the League, while the leaders of the Muslim majority provinces came humbly to Jinnah in 1937 and reluctantly agreed to acknowledge the League's hegemony over them. Iqbal, in his presidential address of 1930, had remarked,

"One lesson I have learnt from the history of Muslims. At critical moments in their history it is Islam that has saved Muslims and not vice versa." The question whether the League saved Islam is not worth asking, but it is clear that Islam did save the Muslim League: in 1937, the League had won only 4.6 percent of the total Muslim votes; in 1946, it polled 75 percent.

By 1940 Jinnah had indeed brought the League quite a way, but in the process the vision of Iqbal had also gone through a transformation, perhaps of a kind that Iqbal might not have approved of. In 1930, before an audience of less than 75 people, Iqbal had said, "I would like to see the Punjab, North-West Frontier Province, Sind and Balochistan amalgamated into a single state. Self-Government within the British Empire, or without the British Empire, the formation of a consolidated North-West Indian Muslim state appears to me to be the final destiny of the Muslims at least of North-West India."

In 1940, the Pakistan Resolution, presented before a crowd of over 50,000 people, demanded that "geographically contiguous units (be) demarcated into regions which should be so constituted, with such territorial readjustments as may be necessary, that the areas in which the Muslims are numerically in a majority, as in the North Western and Eastern Zones of India, should be grouped to constitute 'Independent States' in which the constituent units should be autonomous and sovereign." When someone suggested during the debate that followed that instead of the vague word "zones" the names of the provinces should unambiguously be indicated, Nawabzada Liaquat Ali Khan, the permanent Honorary Secretary of the League and the right hand man of Jinnah, replied amidst a burst of applause, "It is for a reason that we have not mentioned the names of the provinces. If we say the Punjab that would mean the boundary of our state would be at Gurgaon, whereas we want to include in our proposed dominion Delhi and Aligarh, which are centres of our culture and education. Rest assured that 'territorial adjustments' does not mean that we will have to give away any part of the Punjab."

Is it still fair to Iqbal to identify his vision with Jinnah's reality? Jinnah's presidential address in Iqbal's home city contained not one mention of Iqbal's scheme or the reasons he gave for it; instead Jinnah anchored his ideological remarks in a letter from Lajpat Rai to C. R. Das written some fifteen years earlier! It is hard not to believe Edward Thompson when he asserts that Iqbal, near the end of his life, had very serious reservations about the proposed Pakistan.

"In The Observer I once said that he (Iqbal) supported the Pakistan plan. Iqbal was a friend, and he set my misconception right. After speaking of his despondency at the chaos he saw coming 'on my vast undisciplined and starving land' he went on to say that he thought the Pakistan plan would be disastrous to the British Government, disastrous to the Hindu community, disastrous to the Moslem community. 'But I am the President of the Moslem League and therefore it is my duty to support it.'"

The Pakistan that came into existence in August 1947 was not the consolidated state that Iqbal had envisioned in 1930; it certainly did not consist of the "Independent States" that the resolution of 1940 called for; in its cut-up form it was not even the "independent state" of the resolution of 1946. Neither did it come about through some smooth transition that Jinnah may have envisaged. It was a truncated Pakistan and its emergence was preceded by the worst communal carnage that the subcontinent had ever experienced. Jinnah may have had near-dictatorial powers within the Muslim League, but he had himself become a prisoner of the rhetoric about Pakistan that he had allowed to be let loose around him.

By 1945-46, the Pakistan concept had taken on a life of its own, independent of what Jinnah may or may not have felt about it. Inflamed communal passions, the urgency of the British to conclude their rule in India, the resolve of the Sikhs to ensure their own right of self-determination, the growing determination of the Congress leaders to obtain a strong unitary India, no matter what its size—on all this Jinnah had no control. Pakistan became inevitable, not because that was the destiny of Islam in India, but because of the particular configuration of a number of diverse forces at a certain moment in history. By the same token, after 1947, Jinnah, in spite of the accumulation of power in his hands, could not have curbed the conflicts that soon began to appear within

Pakistan even if he had lived longer, for if Pakistan was inevitable then Bangladesh was inevitable too. If one is not careful in choosing one's means one may discover that they have chosen the end for him.

This is not to denigrate the role of Iqbal's vision and Jinnah's leadership in the creation of Pakistan. It is merely to suggest that by defining the existing reality of Pakistan too much in terms of the popular equation "Iqbal plus Jinnah equals Pakistan," the people of that nation are not likely to resolve the dilemma concerning their political and cultural identity which has plagued them during their short but eventful history. The new boundaries, the existence of strong ethnic and regional groups, the minuscule size of the non-Muslim population, the prevalent socioeconomic conditions—all demand that a new, totally fresh start should be made. To make such a start the people of Pakistan will have to do two things. First, they will have to use critical scrutiny to thaw away the charisma that seems to have frozen around Iqbal and Jinnah, and make them more real and human and thus more relevant. To paraphrase the words of Bertolt Brecht's Galileo: Unfortunate is not that country that lacks in heroes but that which needs heroes. Secondly, they will have to delve deep into themselves as they are now, and not as they think they were in the past, recent or remote. After all Iqbal did tell them:

"Why should I ask the 'wise men' what my beginning was? I am busy discovering what my destiny is." Unlike other Muslim League stalwarts of his day Allama Iqbal's main contribution to the Pakistan Movement is mainly in the evolution of Muslims of India's demand for a separate homeland. This idea first expounded by Maulana Abdul Haleem Sharar in Weekly 'Muhazzab', Lucknow (August 23, 1890) and advocated by Khairi Brothers (Jabbar Khairi and Sattar Khairi) in Stockholm's Socialist International (1917), Chaudhry Rehmat Ali in his book 'Pakistan' (1915), Sardar Muhammad Gul Khan, (1922) and Nawab Zulfiqar Ali Khan (1929). Even Lala Lajpat Rai, a Hindu leader from the Punjab supported the idea of Muslim India comprising four regions. Allama Iqbal not only agreed with Sir Syed Ahmed Khan's two-nation theory, but he is the only Muslim leader who intensely thought over and ventilated Muslims' demand for separate homeland in his poetry and writings. The first phase of Iqbal's poetry (1898 – 1905) is for a concept of homeland which overrides any distinctions of creed. He was a staunch nationalist tilting towards the Islamic concept of Oneness of Being (Wahdat-ul-Wujood).

However, a significant change occurred in his thought with the increasing fury of the Congress protest against the partition of Bangal in 1905 which had provided a sense of security to the Bengali Muslims. The partition was actively supported by the All India Muslim League, formed in 1906 with its headquarter in Aligarh. Iqbal has given vent to his feeling of disgust over the Congress protest in his poem 'Abdul Qadir Ke Nam' in 1906. This poem signifies a break from his ardent belief in Indian nationalism. He clearly adopts in this poem a new concept of Muslim Millat.

Alas! See that a new darkness has engulfed the eastern horizon.

Let us spreads light with flames of our voice

Look! In the holy land, the lovers way of life has been renounced

Let us inspire other Qais (the lover) with new dreams

Later on we see in 1908 that he composes a Tarana-i-Milli (The Anthem of the Islamic Community) Translated by: D. J. Mathews.

Even some ghazals composed during this period signify a change which has occurred after his European sojourn with the growing belief that Asia will eventually rise for its as proved by the Japanese victory over Russia in 1903. In his poem on Wataniat (Territorial Nationalism) and in his 'Stray Reflections' (1910) Allama Iqbal is seen providing intellectual muscles to the vague and abstract notion of what the Muslim Millat could do in its hour of trial. In his analytic article Political Thought in Islam which appeared in Hindustan Times, Vols. 42-43 (1910-1911) Iqbal wrote: ... Nationality, with Islam, is not the highest limit of political development. For the general principles of the Law of Islam rests on human nature, not on the peculiarities of a particular people. The inner cohesion of such a notion would consist not in ethnic or geographic unity, nor in the unity of language or social tradition, but in the unity of religious and political ideal. Or, in the psychological fact of like mindedness.

Now, if we closely study Iqbal's thought from 1905 – 1908, we see that most of the Muslim leaders have expressed these strands of thought in their own way but no one seems to be escaping from the stamp of Sir Syed Ahmed Khan and Allam Iqbal's arguments in favour of Muslim Nationalism or against Indian nationalism. Iqbal as we know was not a great supporter of the Caliphate Movement because he thought that the symbol of Muslim aspirations was himself a captive of Imperialism. We can see his support to Mustafa Kamal in the "Reconstruction of Islam" to vouchsafe the result of this statement. Hence the whole hullabaloo about Khilafat, Hijrat and Non-Cooperation for Iqbal was only grist to the mills of Indian nationalism. These movements amounted to undermine of the success of Muslim nationalism. M. A. Jinnah was also a bit lukewarm about the Caliphate agitation simply because of the fact that Mahatma Gandhi, through his support to the Khilafat Movement, was weaning the Muslims away from the focus of their priorities.

Iqbal didn't want to enter regular politics but, in 1926, some Muslim leaders of Punjab prevailed upon him to contest election for Punjab Assembly for the Lahore Urban Muslim Constituency. He was officially declared as a member of the Assembly on December 05, 1926. Soon thereafter he joined the Unionist Party of Mian Fazl-i-Husain.

Later on he joined the Muslim League in January 1927. Though his sympathies for Muslim League were evident right from 1906. Thereafter he became a Member of Punjab Muslim League Council on November 13, 1927. It was possible in those days to be associated with two parties. Iqbal, however, continued to oppose the brazen-faced feudalism. Allama Iqbal's views were, in consonance with the Muslim League right from 1906 when he wrote his poem 'Abdul Qadir Ke Nam'. Iqbal proved himself to be a great champion of the Muslim urban population which remained neglected for years owing to the Unionist Party's support among the Muslim feudal, and Hindu-Sikh mercantilist lobby. However, the records of the Punjab Assembly show Iqbal's strong support for universal education, Muslim Quota in services, increased aid to Muslim schools, healthcare transfer of Income Tax from the Centre to the

Province and economic development of Punjabi Muslims will be gratefully remembered by the posterity.

However, in early 1927, the central Muslim League faced an inner dissention over the Simon Commission. Mian Muhammad Shafi's group favoured the Simon Commission and M. A. Jinnah's faction opposed it. Iqbal, being a close associate of Mian Muhammad Shafi, found himself arraigned against Jinnah's faction. There was a split in the Muslim League. It was for the first time that the Annual Conference of Shafi Group was held in Lahore and that of the Jinnah Group in Calcutta. Shafi League then changed its faction's name to All Parties Muslim Conference and persuaded the Aga Khan, Nawab Chatari and Dr. Sir Ziauddin to join its first session, held on December 31, 1928. Maulana Muhammad Ali Jauhar and Maulana Hasrat Mohani also attended the Conference.

The Jinnah group appointed a committee to draft a constitution for India. However, the tenacity of the Congress not to budge from the Nehru Report – which had made short shrift of the Lucknow Agreement, disappointed Jinnah. In March 1929, Mian Shafi and Jinnah met at Delhi in December 1930 and agreed to unite the two groups of Muslim League. Jinnah and issued a statement to the League Council that the Nehru Report was not acceptable to the Muslims. Iqbal and Jinnah became the leaders of the United Muslim League.

Muslim League's turning point: The 1930 Session had Allama Iqbal as its President and it was his address in Allahabad which could truly be called the Turning Point in the Muslim politics of the subcontinent. Almost all historians and chroniclers of the Pakistan Movement have regarded this Address on December 29, 1930 as a masterpiece for its clarity of exposition of the communal problem of the subcontinent. It is a pity that only one book 'Talash-i-Iqbal' has provided Urdu readers the most authentic translation of this address so far. Iqbal's argument was: "The religious ideal of Islam is organically related to the social order which it has created. The reflection of the one will eventually involve the rejection of the other. Therefore, the construction of a polity on national lines, if it means a displacement of the Islamic principle of solidarity, is simply unthinkable to a Muslim – I would like to see the Punjab, NWFP, Sind and Balochistan amalgamated into a single state. Self-government within the British Empire or without the British Empire appears to me the final destiny of the Muslims, at least of North-West India – I therefore demand the formation of a consolidated Muslim state in the best interest of India and Islam". (Note: The state of Jammu & Kashmir could not to be referred to in this state as its accession related the Maharajah's formal accession to either of the two states in any scheme of Transfer of Power. Hence it was not to be treated as an Indian province under the administrative control of the British government).

Assuring full cooperation to other nations of the India, subcontinent, Iqbal had observed: "And as far as I have been able to read the Muslim mind, I have no hesitation in declaring that if the principle that Indian Muslim is entitled to full and free development on the lines of his own culture and tradition in his own Indian homeland is recognized as the basis of a permanent communal settlement, he will be ready to stake his all for the free down of India – the need not alarm the Hindus or the British…"

But the idea alarmed the British as well as the Congress. The British Prime Minister Ramsay MacDonald "was highly displeased with the views expressed by Iqbal". A dispatch, published in Daily Leader, Allahabad, the next stated that the British as well as Indian circles in the Round Table Conference expressed resentment against what is called an assault made by Iqbal on the idea of an all India Constitution being worked over there. Iqbal further elaborated this point in his address to the National League of London on December 10, 1932. "The point of Muslims of India is that as a people representing a distinct historical tradition and homogeneity, which is not possessed by any other community in India, as such people they want to live and develop on their own cultural lives. We are 80,000,000 in India and we want to protect our own culture and our own historical tradition.

It is on Allama Iqbal's above quoted statements and other speeches that the publicity booklets, prepared by Pakistan Study Circle, Bombay, have mainly drawn upon in 1945-1946. Allama Iqbal was Secretary of Punjab Muslim League during the crucial

1936 elections to the Provincial Assemblies under the government of India Act 1935. It was during this period that: We come across his differences with the Quaid-i-Azam on the Jinnah-Sikandar Pact Allama Iqbal saw it as a sign of weakness of the AIML and a compromise on the political strength of the Muslims.

On the contrary the Quaid-i-Azam held the view that this Pact would strengthen the bargaining position of the Muslim League as the representative of one of the most popular Muslim majority province. Allama Iqbal, later on, agreed with the Quaid-i-Azam and supported the Muslim League candidates despite his illness. However, it was eventually proved beyond any doubt that the Unionists were not prepared to honour their commitment to lend their full support to in its dealing with the Congress and the British the Muslim League. This fact is evident from the fact that very few Muslim seats were won by the Muslim League in the election. Truly Allama Iqbal, as a Muslim League leader, was much move ahead of most of the Muslim League leaders. He sounds a bit idealist but deep down he was a pragmatist. In a letter to M. A. Jinnah dated May 28, 1937 he wrote: The League will have to finally decide whether it will remain a body representing the upper classes or Muslim masses... the problem of bread is becoming more and more acute. The Muslim has begun to feel that he has been going down and down during the last 200 years. Ordinarily he believes that his poverty is due to Hindu money-lending or capitalism... The atheistic socialism of Jawaharlal is not likely to receive much response from the Muslims. The question therefore is how is it possible to solve the problem of Muslim poverty?

The above letter, emphatically, proves that the poet-philosopher, who looked upon Quaid-i-Azam as the only leader of Muslims India to lead them towards the goals of the flowering of Islamic values and eradication of their poverty, was no one else but Iqbal and his contribution to the Muslim League was seminal in so far as philosophical mentorship was concerned. Iqbal was wedded to the idea of change and adaptability in response to the modern challenges – a view which has always been contested by these who are averse to the idea of moving with the times and his Allahabad Address proves that he was a pragmatic politician.

IQBAL AND JINNAH

The year 2002 is the Allama Iqbal year as declared by the government of Pakistan. December 25 is the birthday of the Quaid-i-Azam, M. A. Jinnah. It is, therefore, appropriate on this day to recall the interaction between them with regard to the implementation of the Pakistan idea. Iqbal and Jinnah, the two founding fathers of Pakistan, were two distinctly different personalities. For this reason alone a study of their interaction in a common cause is of great interest to students of our history. We have direct evidence of Iqbal's views recorded by him in his letters to Jinnah, but unfortunately Jinnah's replies to these letters are not available.

We have, therefore, to depend for evidence of Jinnah's responses either directly from his observations in his foreword to these letters or indirectly from Iqbal's letters themselves.

Iqbal was responsible for giving the concept of a Muslim homeland but he passed away in April 1938, two years before the movement for it was actually set afoot by Jinnah in March 1940. Iqbal, as president of the Punjab Provincial Muslim League, had been in touch with Jinnah in the years 1936-37 through correspondence. It was during this period that he exercised effective influence on Jinnah's thinking about the future of Muslim India and the constitutional dispensation that he had proposed earlier.

This is evident from Letters of Iqbal to Jinnah published for the first time in 1942 with a foreword from Jinnah in which he says: "I think these letters are of very great historical importance, particularly those which explain his views in clear and unambiguous terms on the political future of Muslim India. His views were substantially in consonance with my own and had finally led me to the same conclusions as a result of careful examination and study of the constitutional problems facing India, and found expression in due course in the united will of Muslim India as adumbrated in the Lahore resolution of the All India Muslim League, popularly known as the 'Pakistan Resolution' passed on March 23, 1940."

It is an important declaration coming as it does from the founder of the country giving due credit to his illustrious predecessor for moulding "the united will of Muslim India" for a demand to divide the subcontinent on the basis of Hindu/Muslim majority areas.

Iqbal had given a lead to the people in this direction in his presidential address to the Muslim League session at Allahabad in December 1930. He argued that the principle of European democracy could not be applied to India without recognizing the fact of communal entities. He voiced the demand for a separate Muslim state because "the life of Islam as a cultural force in this country (India) very largely depends on its centralization in a specific territory."

He specified the territory by saying, "I would like to see the Punjab, North-West Frontier Province, Sindh and Balochistan amalgamated into a single state... the formation of a consolidated North-West Indian Muslim state appears to me to be the final destiny of the Muslims, at least of North-West India."

In his letter of May 28, 1937 to Jinnah, Iqbal, while discussing the problem of Muslim poverty refers to socialism or social democracy (he uses these terms synonymously) and argues that if Hinduism accepts Jawaharlal Nehru's socialism it must cease to be Hinduism, and goes on to assert: "For Islam the acceptance of social democracy in some suitable form and consistent with the legal principles of Islam, is not a revolution but a return to the original purity of Islam."

Iqbal concludes by suggesting that in order to make it possible for Muslim India to solve the problems it faced, poverty being one of them, "It is necessary to redistribute the country and to provide one or more Muslim states with absolute majorities. Don't you think that the time for such a demand has already arrived? Perhaps this is the best reply you can give to the atheistic socialism of Jawaharlal Nehru."

We may pause here to take note of Jinnah's reaction to Iqbal's suggestion. A master of timing his political moves, Jinnah obviously thought it was not the appropriate time because the Muslims were not yet sufficiently organized and disciplined. Iqbal expresses his agreement with him in his next letter of June 21, 1937, in the context of a suggestion by some Muslims in Punjab to hold a

North-West India Muslim conference presumably for the purpose of making Iqbal's proposal public.

Jinnah seems to have turned down the suggestion because the time for holding such a convention was not ripe. However, Iqbal goes on to say: "But I feel that it would be highly advisable for you to indicate in your address (at the Lucknow session of the Muslim League) the line of action that the Muslims of North-West India would be finally driven to take."

The difference between Iqbal's and Jinnah's perception and approach in the matter is obviously the difference between a man inspired by a vision and a cautious politician waiting for the appropriate time. It so happened that in the following three years the Muslims had ample experience of the working of the Congress governments in the Muslim minority provinces which went a long way to galvanize the Muslim public opinion against the Congress and its concept of composite nationalism. The sentiment of Muslim nationalism of which Iqbal was a catalyst and a symbol received a further impetus. Finally, it was in March 1940 that Jinnah decided to translate Iqbal's vision into a formal demand and the Muslim League passed the Pakistan Resolution.

As we have seen in the letter of May 28, 1937, Iqbal had made reference to "one or more Muslim states with absolute majorities." He is however, more specific in his letter of June 21, 1937 when he says: "Why should not the Muslims of North-West India and Bengal be considered as nations entitled to self-determination just as other nations in India?" Here he does not only include Bengal, the other Muslim majority area in the subcontinent but also treats it as a separate nation from the Muslims of North-West India. This is in line with his thinking about the "redistribution of the country on the lines of racial, religious and linguistic affinities" which he had asked for earlier in the same letter.

Could one, therefore, surmise that the use of the word states in the plural in the Lahore Resolution was an echo of what Iqbal had suggested to Jinnah in his letters? Later, under some political exigency, Jinnah changed his mind as it was in the Muslim League Legislators Resolution at the Delhi Convention of April 1946 that the word state in the singular with Pakistan as its name was used.

However, the emergence of Bangladesh in 1971 as a separate and independent state after a bloody war which could have been avoided if better sense had prevailed with our military and political leaders of the day, has proved the validity of the original concept put forward in Iqbal's letters and the Lahore Resolution.

A divergence of opinion seems to have emerged between Iqbal and Jinnah on the question of the Sikander-Jinnah agreement reached at the Lucknow session of the Muslim League in 1937. Sir Sikander Hayat Khan, as the head of the Unionist Party, was the chief minister of Punjab at that time. The Unionist Party was a purely Punjabi party consisting mainly of Muslim feudals having support of some Hindu and Sikh feudals. Iqbal had apprehensions about Sir Sikander's intentions. He reported to Jinnah in his letter of October 30, 1937, that the idea, as one of Sir Sikander's party members had told him, was to slacken the activities of the provincial League.

On November 1, 1937, Iqbal again wrote to Jinnah informing him of his talk with Sir Sikander and some members of his party "about the differences between the League and the Unionist Party. Statements have been issued to the press by both sides, each side presenting its own interpretation of the terms of the Jinnah-Sikander agreement. This has caused much misunderstanding."

In his next and last letter written on November 10, 1937, Iqbal is far more candid and frank in expressing his apprehensions and in fact goes on to denounce the Sikander-Jinnah Pact itself - a handiwork of Jinnah himself. Here is what he has to say: "After having several talks with Sir Sikander and his friends I am now definitely of the opinion that Sir Sikander wants nothing less than the complete control of the League and the Provincial Parliamentary Board... Sir Sikander tells me that you agreed to their majority in the Board... I personally see no harm in giving him the majority that he wants but he goes beyond the pact when he wants a complete change in the office holders of the League, especially the secretary who has done so much for the League.

"He also wishes that the finances of the League should be controlled by his men. All this to my mind amounts to capturing of the League and then killing it. Knowing the opinion of the province as I do, I cannot take the responsibility of handing over the League to Sir Sikander and his friends. The pact has already damaged the prestige of the League in this province: and the tactics of the Unionists may damage it still further. They have not so far signed the creed of the League and I understand do not mean to."

Iqbal's attack on Sir Sikander was actually part of his fight against the domination of the feudal landlords in the Punjab Provincial Muslim League - a point which has been forcefully brought out by Dr. Ashique Hussain Batalvi in his book on the last two years of Iqbal's life. One does not know about Jinnah's immediate reaction to Iqbal's criticism. But in his foreword to Letters of Iqbal to Jinnah written in 1942, Jinnah touches upon the subject.

Referring to Iqbal's "conspicuous part" in the success that the Muslim League had achieved, Jinnah observes: " He had his own doubts about Sikander-Jinnah pact being carried out and he was anxious to see it translated into some tangible results without delay so as to dispel popular misapprehension about it, but unfortunately he has not lived to see that Punjab has all round made a remarkable progress and now it is beyond doubt that the Muslims stand solidly behind the Muslim League organization."

Actually the divergence of opinion on the Pact in question is again an indication of the difference of perception and approach between Iqbal and Jinnah. Iqbal was against the dominance of the feudal landlords in principle because he believed in turning the Muslim League into a mass organization as he has repeatedly emphasized in his letters.

Jinnah, on the other hand, was looking for the appropriate time to do so and was prepared, in the meanwhile, to take advantage of any compromise formula which he could evolve with the feudals who enjoyed power and influence in Punjab. Looking at it form this point of view the Sikander-Jinnah Pact was a tactical move, on Jinnah's part, to tide over the situation created by the overwhelming success of the Unionist Party in the Punjab election of 1936 in which the Muslim League secured no more than two seats.

The situation started changing after the Lahore Resolution which adopted a scheme for the division of the Subcontinent. Iqbal's vision when translated into a policy objective of the Muslim League inspired and enthused the entire Muslim nation and the Pakistan movement became a mass movement.

Finally the Unionist party was wiped out and the Muslim League swept the polls in the 1946 election in the Punjab as well as in the Muslim majority areas and Pakistan became a distinct possibility. To sum up, it was the interaction of Iqbal and Jinnah, the visionary and the practical politician, which was responsible for the creation of Pakistan·at the leadership level.

IQBAL FINDS A SAVIOUR IN JINNAH

The year 1930 was a great landmark in the history of Muslim India. A definite goal-the establishment of a sovereign state _ had been clearly defined and clarified. It was now possible to channelies their energies on constructive lines. Uptil now their various movements had been rather wayward or unrealistic or without a clear goal. The only exception was Syed Ahmed Khan's Aligarh Movement and the achievement and retaining of separate electorates in the teeth of Hindu and British opposition. This movement was sure and steady, linking up with Iqbal's 1930 Allahabad address. But in the first half of the nineteenth century the Wahabi struggle, first against the Sikhs and then against the British, was not properly organized. In principle it was in accordance with the Quranic ideology.

The Wahabi leaders rightly believed that no Muslim can be a Muslim under a non-Muslim role, be it Sikhs, Hindus or British. He must have an Islamic state of his own. But not being well planned, the movement suffered defeat at Balakot in 1831 at the hands of the Sikhs, and Syed Ahmed Shaheed of Bareilly and Islamil Shaeed of the house of Shah Waliullah were killed. Later the Wahabis were ruthlessly eliminated by the British. Thus this attempt at freedom failed. Then the First War of Independence in 1857 with Bahadur Shah Zafar, the last Mughal Emperor, as the rallying point for the revival of the Mughal Empire, was again brutally crushed. It was at this stage that Syed Ahmed Khan had realised that neither could the desirable. He also realised that an armed struggle could not overthrow the British. People had to be awakened and prepared for a struggle in the future, armed or otherwise. Next came the Balkan Wars and the agitational politics of the younger leadership. This reached its climax in the post-World War I years in the form of Khilafat Movement. Its aims and objects were unrealistic and methods doomed to failure, the result was frustration and hopelessness. However in 1930 the Muslims entered an new phase.

Iqbal had defined the goal, but being essentially a thinker and a theorist, he felt incapable of playing a practical role in its achievement, He realised his potentials and his limitations. Such is the stuff that great men are made of. So he watched an studied the personalities around. His man must not only be sincerely convinced of the "Pakistan Idea", but had to be of high intellectual and moral courage to face fierce opposition and to be able to swim against the tide of the popular fashionable concepts and institutions of the West. It is easy to be popular, it is not easy to be a leader. Iqbal knew that his objective was an uphill task. There was going to be a sever battle of ideologies between his Islamic national group and western national group, be they Hindus, British and even Muslims. No small man could cope with what lay ahead. Even to preserve the separate electorates had been no mean task.

It had been opposed tooth and nail. The issue had been debated again in the Round Table Conferences in London after the virtual failure of the Simon Commission. Iqbal attended the Second Round Table Conference (September 1931-December 1931) as a member of the Minorities Committee. The discussion came to no conclusion. He faced opposition from Mr. Gandhi and other Hindu leaders, as well as the British. Iqbal's comments on it were "..... the discussion at the Round Table Conference of the Communal question has demonstrated, more than ever, the essential disparity between the two great cultural units of India, yet the Prime Minister of England apparently refuses to see that the problem of India is international and not national. Obviously he does not see that the model of British democracy cannot be of any use in a land of many nations" This failure resulted in the British offer of what is known as the Communal Award in August 1932. Even this communal Award which did not fully concede all Muslim demands was opposed by the Hindus in the discussions on it in the Central Legislative Assemble in India. Later in 1934, 19 of June, commenting on the resolution of Congress Working Committee on the Communal Award, he said: "The Congress Working Committee has tried by the resolution to hide its inner communalism, but in the very act of doing so has unveiled its designs to such an extent that no Muslim will fail to see through this game. At this critical juncture I would advise the Muslims of India to stand boldly by the Communal Award even though it does not concede all their demands. This is the only course they can adopt as a practical people." Thus the struggle for Muslim representation continued.

It was during this period that Iqbal had his momentous meetings with Jinnah in England where both had gone in connection with the Round Table Conferences. Iqbal got Jinnah interested in his objectives, declared by him in 1930 and his world-view of humanly destiny, establishment of Pakistan being only a stepping-stone towards it And then a keen observer that he was Iqbal discovered in Jinnah the man he was looking for. He expressed this discovery in his letter to Jinnah on the 21 of June, 1937. "I know you are a busy man; but I do hope you won't mind my writing to you so often, as you are the only Muslim in India today to whom the community has a right to look up for safe guidance through the storm which is coming to the North-West India, and perhaps to the whole of India." Earlier on the 28 May, 1937, he had said: "Muslim India hopes that at this critical juncture your genius will discover some way out of our present difficulties." And how right he was in his choice. Thus was the great giant among Indian politicians converted to Islamic nationalism and Quranic ideology.

As far as the evolution of the Pakistan Idea is concerned Jinnah's participation begins only during these years. Until this time, ideologically speaking, Iqbal and Jinnah were in the opposite camps. Jinnah all these years had been imbued with western concepts like Iqbal himself in his young days. But the potential barbarism and danger of territorial nationalism had dawned upon him early in life. He had, thrown overboard those western gods, and had been preparing his nation for its rightful role. If Jinnah had also been converted earlier, the impact of his personality and leadership would have helped the movement to gain momentum and given more power and effect for the ideas to sink in.

But as Hector Bolitho puts it, he "was not yet sixteen when he sailed across the Arabian Sea towards the western world... when the first generation of Aligarh students was already helping Muslims towards a larger life and freedom of heart, Jinnah was still tramping between Lincoln's Inn, the British Museum and his lodgings in Russel Road," Further on he says: "If Muhammad Ali Jinnah had gone to Aligarh in 1892, instead of venturing across the seas to England and Lincoln's Inn, his belief in the parting of the Muslims and Hindus might have developed much earlier." These remarks are very apt. It is a pity that the major part of his political life he wasted in bringing about Hindu-Muslim unity, so much so, that he was given the title of 'Ambassador of Hindu-Muslim Unity'.

Right up to 1930 he continued to make these untiring efforts, putting his full energies, time and money into it. His membership of the Muslim League in 1913 was subordinate to the National Congress in accordance with his belief in western territorial nationalism; he was the architect of the Lucknow Pact in 1916 between the League and the Congress; his efforts for the revision of Nehru Report in 1928 was yet another attempt. These are the noteworthy instances, actually every moment of his life was devoted to this idea.

It was during the Round Table Conferences that he received the "shock of his life: on the attitude of the Hindu leaders. The intensity of the shock was of such magnitude that in disgust he decided to stay back in England in a self imposed exile. Very unhappy and wondering how the tangle of "India for Indians" could be solved. His political career upto now had set a high standard in policies, recognised by friend and foe. Sarojini Naidu says: ".... he commands unanimous respect and esteem by his personal dignity of character and his fearless and vigilant championship of Indian rights and demands. Further on she adds:

"... true criterion of his greatness...lies in a lofty singleness and sincerity of purpose and the lasting charm of a character animated by a brave conception of duty and austere and lovely code of private honour and public integrity... by the rare significance of his patriotic service, that he holds today his unique place in the front rank of our national leaders."

Right from his boyhood his dictum was "stand up from the dust so that your clothes are unspoiled and your hands clean for the tasks that fall to them." Even an unsympathetic writer Lal Bahadur gives glowing account of his "feeling for common welfare" and "liberalism". The "Jinnah Hall in Bombay, built by the spontaneous response of the citizens of that city, still stands as a monument of his fearlessness and boldness.

Lord Chelmsford said of him, "Jinnah is a very clever man, and it is of course an outrage that such a man should have no chance of running the affairs of his own country." Yes. This was the man Iqbal was looking for As mentioned earlier Iqbal's meetings with him and letters to him brought about a complete transformation in his world-view.

Jinnah admits this in his foreword to "Letters from Iqbal to Jinnah". He says "I think these letters are of very great historical importance, particularly those which explain his views in clear and unambiguous terms on the political future of Muslim India. His views were substantially in consonance with my own and had finally led me to the same conclusions as a result of careful examination and study of the constitutional problems facing India, and found expression in due course in the united will of Muslim India as adumberated in the Lahore resolution of the All India Muslim League, popularly known as the 'Pakistan Resolutions', passed on 23 march, 1940."

In the various letters Iqbal repeats the need for what later materialized in the Lahore Resolution. On the 20 March 1937 he wrote "... you must restate as clearly as possible the political objective of the Indian Muslims as a distinct political unit in the country." On 28 May 1937 he wrote: "... the enforcement and development of the Shariat of Islam is impossible in this county without a free Muslim state or states." In the same letter he explained" ...it is necessary to redistribute the country and to provide on or more Muslim States with absolute majorities. Don't your think the time for such a demand has already arrived?" On 21 June 1937 he questioned "Why should not the Muslims of North-West India and Bengal be considered as nations entitled to self determination just as other nations in India and outside India are?"

Thus was achieved complete consonance in ideas and objects between Iqbal and Jinnah. From now onwards Jinnah worked with the same sincerity, integrity, boldness and singlemindedness. To disagree with him is one thing, but no one has been able to deny these qualities in him, so unusual in the generally accepted Machiavellian politics.

The decade of the thirties was very important. The announcement of the 1935 act brought matters to a head. It created more problems for Muslim India by depriving Punjab and Bengal of their Muslim majorities and establishing a perpetual Hindu majority in the Central Federal Scheme. The time was now to act. Thus Jinnah returned to India from England, basically on the pursuasion of Iqbal on October 24, 1935.

These were very difficult days, Jinnah saw on his return that even in Muslim majority areas-Bengal, Punjab, Sind and NWFP-parties had been formed by Muslim upper and middle classes that did not cooperate with the Muslim League. There was Krishak Proja Party of Fazalul Haq in Bengal, Unionist Party of Fazl-e-Hussain in the Punjab, Abdullah Haroon in Sind, and the Congress forces in NWFP under Khan Abdul Ghaffar Khan and his brother Dr. Khan. "But in the midst of all this darkness there shone a flickering light in Lahore: he was the only consolation of Jinnah." Of Course this light was Iqbal.

At this stage it was felt necessary to form the Central Parliamentary Board of the all India Muslim League with its provincial branches to rally round the Muslim opinion to contest the approaching elections under the India Act of 1935. This was the first step of its kind. The first meeting of the Parliamentary Board was held in June 1936. Jinnah received the following advise from Iqbal: Indirect election to the Central Assembly has made it absolutely essential that Muslim representatives returned to the Provincial Assemblies should be found by an all-India Muslim Policy and programme so that they should return to the Central assembly only those Muslims who would be pledged to support the specific Muslim questions connected with the central subjects and arising out of their positions as the second great nation of India."

It was on the basis of this policy and programme that when Jawaharlal Nehru declared in Calcutta that the parties that mattered in India were the Congress and the British, Jinnah retorted: "There is a third party, namely, the Muslims." The battle was now on. The Congress tried to enlist the Muslim masses, for it got panicky at the programme and success of the Muslim League. The All India Muslim League claimed to be the representative party of Muslim India not as on national organization against another. As such its thorough reorganization was also essential.

Thus Iqbal wrote to Jinnah on 20 March, 1937,:..... we must not ignore the fact that the whole future of Islam as a moral and political force in Asia rests very largely on a complete organisation of Indian Muslim." Again on 28 May 1937 he rote: " The league will have to finally decide whether it will remain a body representing the upper classes of Indian Muslims or Muslim masses who have so far, for good reason, taken no interest in it." Thus in October 1937 the League held its session in Lucknow. This was the "first stage in the reorganization of the Muslim League on a popular basis..." Analysing the political situation he declared with great confidence and hope that.

"The all-India Muslim League has now come to live and play its just part in the world of Indian politics and the sooner it is realised and reckoned with the better it will be for all concerned." Iqbal had been planning all along for this kind of a challenge. His objective was being realized. Lucknow Sessions initiated among Muslims a spirit of self-reliance and independence. In the words of Jinnah himself; " The Lucknow Sessions furnished an unmistakable evidence of the popularity that League commanded among Muslims of all groups and ranks." This Jinnah was able to write in reply to Gandhi's letter on the 3 March, 1938. "We have reached a stage when no doubt should be left that you recognize the All-India Muslim League as the one authoritative organization of Muslims of India and, on the other hand, you represent the Congress and other Hindus throughout the country."

These months and dates are significant because Iqbal was ill and dying, but he knew that this goal was safe in the best of possible hands. Till the last moments of his life his gaze was fixed on the human destiny and the human beings for whom he felt so deeply. In his New Year message broadcast from the Lahore station of All India Radio on the 1 January, 1938 he spoke thus: "Only one unity is dependable and that unity is the brotherhood of man, which is above race, nationality, colour or language. So long as this so-called democracy, this accursed nationalism and this degraded imperialism are not shattered, so long as men do not demonstrate by their actions that they believe that the whole world is the family of God, so long as distinctions of race, colour and geographical nationalities are not wiped out completely, they will never be able to lead a happy and contented life and the beautiful ideals of liberty, equality and fraternity will never materialize. He took up cudgels against the statement of Maulana Hussain Ahmed Madani on "Islam & Nationalism" published in "Ehsan" on the 9 of March 1938, about a month before his death on the 21 April. The Maulana had said that "nations are formed by lands." III and bedridden he gave a befitting reply. However the role of the Maulanas will be treated in a separate chapter.

Iqbal's death was a great loss. Jinnah's message ran as follows: "To me he was a friend, guide and philosopher and during the darkest moments through which the Muslim League had to go he stood like a rock, and never flinched one single moment."

Iqbal and Jinnah had made a beautiful team together. Their mutual confidence and admiration was a tremendous source of inspiration to the Muslim messes. While Iqbal had been lovingly acclaimed as the national poet of Muslim India, Jinnah was now their beloved "Quaid-e-Azam". (The Great Leader) This universal recognition of Jinnah as the symbol of Muslim nationalism and the development of the League as an organisation that could not be exploited by anybody, successfully led the nation to the historical

Lahore Session of 1940, on the 22 of March, though the Unionists under Sikandar Hayat Khan, the Chief Minister of the Punjab, created all kinds of obstacles by disrupting and killing the Khaksars a few days earlier. At the Session, Jinnah declared. "The problem in India is not of an inter-communal but manifestly of an international character and it must be treated as such.... This misconception of Indian nation has gone far beyond the limits and is the cause of most of our troubles and will lead India to destruction if we fail to revise our notions in time.

The Hindus and Muslims belong to two different religious philosophies, social customs literature. They neither intermarry nor inter-dine, and indeed, they belong to tow different civilizations which are based on conflicting ideas and conceptions. Their outlook on life and of life are different. It is quite clear that Hindus and Muslims derive their inspiration from different sources of history. They have different epics and different episodes. Very often the hero of one is a foe of the other, and like-wise, their victories and defeats overlap. To yoke together two such nations under a single state, one as a numerical minority and the other as majority, must lead to growing discontent and final destruction of any fabric that may be so built up for the government of such a state.

On the next day, 23 March, the following resolution was passed. "Resolved that it is the considered view of this session of the All-India Muslim League that no constitutional plan would be workable in this country or acceptable to Muslims unless it is designed on the following basic principle, namely, that geographically contiguous units are demarcated into regions which should be so constituted, with such territorial readjustments as may be necessary that the areas in which the Muslims are numerically in a majority as in the North-Western and Eastern zones of India should be grouped to constitute "Independent States" in which the constituent units shall be autonomous and sovereign."

Iqbal's plans were now given a form an a shape and became the manifesto of the All-India Muslim League. Iqbal knew that only Jinnah could do it, and he had done it. Jinnah himself said to Matlub Hussain Sayyid, "Iqbal is no more amongst us, but had he been alive he would have been happy to know that we did exactly what he wanted us to do." Following is the complete test of the Lahore Resolution (Late called Pakistan Resolution). Text of the Pakistan resolution passed at the twenty-seventh annual session of the all-India Muslim league, Lahore, 24 march, 1940:

1. While approving and endorsing the action taken by the Council and the Working Committee of the All-India Muslim League, as indicated in their resolutions dated the 27 of August, 17 & 18 September, 1940 on the constitutional issue, this Session of the All-India Muslim league emphatically reiterates that the scheme of federation embodied in the Government of India Act, 1935, is totally unsuited to, and unworkable in the peculiar conditions of this country and is altogether unacceptable to Muslim India.
2. If further records its emphatic view that while the declaration dated the 18 of October, 1939 made by the Viceroy on behalf on His Majesty's Government is reassuring in so far as it declares that the policy and plan on which the Government of India Act, 1935, is based will be reconsidered in consultation with the various parties, interests and communities in India, Muslim India will not be satisfied unless the whole constitutional plan is reconsidered de novo and that no revised plan would be acceptable to the Muslims unless it is frame with their approval and consent.
3. Resolved that it is the considered view of the Session of the All-India Muslim League that no constitutional plan would be workable in this country or acceptable to the Muslims unless it is designed on the following basic principles, *viz.*

That geographical contiguous units are demarcated into regions which should be so constituted, with such territorial re-adjustments as may be necessary that the areas in which the Muslims are numerically in majority as in the North Western and Eastern Zones of India should be grouped to constitute "Independent State" in which the constituent units should be autonomous and sovereign.

That adequate, effective and mandatory safeguards should be specifically provided in the constitution for minorities in these units and in the regions for the protection of their religious, cultural, economic, political, administrative and other rights and interests in consultation with them and in other parts of India where the Musalmans are in a minority adequate, effective and mandatory safeguards shall be specifically provided in the constitution for them and other minorities for the protection of their religious, cultural, political, administrative and other rights and interests in consultation with them.

This Session further authorities the Working committee to frame a scheme of constitution in accordance with these basic principles, providing for the assumption finally by the respective regions of all powers, customs and such other matters an may be necessary.

JINNAH'S ADMIRATION AND RESPECT FOR ALLAMA IQBAL

The Quaid-i-Azam Muhammad Ali Jinnah had tremendous respect and admiration for Allama Dr. Muhammad Iqbal and he was an ardent admirer of the power of his inspirational poetry. He often read English translations of his Urdu poems and welcomed English translations of his Urdu poems which he recited in hugely attended public meetings under the aegis of the Muslim League and usually presided over by Jinnah as the Muslim League chief.

The high esteem and deep personal regard in which Jinnah held Allama Iqbal was amply reflected in the moving tribute Jinnah paid to Allama Iqbal on his sad death in April 1938. The Quaid-i-Azam said: "Iqbal was a remarkable poet of worldwide fame and his work will live forever. His services to his country and the Muslims are so numerous that his record can be compared with that of the greatest Indian that ever lived. He was the staunchest and the most loyal champion of the policy and programme of the All India Muslim League. To me he was a friend, guide and philosopher and during the darkest moments through which the Muslim League had to go, he stood like a rock and never flinched one single moment."

On the last night of the historic All India Muslim League session in Lahore on March 23, when more than 100,000 representatives of the Muslims of India from every part of the country were gathered in the Minto Park to chart their political destiny and the Pakistan Resolution demanding a Muslim-majority nation state comprising all the Muslim majority areas of the Subcontinent was passed with thunderous applause, the Quaid-i-Azam Muhammad Ali Jinnah stood up, looked in the direction of the Mughal-built Badshahi Mosque near which is Allama Iqbal's tomb and said in resonant words that Iqbal's soul in the Heavens would be pleased that the Muslim League had now accepted as its political goal the course of action he had spelled out in 1930 in his address to the historic All India Muslim League session held at Allahabad. There was a significant difference between the two events. The Muslim League's Allahabad session in 1930 was attended by a few hundred Muslim representatives. But the Muslim League's history-making session in Lahore on March 23, 1940, was attended by more than 100,000 Muslim representatives—making it a turning point in the Sub-continent's Muslim history, paving the ground for the eventual establishment of Pakistan in 1947—Iqbal's dream state of 1930. It is a historical fact that Iqbal's poetry moved the Muslim masses in the Pakistan Movement as much as Jinnah's superb leadership.

At the time when Allama Iqbal presided over the Muslim League session in Allahabad and issued a clarion call for establishing a nation-state comprising the Muslim majority areas of the Subcontinent, Jinnah was away in London, attending a Round Table Conference of Indian leaders convened by the British Prime Minister to help settle the constitutional problem of the Indian Subcontinent. Allama Iqbal wrote a detailed letter to the Quaid in London about the demand for a Muslim nation state in the Subcontinent made in the Muslim League's Allahabad session. It was in London in 1931 during the Second Round Table Conference that Jinnah got to know Allama Iqbal more closely and developed an immense liking for his sincerity and his tireless devotion to the Muslim cause in the Subcontinent. Allama Iqbal visited Jinnah in his Law Chamber in London near Lincoln's Inn. I learnt from Jinnah's chauffeur during his London years Bradbury that Jinnah invited Allama Iqbal to dinner in his posh home in Hampstead. As a host Jinnah took personal interest in the dinner arrangement, asking the butler to get halal meat for every meat dish.

In these days halal meat shops were few in London and Muslims at times ate kosher meat. Islamic scholars permitted Muslims to eat Jewish Kosher meat if halal meat shops were not available. In the postprandial hours, Jinnah and Allama Iqbal talked at length about the Muslims' political future in the Subcontinent and the Round Table Conference (RTC).

According to Bradbury, Allama Iqbal appealed to Jinnah to return to India after the RTC and take up the leadership of the Muslim League and pursue the goal of establishing a Muslim-majority state in North West India.

Allama Iqbal explained to Jinnah the dangers looming up for Muslims in an India subjected to Hindu majority rule. Jinnah at that time wanted the Hindus and the Muslims to struggle unitedly for India's independence instead of splitting India into separate states on communal basis. Jinnah was at one time called the "Ambassador of Hindu Muslim Unity" by the Congress leaders.

But the insulting behaviour of the Congress leaders towards him in the Nagpur session of the Congress forced him to resign from the Congress. This was the parting of the ways for Jinnah and he became more apprehensive than ever before that Muslims would not be treated justly under Hindu majority rule. Allama Iqbal gave more substance to Jinnah's fears. Earlier, Allama Iqbal himself was an advocate of Hindu Muslim unity but later on Congress' injustices to Muslims had changed Iqbal's perceptions.

In the Third Round Table Conference in London in 1932, to which neither Gandhi nor Jinnah was invited, Allama Iqbal played the most dynamic and statesman-like role, advocating constitutional safeguards for the Muslims in India. Allama Iqbal had a number of meetings with Jinnah during which he thoroughly briefed Jinnah in his Hampstead home on the discussions and bickerings in the Third Round Table Conference. Thus was built up the rapport of trust and confidence between Jinnah and Iqbal which enabled Allama Iqbal to fully persuade Jinnah to espouse the Two-Nation Theory and undertake with all his might and conviction the mission of establishing a Muslim Majority state in the Subcontinent.

Although Allama Iqbal had kept his date with his Maker in 1938, the first salvo in the battle for achieving Pakistan was fired in 1940 in the Lahore session of the All India Muslim League under Jinnah's exemplary leadership. Seven years later, the mission of getting the Muslims of India, a nation state of their own in the Subcontinent under the name of Pakistan was fully accomplished with Jinnah as the Head of the new state, as was envisioned by Allama Iqbal.

While watching the attitude of the delegates, especially those of the Congress in the Third Round Table Conference in London, Allama Iqbal felt more than convinced that in an Indian Federation, under Hindu majority rule, the Muslim minority might be treated unfairly and unjustly and the Hindu rulers might throw to the constitutional safeguard provided for the Muslims in the British dispensation. Allama Iqbal addressed during the Third RTC in 1932, a meeting of the London National League which was attended by some British members of Parliament, foreign diplomats and media persons.

In this meeting Allama Iqbal forcefully projected the Muslim viewpoint. He pleaded that the communal issue in India should be settled first before ushering in constitutional reforms on a countrywide basis. Allama Iqbal advocated maximum provincial autonomy so the Muslims in Muslim-majority provinces may effectively safeguard their religion, traditions and cultural heritage. He ably explained that under a Hindu dominated central Government in a federal setup, Muslims could feel endangered by the steamroller of Hindu majority rule. In December 1933, after the Third RTC had concluded in London and the Indian delegates returned to India, Pandit Jawaharlal Nehru issued a statement containing his unjust fulminations against the Muslim delegates in the Third RTC in London. The Muslim delegates who attended the Third RTC in London were exceedingly annoyed by Nehru's attacks on them questioning their patriotism and accusing them of hurting India's struggle for independence from alien rule. The

Muslim leaders urged Allama Iqbal to blast Nehru with a powerful rejoinder. Accordingly, Allama Iqbal issued a hard-hitting statement. Allama Iqbal said: "I must put a straight question to pundit Jawaharlal Nehru. How is India's problem to be solved if the majority community will neither concede the minimum safeguards necessary for the protecting of a minority of 80 million people nor accept the awards of a third party but continue to talk of nationalism which works out only to its won benefit"?

The Congress-dominated newspapers took up the cudgel to defend Nehru vis-a-vis Iqbal but the great poet remained undeterred and issued more statements blasting the overbearing attitude of the Hindu delegates in the RTC. In Jinnah, Iqbal had found the most suitable leader to lead the Muslims of India. Three months before his death in 1938, Iqbal had appealed to Muslims to strengthen Jinnah's hands; they should join the Muslims League. Iqbal called for a united front of India's Muslims against the hostility of Hindus as well as the English, "Without it our demands are not going to be accepted. These demands relate to our national existence," Dr. Iqbal said. Allama Iqbal gave warnings to the Muslims of perilous times ahead and the dire need for Muslims' national unity under the Muslim League and its president, Jinnah. When a book containing the correspondence between Jinnah and Iqbal was published in 1944, Jinnah said in his introduction that before Iqbal's death in 1938 he had agreed with him regarding the establishment of a state for the Muslims in the Subcontinent and this found full expression in the Lahore Resolution of March 1940 popularly known as the Pakistan Resolution.

Among the Muslim leaders of that time in India, Allama Iqbal possessed vast academic honours. He had a Master's degree from the Punjab University, a BA from Cambridge, Bar-at law from UK, a doctorate from the Munich University in Germany and remarkable command over English, Persian, Arabic, Urdu and knowledge of French and German. He was knighted by the British Government for his services to education in India. Literary organisations in many countries bestowed a great many honours on Allama Iqbal. Cambridge has a special Chair devoted to his thought, writings and poetry.

Some Stray Thoughts

Indians, particularly Hindus, are generally thought to be not only superstitious but also great believers in astrology. They also observe auspicious and inauspicious period during 24 hours of a day before starting a work or embarking on a journey. Looking at the great controversy surrounding L. K. Advani's recent visit to Pakistan and the statement he made about Pakistan's founder Muhammad Ali Jinnah as a secularist while paying homage to Jinnah at his mausoleum in Karachi, one is inclined to believe that Advani apparently did not check with the Rahukalam, Gulikakalam and Yamagandakalam either before leaving India or before visiting Jinnah's mausoleum where he made that disastrous statement.

In retrospect, Advani could only say like Julius Caesar, "What I have said I have said. So be it." It is important to remember the saying that "every saint has a past and sinner a future." Likewise, in the present day Indian political world, we can say, "every secularist has a communal past and every communalist has a secular future." Jinnah always thought that Gandhi, Nehru were communal. Why? Even the Indian National Congress dominated by Hindus was also communal! Look at the way socialists are joining hands with BJP under the NDA umbrella. Similarly, Shiva Sena politicians joining Congress. Hence, it is not surprising if Advani found the virtue of secularism in Jinnah.

Indeed, Muhammad Ali Jinnah was a man who stood for democracy, fairness, justice and secularism. That was when he joined the Congress party. Otherwise, he would not have drafted 1916 Lucknow Pact that brought the Congress and Muslim League together on a joint platform demanding independence after World War I. Jinnah wanted a secular Pakistan with Muslim majority and a secular India with a Muslim minority. Alas, while India remained secular with Muslim minority, Jinnah's Pakistan remained a communal, theocratic country with Hindu minority. Call it an irony or a paradox.

Advani's remarks about Jinnah being a secular person was based on Jinnah's 11th August 1947 speech before Pakistan's Constituent Assembly wherein he had urged for treating the minorities in Pakistan with tolerance and religious freedom. In fact, Pakistan became a fundamentalist Islamic State only after Jinnah passed away in 1948, soon after the creation of Pakistan.

Given the complex and cosmopolitan personality of Jinnah, it is rather difficult to understand how a secular democrat, who was never serious about his religion in personal life, could become the profounder of the two - nation theory seeking a homeland for Muslims. Surprisingly, this new homeland could not include all the Muslims of the greater India. In fact, more Muslims were left behind in India than found in the new country Pakistan. One more example of an historical paradox.

The question is, was Jinnah successful in providing an exclusive homeland for all the Indian Muslims by creating Pakistan? The answer, of course, is no. The division only left the Hindu—Muslim problem of the sub - continent unresolved. If that is so, could it not have been better for both Hindus and Muslims to have continued to live with this problem without dividing the country? In fact, with one-fourth population of the undivided country, Muslims would have had not only greater representation but also a greater say in the administration of undivided India.

Be that as it may, there is an attempt to lay the blame for partition as much on Jinnah as on Nehru by some Hindutva politicians for many reasons. One important reason was that in the aftermath of the 1937 election, which Congress had won with a thumping majority, Jinnah had hoped that Nehru might generously respond to the request made by the Muslim League to form coalition Governments in large provinces, particularly United Province (now Uttar Pradesh), because there was an electoral understanding between the Congress and Muslim League. But Nehru rejected all coalition attempts by Muslim League.

Sheikh Abdullah, in his book Flames of the Chinar says, "despite the understanding when the Congress won a landslide victory, it went back on its undertaking and announced certain pre - conditions to forming a coalition with the League. These preconditions were not acceptable to Muslim League. This led to renewed friction between Hindus and Muslims. When the Congress Ministry resigned in 1939, the Muslim League promptly formed Governments in Bengal, Sindh and Assam."

Probably, the seeds of partition were sown at this juncture in 1939. Nehru might have underestimated the Muslim League's political power and influence with the British rulers in the face of overwhelming victory of Congress in that 1937 election. Nehru might have also failed to read Jinnah's mind. What followed proves the point.

One might argue that Nehru was, in fact, right in not considering the overtures from the Muslim League for two reasons. One, when Congress had absolute majority to form the Government, why a coalition? Two, if Muslim League's overtures were accepted and coalition Government formed, the Congress would only be helping Muslim League to strengthen itself further. The Congress could do this only at its own peril.

Need a present day example? Well, look at the Congress - JD (S) coalition in Karnataka. JD (S) is getting stronger by the day while Congress is getting weaker! When Jinnah became the President of Muslim League after 1934, he was only a Muslim nationalist and had not yet become a Muslim communalist. Probably, after 1937 experience, he became a Muslim communalist propounding a two - nation theory and demanding a separate country for Muslims. Whatever it is, L.K. Advani, by his reappraisal of Jinnah's ideas of nationalism, secularism and communalism, has once again opened up the debate to find out who the real Jinnah was and who was responsible for making him what he was — creator of Pakistan.

Jinnah, born in Karachi to a liberal Muslim family, studied in London and joined the Indian National Congress. He helped the grand old man of Congress Dadabhai Naoroji win his first seat in the House of Commons. Jinnah had the greatest respect for the then Congress President Gopalakrishna Gokhale and had even defended him in a case relating to freedom struggle and, of course, had won. As we all know, Gokhale was Gandhiji's political Guru. While in Congress, Jinnah was such a staunch nationalist that religion did not vitiate his vision for India's freedom.

In Bombay, there stands even today inside the compound of the Indian National Congress building, an auditorium known as P.J. Hall which was originally known as, "People's Jinnah Memorial

Hall". It was a tribute to young Jinnah's nationalist fervour and determination to achieve what he wanted to achieve— abort an attempt by the sycophants of the then Governor of Bombay, Lord Willingdon, a Tory despot, on the eve of his departure.

History says that on Dec. 11, 1918, Jinnah rallied more than 300 youthful Congress supporters and fearlessly shouted down the Sheriff of Bombay who tried to convene that meeting. The meeting was called off. So the P. J. Hall today commemorates that event which took place under the leadership of Jinnah. Now, let me reproduce here what Sheikh Abdullah, the Lion of Kashmir, and M. C. Chagla, the jurist, judge, diplomat, Central Cabinet Minister and above all one who worked in the legal chambers of Jinnah as his junior, thought of Jinnah. This might give an insight into the personality of Jinnah and help everyone, opposing or supporting L. K. Advani, to do a bit of rethink on their individual opinions.

Sheikh Abdullah: "While our movement was gaining popularity in Kashmir, events of far - reaching importance were taking place in the country (1935). In India, Muhammad Ali Jinnah, after a long spell of silence, was challenging the representative status of the Congress. Jinnah had a very high opinion of himself and wanted to carve an eminent place for himself at the national-level.

The entire sub - continent had to suffer the consequences of his inflated ego. The Congress and the Muslim League were spelling out their politics regarding the State. Since the Congress viewpoint conformed with our ideology we were, naturally, drawn towards it. In the same year (1935), Jinnah visited Kashmir for the first time. The Muslim Conference organised a reception in his honour.

Replying to the address of welcome, Jinnah said that Muslims, being the majority in the State, must be fair in their treatment of the minorities. A certain group of loyalists, however, rejected the idea because the unity of the people was considered hazardous for the autocratic rule of a Hindu Maharaja.

The Cripps Mission was doomed to fail. The Congress party rejected its proposals and launched the 'Quit India' movement in 1942. Rejection of the Cripps proposals was in my view, not in the best interest of the country. M. A. Jinnah and the Muslim League had already accepted them. Had the Congress party accepted them as well, the partition of the country might have been avoided. In 1935, when Muhammad Ali Jinnah visited Kashmir, he had already acquired a national reputation. In addition to his political sagacity, he was generally admired for his legal acumen. His sister, Fatima, accompanied him wherever he went. Mirza Mohammed Afzal Beg and I called on him with a request to take a case on behalf of a friend.

This was our first meeting. Since Eid-e-Miladun Nabi, the Prophet's birthday, was to be commemorated at a meeting held in the Shahi Masjid, we invited Jinnah to preside over it. He spoke in English and exhorted the Muslims, as the majority community, to respect the sentiments of the non - Muslims. We strove to save Kashmir from the inevitable fallout of the two-nation theory. Even Muhammad Ali Jinnah, chief torchbearer of the two - nation theory, was aware of the dangers of this campaign of hatred.

The day after Pakistan came into existence, he announced that there would be no distinction between Muslims and non - Muslims. Obviously, Jinnah had to accept the truism that mutual hatred cannot form the basis for national reconstruction." Probably, Advani had all this in his mind when he spoke at Jinnah's mausoleum at Karachi in Pakistan. Jinnah about Muslims in Indian States: "They will look after themselves. I am not interested in their fate".

Advani speak... At Jinnah's mausoleum in Karachi on June 4, 2005: "His August 11, 1947 address is a forceful espousal of a secular State in which, every citizen would be free to practice his own religion. My respectful homage to this great man".

On June 5, 2005: "Partition can not be undone, but some of the follies of partition can be undone and they must be undone."

Among those who knew Muhammad Ali Jinnah, not only from close quarters but also for a considerable length of time, can be counted M. C. Chagla (1900-1981), Jurist, Judge, Diplomat, who had represented India in the United Nations, arguing on Kashmir, and of course, Central Cabinet Minister. He was Central Education Minister and later External Affairs Minister as well.

Chagla had known Jinnah in Bombay and had come into close contact with him during his days of student activities. Jinnah was the President of the Muslim Students Union with which Chagla was associated. Jinnah used to often address the students in his capacity as the President. According to Chagla, "His (Jinnah's) theme always was that the students should work for inter - communal unity without which we would not be able to shake off the British yoke and attain freedom for our country".

Chagla next saw Jinnah in London where a Joint Select Committee, appointed by the British Parliament to consider the Government of India Bill dealing in the Indian Constitution, was going on. Before Chagla left for England, Jinnah had promised to take him in his chambers.

Here is what Chagla says about Jinnah: "What attracted me to Jinnah was the force of his personality and more than that his sterling nationalism and patriotism. If at that time anyone had told me that Jinnah would one day be responsible for the partition of our country I would have thought him mad. I joined his chamber and remained with him for about six years".

Here is another face of the same Muhammad Ali Jinnah that M. C. Chagla saw soon after: "During the first eight years or so, I hardly had any practice at the Bar. I was in dire circumstances, but do not remember in all those years Jinnah ever enquiring of me, how I managed my finances or how I fared at the Bar. I have never come across any man who had less humanity in his character than Jinnah. He was cold and unemotional, and apart from law and politics he had no other interests. I do not think he ever read a serious book in all his life. His staple food was newspapers, briefs and law books".

Well, having learnt this special character of Jinnah from his protege, it is worth remembering Jinnah once remarking about leaving the Indian Muslims to their fate following the partition. According to Chagla, Muhammad Ali Jinnah still remains an enigma. Poor Advani, not realizing this enigmatic character of Jinnah's personality, had hastened to utter platitudes landing himself in trouble. Chagla had this to say in the book Roses in December, an autobiography, about this enigmatic man who was capable of blowing hot and cold and who could at one time be a nationalist and at another time a communalist:

"So long as Jinnah remained a nationalist and Muslim League continued the old policy, I remained with Jinnah and also with the League. But, as soon as Jinnah became communal minded and started his two - nation theory, I parted company both with him and with the League. The evolution of Jinnah from a national to a communal leader remains an enigma."

Here is what Jawaharlal Nehru thought of Jinnah, according to M. C. Chagla: "Jawaharlal Nehru disliked Jinnah as a man because he thought Jinnah was all arrogance and pomposity. He also described Jinnah as someone essentially uncultured and almost illiterate. He thought Jinnah's reading never extended beyond the daily newspaper and that he had not a single intelligent or enlightened idea in his head." Jinnah was dropped from the third Round Table Conference for obvious reasons. It was at this point; Jinnah decided that if he were to have a place under the sun, he would have to stand on a communal platform. So it was.

The British bureaucracy, known for its divide and rule policy, also threw in its weight, consciously or unconsciously, on Jinnah's side, says Chagla. Here is the final damning picture of Jinnah, the merciless, ruthless man that Advani was eulogizing on June 4 and 5, 2005 in Karachi. Let me quote Chagla and be done with my stray thoughts on the subject. Chagla writes: I remember once asking Jinnah: "You are fighting for Pakistan mainly in the interests of the Muslim majority States. But what happens to the Muslims in the States, particularly like Uttar Pradesh, where they are in a small minority?"

I will never forget the answer he gave me. He looked at me for a while and said: "They will look after themselves. I am not interested in their fate."

If one reads M. C. Chagla's autobiography Roses in December, it is impossible for any sane Indian to think that Muhammad Ali Jinnah is Quaid-e-Azam [A great leader — Quaid (leader), Azam (Great)]. The truth is, as one of many ironies of history, it was Gandhiji who gave Jinnah the appellation of Quaid – e - Azam. Chagla says, Jinnah gratefully and proudly accepted this appellation of honour. If Chagla could find fault with Jinnah's nationalism, Jinnah's secularism and Jinnah's division of India, small wonder, how could L. K. Advani, President of Hindutva Party like BJP find virtue in the man for the same reason? Akhanda Bharath is the dream of RSS, Vishwa Hindu Parishat and the Hindu Jagaran Manch. How could that dream be converted into a nightmare in his anxiety to be polite and courteous to his hosts in Pakistan, only Advani should explain.

Could be Advani thought, in the light of the on-going peace process between India and Pakistan, it was the right time and right place to impress upon the Pakistan Government and also people that despite the division of the country on communal lines, their great leader, Quaid-e-Azam, was in fact a secular person and hence wanted Pakistan to treat the Hindus and other minorities as equal citizens of the newly-born Muslim majority State.

Therefore, present Pakistan Government and also the people should follow the example of Quaid-e-Azam rather than that of their dictator late Zia-ul-Haq who declared Pakistan to be an Islamic State and who got removed Quaid-e-Azam's August 11, 1947 "secular" speech from school and college text books altogether. Rewriting history!

Advani might have also thought that such a remark by him might open a dialogue "about our common past for true reconciliation in the future" as the celebrated writer Prem Shankar Jha wrote in Outlook magazine and further, hopefully, in the remote future good sense will prevail both in India and Pakistan leading to an Akhanda Bharath! If this was his thinking then Advani is a great visionary unlike Nehru. Be that as it may, Chagla has given the following definition for secularism, which is worth recalling here:

"That brings me to the question of secularism. Today, secularism has been written into our Constitution in indelible lines. As a legal concept, secularism means equality before the law, and no distinction between one citizen and another as far as the application of laws is concerned. It also means equality of opportunity and a refusal to classify citizens into first class citizens and second-class citizens. But, in my opinion, secularism is much more than that. Secularism is an attitude of the mind and a quality of the heart. It is a matter of temperament, of outlook, even of feeling. A man with a secular outlook looks upon all persons as human beings pure and simple, equally estimable or precious not only in the eye of the law, but in the eye of God. You refuse to classify people according to the religious labels, which you attach to them.

You do not think of a man as a Hindu, a Muslim or a Christian, but merely as a human being. You make friends with him as a human being and you deal with him as a human being. You are not conscious of the religion he professes.

"I remember when I went to the United States as Ambassador, when I was asked at my first Press Conference whether I was a Muslim, I answered: "How is it any business of yours what my religion is? That is purely my personal affair. All that you have a right to know is that I am an Indian and proud to be an Indian. When I meet an American I do not ask him "Are you a Protestant or a Catholic or a Jew?" To me he is a citizen of the United States, and I treat him as an American. I do not understand why you take this attitude when you are dealing with the people of India."

I am sure, from what we know of Jinnah after 1937, he could not be called a secularist nor a nationalist no matter what he was mouthing before his brothers of Muslim League comprising mostly reactionary Nawabs and Zamindars as its members rather than the Muslim masses. The division of India, which was too artificial, both demographically and geographically, invited history's greatest bloodbath and migration of people across the border.

The man who delivered his famous "secular" speech on Aug. 11, 1947 did not have the responsibility to ask the Muslims of Pakistan to stop violence against Hindu minority and issue shoot – at - sight order if necessary. Jinnah did not even ask the Hindu minority not to flee the country, which was their home just a while ago, according to the former Minister and author Rafiq Zacharia who recently appeared on TV channel NDTV 24X7.

Sometimes, when you look at the twists and turns of history, you will be left wondering about ifs and buts of history in the same way Shakespeare wondered about the fate of Rome and Egypt if only the nose of Cleopatra was slightly different in shape. Sheik Abdullah, ruminating on these historical relationships between individuals and events, says that, "some believe that individuals make history, while others contend that historical forces create individuals. I believe, the reality lies somewhere between these two lines. Unless given an opportunity, individuals cannot prove themselves."

In case of Jinnah, this is very true. He was given the opportunity by the Muslim League, the British and unwittingly also by the Congress and he proved himself as the creator of Pakistan. Well, despite all those propitious circumstances, he still would have missed the opportunity of creating Pakistan if he had succeeded in England, where he had gone in 1931 to stay permanently and practice in the Privy Council. In Dec. 1931, Jinnah left India for England. Jinnah, of course, could not succeed and returned to India in 1934 only to become, to India's misfortune, the President of Muslim League. The Muslim Students Union gave him a warm welcome and in his speech Jinnah spoke of rendering some service "to my country, my motherland." In a way, Jinnah came to India, Jinnah divided the people and then Jinnah divided the country. With this, did he solve the problems of the Muslim majority States or the Muslim minority States or of all the Muslims in this subcontinent, as it existed during the pre-independence period? No. The problem persists on either side of the border.

Therefore, both politicians and statesmen should understand Jinnah as a person who spoke of secularism, freedom of religion and minority rights merely from his lips without conviction. Sadly, Advani did not understand the true nature of Jinnah for whatever reason. Chagla narrates an interesting story about Jinnah's fondness for a food item that is prohibited for Muslims which in a way reflects his liberal view of private life in contrast to his public life. Let me quote:

"Just before one O' clock Mrs. Jinnah drove up to the Town Hall in Jinnah's luxurious limousine, stepped out with a tiffin basket and coming up the steps of the Town Hall said to Jinnah: "J" — that is how she called him — "guess what I have brought for you for lunch." Jinnah answered: "How should I know?" and she replied: "I have brought you some lovely ham sandwiches." Jinnah, startled, exclaimed: "My God! What have you done? Do you want me to lose my election? Do you realise I am standing from a Muslim separate electorate seat, and if my voters were to learn that I am going to eat ham sandwiches for lunch, do you think I have a ghost of a chance of being elected?"

At this, Mrs. Jinnah's face fell. She quickly took back the tiffin basket, ran down the steps and drove away. Then Jinnah turned to me and said: "Let us go and get something to eat somewhere." We decided to go to Cornaglia's, which was a very well known restaurant in Bombay, not far from the Town Hall. We sat down, and Jinnah asked me what I would like to have. I said: "I will have some coffee." He then added, "What would you like to eat? I remarked that they had some very good pork sausages there, so Jinnah ordered two cups of coffee, a plate of pastry and a plate of pork sausages."

The story does not end here as it has yet another interesting follow-on. Be that as it may, according to Chagla, "Mrs. Jinnah was a real nationalist and kept Jinnah on the right track as long as she was alive. Mrs. Jinnah also had a sense of humour... After her death Jinnah's soul companion at home was his sister Fatima who was more communal minded and partly responsible for the transformation brought about in Jinnah subsequently... She enjoyed Jinnah's diatribes against the Hindus, and if anything, injected an extra dose of venom into them." Indeed, it is truly said that there is always a woman behind every successful man!

Tail piece: The root of the name Gandhi comes from Gandh (sandalwood) and the one who does business in sandalwood and other items related to perfumes was called, as per the practice of those days, as Gandhi — a surname derived from a person's profession. Indeed, in a way, Gandhiji spread his fragrance all over the world thus being worthy of his surname literally and also figuratively. I do not know the root of the name Jinnah!

IQBAL AND THE QUAID-I AZAM

Who could understand Allama Iqbal better than the Quaid-i Azam himself, who was his awaited "Guide of the Era"? The

Quaid-i Azam in the Introduction to Allama Iqbal's letters addressed to him, admitted that he had agreed with Allama Iqbal regarding a State for Indian Muslims before the latters death in April, 1938. The Quaid stated: *His views were substantially in consonance with my own and had finally led me to the same conclusions as a result of careful examination and study of the constitutional problems facing India and found expression in due course in the united will of Muslim India as adumbrated in the Lahore Resolution of the All-India Muslim League popularly known as the "Pakistan Resolution" passed on 23rd March, 1940.*

Furthermore, it was Allama Iqbal who called upon Quaid-i Azam Muhammad Ali Jinnah to lead the Muslims of India to their cherished goal. He preferred the Quaid to other more experienced Muslim leaders such as Sir Aga Khan, Maulana Hasrat Mohani, Nawab Muhammad Ismail Khan, Maulana Shaukat Ali, Nawab Hamid Ullah Khan of Bhopal, Sir Ali Imam, Maulvi Tameez ud-Din Khan, Maulana Abul Kalam, Allama al-Mashriqi and others. But Allama Iqbal had his own reasons. He had found his "Khizr-i Rah", the veiled guide in Quaid-i Azam Muhammad Ali Jinnah who was destined to lead the Indian branch of the Muslim *Ummah* to their goal of freedom. Allama Iqbal stated: I know you are a busy man but I do hope you won't mind my writing to you often, as you are the only Muslim in India today to whom the community has right to look up for safe guidance through the storm which is coming to North-West India, and perhaps to the whole of India. Similar sentiments were expressed by him about three months before his death. Sayyid Nazir Niazi in his book *Iqbal Ke Huzur*, has stated that the future of the Indian Muslims was being discussed and a tenor of pessimism was visible from what his friends said. At this Allama Iqbal observed:

There is only one way out. Muslim should strengthen Jinnah's hands. They should join the Muslim League. Indian question, as is now being solved, can be countered by our united front against both the Hindus and the English. Without it our demands are not going to be accepted. People say our demands smack of communalism. This is sheer propaganda. These demands relate to the defence of our national existence.

He continued: The united front can be formed under the leadership of the Muslim League. And the Muslim League can succeed only on account of Jinnah. Now none but Jinnah is capable of leading the Muslims.

Matlub ul-Hasan Sayyid stated that after the Lahore Resolution was passed on March 23, 1940, the Quaid-i Azam said to him: Iqbal is no more amongst us, but had he been alive he would have been happy to know that we did exactly what he wanted us to do.

But the matter does not end here. Allama Iqbal in his letter of March 29, 1937 to the Quaid-i Azam had said: While we are ready to cooperate with other progressive parties in the country, we must not ignore the fact that the whole future of Islam as a moral and political force in Asia rests very largely on a complete organization of Indian Muslims.

According to Allama Iqbal the future of Islam as a moral and political force not only in India but in the whole of Asia rested on the organization of the Muslims of India led by the Quaid-i Azam. The "Guide of the Era" Iqbal had envisaged in 1926, was found in the person of Muhammad Ali Jinnah. The "Guide" organized the Muslims of India under the banner of the Muslim League and offered determined resistance to both the Hindu and the English designs for a united Hindu-dominated India. Through their united efforts under the able guidance of Quaid-I Azam Muslims succeeded in dividing India into Pakistan and Bharat and achieving their independent homeland. As observed above, in Allama Iqbal's view, the organization of Indian Muslims which achieved Pakistan would also have to defend other Muslim societies in Asia. The carvan of the resurgence of Islam has to start and come out of this Valley, far off from the centre of the *ummah*. Let us see how and when, Pakistan prepares itself to shoulder this august responsibility. It is Allama Iqbal's prevision.

Muhammad Ali Jinnah in the famous Jinnah House, which Pakistan is now demanding, on Mount Pleasant Road on Malabar Hill in Mumbai. L.K. Advani was by no means the first of the adventurers who tried their skills in self-promotion by holding forth on Muhammad Ali Jinnah, professing to retrieve "the real

Jinnah" from the morass of hagiography in Pakistan and demonisation in India. Politicians, journalists and academics of varied hues participated in this sport. Amazingly, there is yet not one comprehensive collection of his writings and speeches from 1906, when he entered public life, till his death in 1948, let alone a definitive biography. If a Pakistan academic, Akbar S. Ahmad, involved in an unsavoury controversy over a film on Jinnah, likened him to Saladin *(sic)*, Stanley Wolpert, an American academic, who claimed to have toiled for more than a quarter of a century over his biography, appointed him as "Managing Director of the Tata Enterprises" *(sic)* and hailed Z.A. Bhutto as a "Sufi mystic". He could not tell M.O. Mathai and John Mathai apart. Jinnah's close friend Kanji Dwarkadas was made a "Parsi" and Sir Abdullah Haroon "a princely ruler" of Khairpur state.

Any biography, to be worth the name, must provide an intelligent explanation for Jinnah's famous speech of August 11, 1947. Wolpert's failure in this test is abject: "What was he talking about? Had he simply forgotten where he was? Had the cyclone of events so disoriented him.... ?" Disorientation would be too charitable an explanation for Wolpert's comments.

As the Advani episode revived interest in Jinnah, protagonists on both sides entered the lists. On one point Indians and Pakistanis heartily concur. Jinnah was politically born on March 23, 1940, when the Muslim League passed a resolution demanding partition of India on the basis of religion. Neither side is interested in his superb record before that. How does one evaluate a political leader whose later career and credo seem so radically different from those that marked him most of his life, with only a brief twilight period to separate the two? It is unhistoric to read the two completely apart. It is equally wrong to rewrite the record of 1906-1940 because of what ensued thereafter, all the more so if one has not cared to understand the first phase correctly.

Churchill's personality as war leader had shades of the distrusted Churchill of old; but facets of greatness emerged prominently only during the Second World War. Jinnah's secularism is not to be underestimated because he later espoused the poisonous two-nation theory; nor is his culpability, on this score, affected by the creditable record earlier. The crucial question, surely, is whatever led a man of his sterling qualities and unblemished patriotism to advocate India's partition and espouse a theory whose poison spread far and deep? The partition of India must rank in any list of 10 of the greatest tragedies in the history of man. A heavy responsibility devolves on any who brought it about.

IQBAL AND POLITICS

These thoughts crystallised at Allahabad Session (December, 1930) of the All India Muslim League, when Iqbal in the Presidential Address, forwarded the idea of a Muslim State in India: I would like to see the Punjab, North-West Frontier Provinces, Sind and Balochistan into a single State. Self-Government within the British Empire or without the British Empire. The formation of the consolidated North-West Indian Muslim State appears to be the final destiny of the Muslims, at least of the North-West India.

The seed sown, the idea began to evolve and take root. It soon assumed the shape of Muslim state or states in the western and eastern Muslim majority zones as is obvious from the following lines of Iqbal's letter, of June 21, 1937, to the Quaid-i Azam, only ten months before the former's death: A separate federation of Muslim Provinces, reformed on the lines I have suggested above, is the only course by which we can secure a peaceful India and save Muslims from the domination of Non-Muslims. Why should not the Muslims of North-West India and Bengal be considered as nations entitled to self-determination just as other nations in India and outside India are.

There are some critics of Allama Iqbal who assume that after delivering the Allahabad Address he had slept over the idea of a Muslim State. Nothing is farther from the truth. The idea remained always alive in his mind. It had naturally to mature and hence, had to take time. He was sure that the Muslims of subcontinent were going to achieve an independent homeland for themselves. On 21st March, 1932, Allama Iqbal delivered the Presidential address at Lahore at the annual session of the All-India Muslim Conference. In that address too he stressed his view regarding nationalism in India and commented on the plight of the Muslims under the circumstances prevailing in the subcontinent. Having attended the Second Round Table Conference in September, 1931 in London, he was keenly aware of the deep-seated Hindu and Sikh prejudice and unaccommodating attitude. He had observed the mind of the British Government. Hence he reiterated his apprehensions and suggested safeguards in respect of the Indian Muslims: In so far then as the fundamentals of our policy are concerned, I have got nothing fresh to offer. Regarding these I have already expressed my views in my address to the All India Muslim League. In the present address I propose, among other things, to help you, in the first place, in arriving at a correct view of the situation as it emerged from a rather hesitating behaviour of our delegation the final stages of the Round-Table Conference. In the second place, I shall try, according to my lights to show how far it is desirable to construct a fresh policy now that the Premier's announcement at the last London Conference has again necessitated a careful survey of the whole situation.

It must be kept in mind that since Maulana Muhammad Ali had died in Jan. 1931 and Quaid-i Azam had stayed behind in London, the responsibility of providing a proper lead to the Indian Muslims had fallen on him alone. He had to assume the role of a jealous guardian of his nation till Quaid-i Azam returned to the subcontinent in 1935. The League and the Muslim Conference had become the play-thing of petty leaders, who would not resign office, even after a vote of non-confidence! And, of course, they had no organization in the provinces and no influence with the masses.

During the Third Round-Table Conference, Iqbal was invited by the London National League where he addressed an audience which included among others, foreign diplomats, members of the House of Commons, Members of the House of Lords and Muslim members of the R.T.C. delegation. In that gathering he dilated upon the situation of the Indian Muslims. He explained why he wanted the communal settlement first and then the constitutional reforms. He stressed the need for provincial autonomy because autonomy gave the Muslim majority provinces some power to safeguard their rights, cultural traditions and religion. Under the central Government the Muslims were bound to lose their cultural and religious entity at the hands of the overwhelming Hindu majority. He referred to what he had said at Allahabad in 1930 and reiterated his belief that before long people were bound to come round to his viewpoint based on cogent reason.

In his dialogue with Dr. Ambedkar Allama Iqbal expressed his desire to see Indian provinces as autonomous units under the direct control of the British Government and with no central Indian Government. He envisaged autonomous Muslim Provinces in India. Under one Indian union he feared for Muslims, who would suffer in many respects especially with regard to their existentially separate entity as Muslims. Allama Iqbal's statement explaining the attitude of Muslim delegates to the Round-Table Conference issued in December, 1933 was a rejoinder to Jawahar Lal Nehru's statement. Nehru had said that the attitude of the Muslim delegation was based on "reactionarism." Iqbal concluded his rejoinder with: In conclusion I must put a straight question to punadi Jawhar Lal, how is India's problem to be solved if the majority community will neither concede the minimum safeguards necessary for the protection of a minority of 80 million people, nor accept the award of a third party; but continue to talk of a kind of nationalism which works out only to its own benefit? This position can admit of only two alternatives. Either the Indian majority community will have to accept for itself the permanent position of an agent of British imperialism in the East, or the country will have to be redistributed on a basis of religious, historical and cultural affinities so as to do away with the question of electorates and the communal problem in its present form.

Allama Iqbal's apprehensions were borne out by the Hindu Congress ministries established in Hindu majority province under the Act of 1935. Muslims in those provinces were given dastardly treatment. This deplorable phenomenon added to Allama Iqbal's misgivings regarding the future of Indian Muslims in case India remained united. In his letters to the Quaid-i Azam written in 1936 and in 1937 he referred to an independent Muslim State comprising North-Western and Eastern Muslim majority zones. Now it was not only the North-Western zones alluded to in the Allahabad Address.

There are some within Pakistan and without, who insist that Allama Iqbal never meant a sovereign Muslim country outside India. Rather he desired a Muslim State within the Indian Union. A State within a State. This is absolutely wrong. What he meant was understood very vividly by his Muslim compatriots as well as the non-Muslims. Why Nehru and others had then tried to show that the idea of Muslim nationalism had no basis at all. Nehru stated: *This idea of a Muslim nation is the figment of a few imaginations only, and, but for the publicity given to it by the Press few people would have heard of it. And even if many people believed in it, it would still vanish at the touch of reality.*

Bibliography

Afzal, M. Rafique: *Quaid-i-Azam Muhammad Ali Jinnah: Speeches in the Legislative Assembly of India, 1942-30*, Lahore, Research Society of Pakistan, 1976

Ahmad, Riaz: *Iqbal's Letters to Quaid-i-Azam*, Lahore, Friends Educational Service, 1976.

Ahmed, Akbar S.: *Jinnah, Pakistan, and Islamic Identity: The Search for Saladin*, 1997.

Ahmed, Waheed: *Quaid-I-Azam Muhammed Ali Jinnah : Speeches Indian Legislative Assembly 1935-1947*, Quaid-i-Azam Accademy, 1991.

Alva, Joachim: *Leaders of India*, Bombay, Thacker & Co., Ltd., 1943

Bakhsh, Ilahi: *With the Quaid-i-Azam During His Last Days*, Karachi, Quaid-i-Azam Academy, 1978.

Bhattarcharjea, Ajit: *Countdown to Partition: The Final Days*, New Delhi, HarperCollins, 1998.

Chaudhary, M.: *Partition and the Curse of Rehabilitation*, Calcutta, Bengal Rehabilitation Organization, 1964.

Chopra, P. N.: *Towards Freedom: Documents on the Movement for Independence in India, 1937*, Delhi, Oxford UP, 1986.

Dasgupta, Subrata : *The Bengal Renaissance : Identity and Creativity from Rammohun Roy to Rabindranath Tagore*, Delhi, Permanent Black, 2007.

Gilmartin, David: *Empire and Islam: Punjab and the Making of Pakistan*, London, Oxford UP, 1988.

Hasan, Khalid: *Quaid-i-Azam Mohamed Ali Jinnah: A Centenary Tribute*, London, Information Division, Embassy of Pakistan, 1976.

Hasan, Saadat : *Kingdom's End and Other Stories*, Delhi, Penguin, 1987.

Haynes, Jeff: *Religion, Globalization, and Political Culture in the Third World*, New York, St. Martin's Press, 1999.

Jafar, Malik Muhammad: *Jinnah as a Parliamentarian*, Lahore, Afzar Publications, 1977.

Jha, P. S.: *Kashmir, 1947: Rival Versions of History*, Delhi, Oxford UP, 1996.

Johnson, Alan: *Mission with Mountbatten*, London: Hale, 1982.

Kaushik, Asha : *Globalization, Democracy and Culture : Situating Gandhian Alternatives,* Jaipur, Pointer, 2002.

Manohar, Lohia, Ram : *Guilty Men of India's Partition*, Allahabad, Navahind, 1960.

Michel, A. A.: *The Indus Rivers: A Study of the Effects of Partition*, New Haven, Yale UP, 1967.

Mir Laik: *In Muhammad Ali Jinnah*, Karachi, Ministry of Information & Broadcasting, 1976.

Mukhtar, Zaman: *Students' Role in the Pakistan Movement*. Karachi, Quaid-iAzam Academy, 1978.

Philips, C. H. and Wainwright, M. D.: *The Partition of India: Policies and Perspectives 1935-47*, London, Allen and Unwin, 1970.

Saint, Tarun K.: *Translating Partition*, New Delhi, Katha, 2001.

Singh, Anita Inder. *The Origins of the Partition of India, 1936-1947*. New Delhi: Oxford UP, 1987.

Tinker, Hugh: *Experiment with Freedom, India and Pakistan 1947*, London, Oxford UP, 1967.

Index

I

L

N

P

S

T

V

❑❑❑